SPIRIT POWER

THINKING FROM ELSEWHERE

Series editors:
Clara Han, Johns Hopkins University
Bhrigupati Singh, Ashoka University and Brown University
Andrew Brandel, Harvard University

International Advisory Board:
Roma Chatterji, University of Delhi
Veena Das, Johns Hopkins University
Robert Desjarlais, Sarah Lawrence College
Harri Englund, Cambridge University
Didier Fassin, Institute for Advanced Study, Princeton
Angela Garcia, Stanford University
Junko Kitanaka, Keio University
Eduardo Kohn, McGill University
Heonik Kwon, Cambridge University
Michael Lambek, University of Toronto
Deepak Mehta, Ashoka University, Sonepat
Amira Mittermaier, University of Toronto
Sameena Mulla, Emory University
Marjorie Murray, Pontificia Universidad Católica de Chile
Young-Gyung Paik, Jeju National University
Sarah Pinto, Tufts University
Michael Puett, Harvard University
Fiona Ross, University of Cape Town
Lisa Stevenson, McGill University

SPIRIT POWER

Politics and Religion in Korea's American Century

HEONIK KWON AND JUN HWAN PARK

FORDHAM UNIVERSITY PRESS   NEW YORK 2022

Fordham University Press gratefully acknowledges financial assistance and support provided for the publication of this book by the Academy of Korean Studies.

Fordham University Press has no responsibility for the persistence or accuracy of URLs for external or third-party Internet websites referred to in this publication and does not guarantee that any content on such websites is, or will remain, accurate or appropriate.

Fordham University Press also publishes its books in a variety of electronic formats. Some content that appears in print may not be available in electronic books.

Visit us online at www.fordhampress.com.

Library of Congress Cataloging-in-Publication Data

Names: Kwon, Heonik, 1962– author. | Park, Jun Hwan, author.
Title: Spirit power : politics and religion in Korea's American
    century / Heonik Kwon and Jun Hwan Park.
Description: New York : Fordham University Press, 2022. |
    Series: Thinking from elsewhere | Includes bibliographical
    references and index.
Identifiers: LCCN 2021061997 | ISBN 9780823299928 (hardback) |
    ISBN 9780823299911 (paperback) | ISBN 9780823299935 (epub)
Subjects: LCSH: Korea—Religion—20th century. | Religion and
    politics—Korea. | Shamanism—Korea. | United States—Influence.
Classification: LCC BL2231 .K85 2022 | DDC 322/.1095190904—
    dc23/eng20220521
LC record available at https://lccn.loc.gov/2021061997

Printed in the United States of America

24 23 22   5 4 3 2 1

First edition

CONTENTS

SPIRIT POWER

INTRODUCTION

In his *Portrait of a Shamaness* (1936), the celebrated Korean writer Kim Dong-li (1913–1995) describes a family tragically disintegrating because of a religious conflict and a clash of civilizations. They live in a poor community on the outskirts of the ancient city Gyeongju. Mohwa, the mother, is an established shaman in the village, and she is fond of rice wine. On her way back from the village drinking house, she sings to trees, animals, the clouds, and the wind—all entities in her lived world which, for Mohwa, are spirited or are spirits themselves. For her, even household objects such as the lantern, cast-iron pots and pokers are spirited and need to be treated as such with respect. Her daughter, Nang-i, is a talented artist, and the story begins with an episode involving the portrait of a shamaness that she had painted. Wearing a ritual dress in striking raw colors, the woman in the painting is performing a *kut*, a shamanic rite. Nang-i has a hearing problem and a special liking for peaches. When Mohwa returns from work, she often brings a peach home for her daughter—a large, juicy "heavenly peach." Nang-i features in her mother's hymns as a princess from the Water World, exiled to the human world as punishment for her free (and unruly) spirit, whom Mohwa has the privilege of looking after while the young lady is in this world.

The story is set in the 1920s, the decade after Korea lost its sovereignty to Japan, Asia's unique player in the circle of modern empires. It begins soon after the March 1919 uprising to protest against Japanese colonial occupation. Known as the March First Movement, this event was a constitutional episode for modern Korea, both South and North, when ordinary Koreans throughout the country (women and men, old and young) took to the street to assert their sovereign rights in peaceful protest marches.[1] It was part of the momentous turn in global history following the end of World War I, which historians consider to mark the onset of decolonization across the colonial world.[2] Korea's then-small yet active Protestant community and its leaders played a prominent role in the mobilization of the March First popular uprising. None of these is mentioned in *Portrait of a Shamaness* (*Munyŏdo*; henceforth, *Portrait*).[3] Nor does the story give any indication of colonial politics or the conflicts in culture and morality generated by the coerced contact with a foreign power. The clash of civilizations highlighted in *Portrait* is not that of indigenous cultural integrity versus overpowering foreign dominance of a colonial character—a pattern that often appears in the scholarship of colonial history and contemporary postcolonial cultural studies.[4] Instead, the clash relates to the unique and exceptional character of Japan's imperial politics: an Asian nation colonizing another Asian country, which was unlike the better-known imperial politics pursued primarily by European nations in non-European (i.e., non-Christian) territories. The crises in values and norms depicted in *Portrait* point to the distance between two moral and religious systems—indigenous Korean shamanism and American missionary Protestantism—which shared a precarious existence under Japan's powerful colonial rule and its politicized religion of Shintoism, albeit each in a distinct way.

Mohwa, as the shamaness, represents one of these two polar positions, whereas her son Uk-i, takes up the other. Uk-i returned home after many years of estrangement, during which he had become a fervent follower of "the path of Jesus," after encountering the Reverend Hyun, an American missionary in Pyongyang. Mother and son clash with each other, and the intensity of their confrontation leads to a tragic conclusion with no possibility of reconciliation. Uk-i sees his mother's profession (and her entire world) as manifest idolatry, and he takes it as his mission to rescue her from the darkness (which he calls *mudang gwisin*, "shamanism demon"); Mohwa sees her son's obsession as the influence of some alien spirits and commits herself to chasing these threatening spirits away. Both fail miserably in their separate, bifurcated attempts.

Many years later, Kim Dong-li (also known as Kim Dong-ni) returned to *Portrait* to rewrite it into a larger epic story, published under the title *Ŭlhwa* (Mohwa's new name) in 1978. One notable feature of this revised version, in comparison with the original 1936 story, is the role of Nang-i, the painter. The daughter plays a more visible role in the new version, both within the polarized family and between the two religious sensibilities in confrontation. Nang-i feels hostile to the Book, the Bible that Uk-i cherishes so dearly, because she sees it as causing her family's troubles. Unlike her mother, however, she is curious about what it has to say and why her stepbrother treasures it so much. She is fascinated by the words of the Book, just as her artistic spirit is drawn to the intoxicating music and dance—the world of ritual performance that is her mother's vocation. Nang-i is aware that in her mother's world there are numerous spirits, whereas in her brother's world there is just one, a singularly meaningful Spirit. However, she questions whether these two worlds are indeed incompatible, and asks if the two can have a parallel existence, both within her family and beyond. In this way, Kim Dong-li speaks, through Nang-i's searching self-reflection which she, however, cannot put into spoken words, into the moral imperative of common existence between the old and the new, and the indigenous and the foreign—the message that was missing (or at least kept hidden) from the 1936 version.

Portrait remains popular today among readers in South Korea and is considered, among literary critics, Kim Dong-li's most powerful work. It has been made into a feature film (1972), popular song (1975), TV drama (1980, based on the 1978 version), and, most recently, an animation (2017). What interests us are the changes in the story from the original version, published at the outset of Japan's militarized colonial incursion into China, to the revised and expanded version that Kim prepared during a time of turbulent Cold War politics in Korea and its environs. One notable change is, as mentioned, from a violent clash of cultures to a cautious search for cultural coexistence as regards shamanism and Christianity. In terms of broad historical background, these changes speak of Korea's transition between two distinct eras of global politics—colonialism and the Cold War. *Portrait* first became available to the public in the heyday of Japan's imperial order in Korea, when this order was rapidly taking on a more belligerent, expansionist character, leading to the outbreak of the Second Sino-Japanese War in 1937 and eventually to the destruction of the Pacific War. The story takes as its background the 1920s, when Korea's shamanism tradition was given an important place in Japan's colonial cultural policy. Delving into the work of Akiba Takashi, a Japanese sociologist and key figure in this domain, Kim Seong-nae explains shamanism's place in colonial politics in terms of a double-bind logic.[5] According to this logic, which is far from unfamiliar to colonial politics at large, Japan's cultural politics in Korea first took Korean shamanism as the nation's most authentic religious culture, and then placed it on a lower tier of cultural evolution in relation to the spiritual achievement of Japan's metropolitan culture. Hence, the double bind in this context refers to an idea of cultural authenticity and integrity that is not translated into political integrity and sovereignty. Such an act of translation became vital for state and nation building in the decolonizing world after the end of World War II; in contrast, at the outset of colonization, ideas of cultural authenticity, combined with an ideology of social evolutionary hierarchy between the colony and the metropolis, were conducive to colonial occupation and for generating the political logic of *mission civilisatrice*.

The second version of Kim Dong-li's story was prepared in the 1970s, another crucial period in Korea's modern cultural history and political genesis. This was when the southern half of the partitioned Korea was racing forward in an era of rapid industrial growth, thereby overtaking its northern adversary in terms of economic power. South Korea's economic advance was grounded, to a significant extent, in the prevailing theory of economic growth at the time as part of the Cold War political struggle, such as that which Walt Rostow propagated in *The Stages of Economic Growth: A Non-Communist Manifesto* (1960). Politically, as indicated in Rostow's title, South Korean society was then in the grip of a powerful anti-communist, authoritarian state hierarchy, headed by Park Chung-hee.[6] President Park was an effective economic modernizer, but he was also an aggressive cultural reformer. The state's culture and "mentality" reform drive involved an all-out assault on what it considered to be backward customs and beliefs—namely, ideas and practices that it believed were antithetical to the execution of societal mobilization for economic take-off. Of these cultural relics that were blamed for dragging the progress of modernizing Korea, shamanism was singled out as the principal target for state disciplinary action.

In both of these epochal episodes, one written in the heyday of colonialism and the other during the height of the Cold War, it is interesting to observe that another powerful actor was in the picture. Kim Dong-li's *Portrait* emblematizes this actor in the Reverend Hyun, an American Presbyterian missionary in Pyongyang (now the capital of North Korea). Pyongyang was a stronghold of American mission activity during the early part of the twentieth century, to the extent that the city was then considered "the citadel of

Christianity in Korea" and even "the Jerusalem of the Orient."[7] In the 1970s, however, Seoul was fast replacing it as the new Jerusalem of the East. South Korea's Protestant church underwent an astonishingly rapid growth in line with the country's economic growth during that decade. Among notable events in this respect was the visit of the renowned American evangelist Billy Graham to Seoul in 1973, a formative episode in Korea's evangelical history as we will see in Chapter 1. It is alongside this transition from Pyongyang to Seoul as the center of Korea's Protestant movement (and the trajectory from Reverend Hyun's mission activity in Pyongyang to Reverend Graham's mass revival rally held in Seoul as emblematic events of this transition) that Korea's traditional religiosity, especially that associated with shamanism, encountered a strong and aggressive gesture of disapproval, being relegated to the status of superstition or idolatry.

The unfolding of this story coincides with the advent of the so-called American Century, the epoch associated with the growing preponderance of American power in global politics since the late nineteenth century. In Korea's modern history, the manifestation of American power was both religious and political. This was primarily in the sphere of religion in the first half of the twentieth century, and, during the second half and after the Pacific War, it was part of the geopolitics of the Cold War. The religious character of American power continued to thrive in South Korea well into the Cold War era, however, and remains entrenched in this place even today, a generation after that global conflict was declared over.

This book explores the manifestation of American power in Korea's modern history with a focus on the religious sphere. Such a focus is familiar in recent scholarship of Cold War history, not to mention in the tradition of American studies. The story of American power in Korean religion that we will tell in this book is not, however, restricted to the sphere of religion that is familiar to these research domains and to America's constitutional history: the global Protestant movement. It may come as a surprise to readers that this power is also found in such apparently unlikely places as the subject of Nang-i's painting—the Korean shamaness and her world of ten thousand spirits.

Although part of this book deals with a broad brush on the presence of American power in Korea's religious history and culture, from the late nineteenth century to the present, its principal focus, in terms of historical investigation, lies in the post–Korean War period. The Korean War was a pivotal episode in the making and shaping of the early Cold War international order; this was also what firmly entrenched the political and cultural power of the United States in the Korean peninsula. The partition of Korea and the ensuing Korean War "played a central role in shaping the attitudes of Koreans toward religion," observed Han Kyung-Koo, South Korea's prominent cultural anthropologist.[8] Of several issues regarding how the experience of war affected the religious social landscape, Han highlights the phenomenon of mass population displacement, especially the relocation of northerners to what is today South Korea. Notable is the exodus of Presbyterians from the North, who subsequently exerted a huge influence on the traditionally weaker southern Protestant community. However, Han urges the reader not to disregard other less institutionalized religions, such as the many traditions of shamanism in northern Korea, and how these locally-grounded religious forms came to terms with their war-caused deracination from their long-familiar locales.

The port city of Incheon, west of Seoul, familiar to visitors to Korea today because of its international airport, is a good place to reflect on the subject of war and religion, as analyzed by Han. Owing to its proximity to the maritime frontier between the two Koreas, Incheon received a large influx of refugees from the North during the war, and it abounds with stories of their painful loss of home and search for a new place to live. Most of these refugees and exiles hailed from two separate regions of northern Korea: Hwanghae and Pyŏngan. Religiously, what stands out are, among others, the northern Presbyterian movement (predominantly from the Pyŏngan region) and the tradition of shamanism (especially from the coastal and maritime Hwanghae region). The ethnographic parts of this book, therefore, focus on the urban space of old Incheon, where relics of exiled northern Presbyterianism are concentrated. It is also where some of our key interlocutors about displaced Hwanghae shamanism have long been based.

However, Incheon abounds with other historical relics. Having long been a gateway for overseas cultures, the city maintains a host of sites of memory relating to Korea's opening its doors to Western cultural and commercial influences at the turn of the twentieth century. These include monuments and other built objects that celebrate the inception of Protestantism, by American Presbyterian and Methodist missionaries, at the end of the nineteenth century. A prominent memorial complex in Incheon relates to the history of the Korean War, focusing on the Incheon Landing in September 1950. This was a critical episode in the three-year conflict. The American who stands out from this historical time is Douglas MacArthur, the Supreme Commander of the United Nations forces during the early phase of the war. In between these two historical events of considerable significance for Korea's modern history—the arrival first of the American missionaries and then of this American general—lies the experience of colonial conquest at the hands of a non-Western Asian empire. Each of these past events and formations (contact with Western culture and power, colonial experience, and the Korean War) had a great impact on the constitution of the two religious forms this book concentrates on—evangelicalism and shamanism—although in distinct ways. We will explore contemporary traces of these powerful waves of history as seen in each religious form, before bringing them together in a dialogue for a wider discussion of religion and political history.

The concept of religion as in Korean religion does not discriminate between a powerful institutional religion with a global reach, such as modern evangelicalism, and a highly localized, diffuse ritual tradition such as Hwanghae shamanism. It incorporates both great and little religious traditions, as it were, and addresses the condition that religious forms of varying operational scales and different historical origins exist in parallel within a common sociohistorical context. At times, however, the term "Korean religion" may refer to the sphere of religiosity that is observed to have a great historical depth and is, therefore, argued to constitute a certain property of indigeneity. This argument has fluctuated in intensity in modern Korean history and has been a political polemic as well as a cultural statement, being closely intertwined with the idea of sovereignty. We embrace these two separate notions of religion—plural and indigenous—for the simple reason that they are both real, meaningful, and relevant to this book's investigative sphere. Relatedly, it needs to be made clear at the outset that when we make comments on the idea of shamanism's indigeneity, this is largely for the purpose of reflecting on the idea's changing political meanings in specific historical circumstances. In short, the expression "Korean religion" is used in this book to address the existence of different (and sometimes conflicting) religious orientations and heritages in Korea's modern history—the horizon of religious pluralism. Furthermore, the expression is used to convey the profound contradictions found in this horizon—the politics of religion that relegated indigenous religious culture to superstition and thereby cast it out of the legitimate public realm of religious plurality. As we will see, this political process has been broad in scope and broadly intertwined with the progression of the American Century. We will also explore how the culture of shamanism has assimilated the materiality of American power, partly as a way to counter the powerful politics of social exclusion (see Chapter 3), in its traditional yet ingenuous way, and identify what we can learn from this development in thinking through the relational world of religion and modern politics.

Our journey begins at the public park in old Incheon, called Freedom Park, where the imposing statue of Douglas MacArthur stands. MacArthur is sometimes referred to as a "man of the American Century," and he is a hero of the Korean War in South Korea's dominant public accounts. In circles of the country's strong evangelical community, he is commemorated as a mighty puritan crusader, chosen by the divine power to defend the Jerusalem of the East from the menace of god-denying communism. In Incheon, the American general has also become an effective helper-spirit among the town's war-displaced performers of Hwanghae shamanism. We will take the statue of MacArthur and Freedom Park as the principal sites of memory, where we will reflect on questions of *power and religion* as they relate to Korea's modern political genesis and its century-long relationship with the United States.

We begin Chapter 1 by explaining how we approach these questions. The conceptual pairing of religion and power is familiar in the history of anthropological research, in which religion, together with ritual, has long been considered a supreme manifestation of collective moral power. However, this is far from the case in the field of modern diplomatic history, with which this book also engages. This field has concentrated primarily on the dynamics of power—secular and material—and, with regard to the Cold War in particular, on the balance and hierarchy of power. Some scholars of Cold War history have recently begun to raise questions about the preponderance of power as an analytical concept, however, while claiming that religious ideas and/or ideas about religion should be seen as part of the competition for power. Reviewing this claim, Chapter 1 provides a broad overview of how the southern half of partitioned Korea became a stronghold of the Protestant movement, unique in East Asia. The unfolding of this phenomenon was closely intertwined with that of the particular relationship of power forged between South Korea and the United States after the Korean War, and hence can be discussed according to the "religion and the Cold War" framework.

The explosive growth of Protestantism is undoubtedly the most notable phenomenon of Korea's Cold War modernity in the religious sphere, especially when seen in relation to the country's drive to economic modernization in the 1970s. The development had considerable ramifications in other religious domains, however, notably in the eclectic, diffused, traditional grassroots religiosity of Korea where shamanism, including some aspects of animism, is an important constituent element. The growth of evangelicalism, later combined with the developmental state's heavy-handed societal enlightenment and purification drive, resulted in a confrontational religious culture in South Korea, which had long been a religiously pluralistic, dominantly and pragmatically secular society. In the investigative sphere of politics and religion, we could focus on Christian faith only, as in contemporary religion and the Cold War scholarship, which concentrates on the American and transatlantic historical horizons. In exploring this subject in a frontier society of Asia's postcolonial Cold War, such as South Korea after the Korean War, we need to throw a wider net. In this perspective, Chapters 3 and 4 deal with the forceful politics of anti-superstition in Cold War South Korea, focusing on the nation's long-established shamanism tradition as the principal cultural antagonist to modern life, material and spiritual, in the view of both the state and the church. Putting a powerful universal religion and a localized popular religious tradition in a common discursive terrain has another analytical implication. Modern anthropology has a long pedigree in the study of indigenous or popular religious forms. Strong in the discipline is the notion that, in order to understand a non-Western society, it is imperative to come to terms with its religious sensibility and morality, since these moral ideas provide structuring principles for its sociopolitical order—namely, as an equivalent to how the system of law operates in a modern state society. In contrast, attention to the Christian experience in non-Western societies has been steadily growing during the past two decades. Investigations in this genre, commonly referred to as the anthropology of Christianity, vary considerably in orientation: Some delve into the politics of conversion to Christianity in the historical contexts of colonial encounter, whereas many others take ethnographic interest in the intimate experience of Christian conversion and the redefining of the self and the world that this process arguably involves.[9] The ethnographic component of this growing research trend surely speaks closely to the contemporaneous global phenomenon: the re-empowerment of the world evangelization movement since around the 1970s, in which South Korea's evangelical community has become an important player second to their US counterparts. This book also interacts with the colonial-historical component of the anthropology of Christianity, although, as noted earlier, what we are dealing with here, as regards Korea's colonial experience, is Japan's political religion based on its formerly locally based, largely animistic beliefs, rather than a manifestly universalizing, doctrinal Abrahamic religion, as is nearly always the case in the existing religious studies of colonial encounters. In short, this book participates in the anthropology of Christianity with two distinct issues: first, the particularity of Korea's colonial historical experience, and second, the postcolonial Cold War history, when church communities in South Korea not only underwent phenomenal growth within the country but also began to actively partake in the world mission to the Asia-Pacific region, Central Asia, Africa, and elsewhere in the global South, thereby affecting the very fields within which current research in the ethnography of Christianity is taking place. This implies that the postcolonial field of global evangelical expansion is one that is as politically charged as the colonial encounter with European missionaries and should be approached with due attention to religion in politics and the politics of religion. In order to achieve this investigative goal, however, we need to bring anthropology closer to Cold War history, not merely to colonial history: an effort that is still in its infancy today.[10]

In this respect, Chapters 3 and 4 further explore the questions of power and religion raised in Chapter 1. They do so in a specific, postcolonial context of global bipolar politics, and the keyword in this investigation is *superstition*—defined in both the religious-moral and political-ideological senses. Before doing this, in Chapter 2 we offer a view of Korea's shamanism tradition, the principal object of containment in the religious sphere of Korea's Cold War political modernity. Shamanism in Korea is a highly localized cultural and religious form, even though its long-established parochialism (in a purely empirical sense) has been weakened in recent times (i.e., with the advent of colonial politics and subsequently with that of postcolonial state-building). Accordingly, our focus is on shamanism as a specific local ritual form rather than a national cultural heritage—the latter being very much an invented tradition, if not a vacuous concept outright. The shamanic tradition we describe is that of a northern Korean region that has been anchored in the coastal town of Incheon since the Korean War. This is a traditional religious form that is nevertheless far from "traditional" if considered from the local perspective, and cannot be considered properly if we ignore the historical experience of radical displacement from the familiar locale. This last, in fact, may apply to all existing local shamanism traditions in Korea that underwent the politics against superstition, which is also a form of dislocation. For the Hwanghae shamanism tradition, however, displacement also meant the war-induced permanent loss of home, and we approach this ritual tradition's intimate association with MacArthur in Freedom Park in the light of this historical experience. We invite readers to join us in getting to know how this American General has become a powerful spirit entity in Incheon's Hwanghae shamanic rituals, believing that this way of discovering a *local* cultural tradition (that is, the idea of the local that, in modern life, unavoidably involves some history of deracination and dislocation) is probably a proper method for getting closer to what shamanism actually is in this part of the human cultural world today. We also submit this discovery as part of an understanding of politics and history, as previously emphasized, rather than knowledge of the religious system per se—following the classical tradition in the anthropology of religion and morality.

Speaking of religion and politics, we reiterate that these two domains of human interest and practice can be much less mutually discrete spheres of values and ideas, even in modern times, than they are understood to be in the dominant ideology of modern political life, as Jürgen Habermas lucidly shows, relegating religion (and kinship) to private business and politics to the public world.[11] This is not merely because even in a most secularistic, power-focused political form, such as Cold War politics, religion and religious ideas play a considerable, if not formative, role; it is also due to the possibility that political ideas are embedded in religious forms, even in such seemingly unlikely places as shamanism. This corresponds with the view of one of Korea's most distinguished observers of its popular religious tradition, Yim Suk-jay (1903–1998), who asserted that a distinct theory of politics can be found in the shamanic culture of Korea.

Following our discussion of religion in political history, including shamanism in Korea's Cold War history, we will turn to Yim's political theory of shamanism. This theory is complex and defies summary capturing, as any good political theory should, so we devote two chapters to it. We also bring in a body of resources from the anthropology of religion in the hope of contextualizing Yim's insights in some of the relevant debates in contemporary anthropology as well as in the history of anthropological thought on religion and moral order. One keyword in Yim's rendering of shamanism's political constitution is *sovereignty*—which addresses the fact that power entities in this religious form (deities, spirit-helpers, and other spirits), whether nominally majestic or humble in origin, are all stubbornly self-determining, sovereignty-claiming-and-respecting beings. We find Yim's bold perspective on shamanism's supernatural political order challenging and worthy of a careful introduction to a wider audience.

In the concluding chapter, we, too, take a somewhat bold step, and relate Yim's portrait of a democratic world society (in the supernatural realm) to a vision for an ideal world society (in human actuality) existing in the history of modern anthropology. On the more modest side, we attempt to see the life of MacArthur in Incheon's spirited landscape in the light of Yim's two-sided portrait of shamanism in the world and the world in shamanism. We hope to have done some justice to this remarkable scholar's original contribution to the anthropology of religion, and we ask readers to judge whether, in so trying, we succeeded in connecting the world of spirits with the world of human affairs, which is the telos of Korea's long shamanism tradition, in the scale and milieu of religion and the global Cold War.

1

RELIGION AND THE COLD WAR

On June 3, 1973, Billy Graham gave a powerful sermon to a million-strong crowd. Being part of the '73 Crusade, a mass spiritual revival movement in South Korea, it was a finale for the week-long "mission assemblies" that had taken place across the country. His sermon was delivered in Yŏŭido Square in Seoul, a former Japanese airfield that is now a public park attracting thousands of townspeople, especially during the cherry blossom season each spring. The place also used to be known as 5/16 Square, referring to the military coup d'état on May 16, 1961, that brought the coup leader Park Chung-hee to power. Reverend Graham began that day's preaching with a look back on his earlier encounter with Korea, during the Korean War:[1]

> Twenty-two years ago, I was here in Korea. It was Christmas time and it was very cold. I have never been so cold in all my life, and I toured along what is now the DMZ [which divides the two Koreas].

Then the preacher, who some call America's greatest evangelist of the twentieth century, went on to describe what he had heard at a place called Heartbreak Ridge:[2]

> I was in Heartbreak Ridge. And on Heartbreak Ridge there were twelve soldiers. They were American soldiers huddled together. An enemy sneaked through the line. He threw a hand grenade in the middle of them. It was going to go off in three seconds. A soldier saw it and jumped on top of it. He grabbed it to hold it to his heart. And it exploded.

The soldier died, the preacher continued, but his sacrifice saved the lives of his fellow soldiers. Citing "Greater love has no one than this: to lay down one's life for one's friends" (John 15:13), Graham then moved on to the real subject of the day—the death of *the* Person. In his earlier media interview, he said emphatically that "Christianity is not a system of ethics. Christianity is not a philosophy. Christianity is a Person, and that Person is Jesus Christ." This followed on from the speech he had delivered on his arrival at Gimpo International Airport on May 25:

> I have come as a representative of the Kingdom of God. I am not here as an American. I represent a higher court than the White House. I am an ambassador of the King of Kings and the Lord of Lords, and I have come in that spirit and as His representative.

Reverend Graham was not merely an ambassador of the Kingdom of God only, however. On May 27, he was invited to South Korea's presidential complex, Blue House, to meet with Park. There, the American preacher conveyed to South Korea's head of state a personal message from Richard Nixon. It is reported that, receiving him, Park said that "the existence of God is denied or strictly regulated in Communist countries." Park added, "The Communist rulers suppress religion to continue their survival because their ideologies are contradictory to the cause of religion."[3] Later, during his sermon in Yŏŭido, Graham mentioned the meeting and asked the crowd to join in a prayer on behalf of Park, whom he called the leader of the Korean people.

The '73 Crusade is regarded as "the greatest turning point" in the history of Korean Protestantism. Reverend Han Kyung-chik, one of the principal organizers of the '73 Crusade and Billy Graham's key Korean contact and counterpart, called for "fifty million [roughly the total combined population of South Korea and North Korea at the time] to Christ!" during his opening speech. The Crusade event as a whole, and Graham's role in it as the ambassador of the Kingdom in particular, are recognized as the vital springboard for the explosive growth of churches and churchgoers in the ensuing decade. In fact, the day of Billy Graham's public performance is still referred to as The Day in some church circles today. For Reverend Graham, the meaning of that day went even further—he claimed it was "one of the most historic moments in the history of the Christian Church."[4]

Crusade '73 in 1973 was followed by Explo '74 in August 1974, which, co-organized by William Bright's Campus Crusade for Christ, focused on the "explosive" evangelization of the youth and students.[5] The official video foot-

Billy Graham and Han Kyung-chik, 1973. Reproduced by permission of the Museum of Christianity, Sungsil University.

age of this event explains the event's objective as the Christianization of the entire Korean nation, which would involve the rescuing of 15 million Koreans (in the North) from captivity in "the tyranny of Red Wolves."[6] A decade later, Yŏŭido witnessed yet another round of mass assemblies. In the summer of 1984, tens of thousands of people crowded the same square to join revival rallies marking the centenary of Protestantism in Korea. Chaired again by Reverend Han Kyung-chik, who gave the closing sermon on August 19, the event attracted more than two million people. The Centenary celebrations included a number of other events—notably, the completion of a museum for Christian martyrs and a memorial dedicated to some of the first American Protestant missionaries to Korea: Henry Appenzeller and Horace and Lillias Underwood. The Centennial Memorial Tower of Korean Protestantism is located in the Incheon harbor, the site where these three missionaries came ashore on Easter Day 1885.

Billy Graham came back to Korea to join this centennial event. However, the atmosphere this time was considerably different from that in the 1973 rally. One of the popular slogans of the Centenary rally was "from a church

Centennial Memorial Tower of Korean Protestantism, Incheon. Photo by
Jun Hwan Park.

that receives to a church that gives." Korea's Protestant movements had ac-
quired considerable confidence by then, having grown exponentially in scale
and influence during the preceding decade. The number of followers nearly
doubled in the 1970s; by the end of the 1970s, about six new churches were
opening up each day.[7] In an address in 1992, Rev. Han reminisced that when
he left Pyongyang in 1945, there were very few churches in Seoul: "I remember there were only about thirty churches in the city of Seoul. But today you
will be really surprised by what God has done."[8] The phenomenon of megachurches was also taking root during the time. Most notable was Yŏŭido
Full Gospel Church, headed by the renowned pastor Cho Young-ki (also
known as David Yonggi Cho). Having relocated in 1973 from the old city
center of Seoul, Cho's church consistently grew by more than 9 percent each
year from 1972 to 1982. By the early 1990s, the church had become the largest super-church in the world, with more than 600,000 followers. The
growth rate of this church during the 1970s corresponded closely to that of
South Korea's economy during the same decade: also averaging about
9 percent. Against this background of monumental growth, the purpose of
the Centenary rallies was not merely to celebrate the evangelization of Korea,
as had been the case in the earlier '73 Crusade rally. Their new slogan was
"global mission" (*segyesŏn'gyo*): extending the gift of Evangel from Korea to

the world at large. This was the intended meaning of the transformation from "a church that receives" to "a church that gives"—a process that indeed became forcefully realized in the ensuing decades, when South Korean evangelicals became increasingly visible and assertive outside Korea. This development affected also some established Korean American church communities in the United States, which, according to some critics, were losing touch with the conditions of ethnic diversity and economic inequality in their locales while aggressively following the message of globalization emanating from their distant former homeland.[9] Reverend Graham came to Korea in 1973 as an ambassador of the Kingdom of God; a decade later, Korea was preparing its own ambassadors ("Asia's apostles" according to the *Washington Post*) to send to Asia, the Americas, Africa, Oceania, the Caribbean, and elsewhere.[10]

RELIGION IN COLD WAR POLITICS

Scholars of Cold War history have begun to pay attention to similar episodes. In *The Kingdom of God Has No Borders*, for instance, Melani McAlister explores Billy Graham's Evangelical Association in the context of the 1974 International Congress on World Evangelization in Lausanne, Switzerland, which was "the largest-ever gathering of evangelical Christian leaders" thus far.[11] In this international event, Reverend Graham appears to have undertaken rhetorical practices similar to those he used during his visit to Seoul the previous year—with phrases such as "When I go to preach the Gospel, I go as an ambassador of the Kingdom of God—not America."[12] The Lausanne meeting is known to be an important threshold in the history of the modern evangelical movement, a turning point in this movement's change of orientation increasingly toward engagement with vexing social issues such as poverty and inequality—parting with their previously dominant exclusive emphasis on individual salvation. This change was, in part, a critical response to "the evangelism-first evangelicals" and the proponents of "church growth theory," despite the fact that all the participants, both those who criticized and those who were challenged, were commonly "biblical literalists and Christian exclusivists."[13] McAlister explains how this partial change of course involved a challenge to the movement's hitherto dominant American leadership (such as Billy Graham and his group) by religious leaders from the Global South, and how this change mirrored the broader transformation in the stage of world politics at that time—the rising voice of postcolonial nations in Africa, the Middle East, and Latin America, which was, in the secular international political sphere, represented most prominently by the then active Non-Aligned Movement.

McAlister details a plethora of challenges initiated by actors in the Global South to the preponderance of American power within the sphere of international evangelicalism. Other scholars concentrate on how American prominence in this particular sphere interacts with the country's power in secular politics. In this light, Andrew Preston offers an epic drama of "America's Mission." The idea of "mission" in this context runs along a tightrope between the secular (pursuit of aggressive and sometimes expansionist liberalism, as in Manifest Destiny—the idea that the United States is a uniquely virtuous nation and, as such, has the calling to save the world) and the religious (reaching and proselytizing the unreached, as Upholders of Spiritual Values and Defenders of the Faith).[14] Hence, the idea of mission has both literal and metaphorical meanings in this context, shifting its semantic life between the two spheres, secular and religious, time and again—despite the founding constitutional creed of separation between church and state. Preston traces the work of America's mission in this double sense of the term chronologically from Abraham Lincoln and Woodrow Wilson to George Kennan and Harry Truman. Others explore it in a more temporally confined and specific way. Focusing on the immediate post–World War II and early Cold War era, Dianne Kirby argues that in an effort to understand Harry Truman's foreign policies, one may not ignore his religious character and his grasp of religious ideas: "President Harry S. Truman made religion an integral part of his Cold War campaign to persuade the American people to abandon isolationism, embrace globalism and world leadership, and roll-back communism."[15] According to her, anti-communism "had no intrinsic positive values," and religious ideals "allowed it to assume doctrinal status in the popular mind as a legitimate ideological concept."[16] Anti-communism was largely a reactive ideology, lacking authentic conceptual properties; Kirby's rendering of Truman's contribution to the building of the Cold War order navigates between this practical need to fill the vacuous conceptual interior of anti-communism with some tangible content, on the one hand, and, on the other, Truman's personal beliefs and dispositions. The element of personal character is also noted regarding religious leaders— for instance, in relation to Pope Pius XII or, concerning the other end of

Cold War history, Pope John Paul II.[17] Kirby proposes that the keyword in this religious political history of the Cold War is "liberation"—the liberation of the faithful from captivity behind the Iron Curtain. McAlister also takes on this notion in her earlier work, dealing with the representation of the Middle East in the mid-twentieth-century American public media. She shows how, in the late 1950s, popular films of the time—such as *The Ten Commandments* (1956) and *Ben Hur* (1959)—contributed to propagating the imperative of political liberation from communist tyranny (and the United States' foreign policies that advocated this) through the idea of freedom of religion, a familiar idea for the American public.[18] McAlister speaks evocatively of her coming of age in a southern state: how she and other youths were asked to take part in a public rally with the Stars and Stripes in one hand and the blue Star of David in the other—the latter being a symbol of religious freedom, not merely the emblem of the state of Israel.

These are exciting developments in the historiography of the Cold War and in modern diplomatic history more broadly. Such developments contribute to enlarging the idea of diplomacy to horizons of transnational interactions beyond the narrowly defined international relations centered on state actors and their interactions. Being part of the so-called culture turn in Cold War history, which seeks to approach ideological forms and rhetorical practices as more than an epiphenomenon of realpolitik or power politics, these researches follow the broader constructivist orientation of international studies.[19] Religion and religious mission were a key domain of the earlier colonial politics in Africa and Asia before this political form was partially subdued by the rise of the Cold War partitioning of the world; thus, the foregrounding of religion with regard to the Cold War also has the effect of considering the global politics of the second half of the twentieth century as less than a rupture from those of the preceding eras. Moreover, the growing scholarship on religion and the Cold War since roughly the beginning of the 2000s also finds its merit as an important means with which one can reflect on contemporary history. The rise of this research domain largely coincides with the explosive growth of public concerns with the threats of politicized or fundamentalist religiosity to modern democracy. These concerns are principally about the place of religion and secularism in modern politics; however, the ways in which these concerns are expressed vary considerably across places.[20] If the guarding of the *laïcité* of the public space is a great concern for some societies, in other political societies where religiously diverse communities cohabit, the main concern may lie instead with the protection of religious minorities or the principle of religious plurality. With the end of the Cold War, some speculated that the fault line of the new world order would no longer be according to clashing secular ideologies but rather between religiously defined civilizational entities and spheres.[21] It is against this background of the alleged return of religion as a structuring force of the human world that the investigation of Cold War history from the angle of religious history finds its critical relevance—that is, by showing how the age of extremes was not merely about clashing secular ideas and ideals and that it was equally about alternative ways to define the place of religion in human life.

Despite these merits, other observers note the problems in bringing religion into Cold War history. The strongest criticism relates to the modernist foundation of contemporary international politics.[22] Although exceptions do exist, this field of social science defines the modern state, the principal actor in the international system, in the image of the modern individual—an autonomous and sovereign being having inalienable rights such as the right to pursue its own interest. These entities are nominally equal to one another but, in reality, entertain unequal relations in terms of wealth and power. It follows that, in understanding the fabric of international society, it is imperative to come to terms with how the principle of equality and the reality of inequality play out in the relational field of state actions and behavior. The modernism of this picture concerns both the playing field (international society) and the players (states). The field is a modern ground in which only subjectively sovereign and relationally equal beings can join. The participating players or actors—that is, the states—have to be cognizant of these rules while in the field, whether or not the same rules are applied internally to their own political societies. It is hard, therefore, to bring religion to this modern, rational, self-interested, and calculating actor, without risking weakening the very foundation of its social existence. If this actor thinks religiously, rather than with the logic of rational choice, and acts accordingly, it would be difficult to understand its past behavioral pattern and predict its future behavior using the given modern scientific tools.

Furthermore, the Cold War world was a peculiar world in which the reality of inequality and the ideal of equality existed within another broader structural condition often referred to as the balance of power, which points to the contest of power between the two superpower state actors of the time:

the USSR and the USA. The last condition is central to the specificity of the Cold War as a political form, whereas the first two conditions typically characterize what went on, within the specific sphere of influence, between the leading superpower state and other smaller or weaker state actors. In this environment, it was difficult to envisage the possibility of a coherent and systemic analysis unless this analysis was grounded in a concept that can apply to both the inter-spheric relations between the two superpowers and the intra-spheric order headed by each superpower. That concept was *power*, mostly the material power (of economic, military, and institutional capability) and only occasionally incorporating the immaterial power of ideological, cultural, and rhetorical persuasiveness. The criticism against the scholarship of religion and the Cold War noted above draws on these specific historical conditions of global bipolar politics, asking whether and to what extent an emphasis on the role of religion in the unfolding of modern international politics helps advance the understanding of the *power politics* of the Cold War.[23]

Related debates exist in anthropology. Notable is Clifford Geertz's famous adage of "power as display" and his related idea of ideology as "symbolic coercion."[24] What Geertz is trying to convey with these expressions is in line with the prevailing ethos of cultural pluralism in modern anthropology, addressing the fact that the idea of power, like many other important things in human life, is not universal but varies across cultural and historical contexts. For the rulers of the nineteenth-century, precolonial Balinese kingdom and their subjects, Geertz argues that political power was, above all, of a demonstrative kind—made and maintained, for instance, in the theatrics of royal rituals. In advancing this idea of power as spectacle, Geertz intends to challenge Max Weber's definition of political power as a monopoly of coercive might—interestingly, against the fact that his widely known semiotic definition of culture (or religion and ideology) draws upon the Weber-inspired image of a spider's web—as webs of meanings that humans spin around themselves and are thereby trapped in.[25] This idea also goes against the prevailing concept of political power in the social sciences of the 1960s and 1970s, the time he advanced these ideas, which concentrated on material power—in his words, on what goes on in the smoke-filled back room of the theater of politics where powers that be discuss how to govern the world, disregarding what is actually happening on the theater's actual, public stage.

The meaning-focused, culturally specific and pluralistic notion of power that Geertz advocated has had considerable influence on the culture turn in the scholarship of Cold War history.[26] In his investigation of the reconstruction of western Europe after World War II, David Ryan writes:

> The culture of the Cold War provided the atmosphere and the tools that enabled Washington to enhance its consensus, achieve its objectives and largely win the battle for the hearts and minds of West Europeans. But far from the idea of a passive transfer of culture, Washington initiated numerous programmes designed to bring about its desired ends. [A] new West was created in which old inconsistencies were forgotten and new identities were advanced.[27]

Following this remark about the transatlantic migration of Cold War culture, Ryan introduces a quote from Geertz's essay "Ideology as a Cultural System":

> The power of a metaphor derives precisely from the interplay between the discordant meanings it symbolically coerces into a unitary conceptual framework and from the degree to which that coercion is successful in overcoming the psychological resistance such semantic tension inevitably generates in anyone in a position to perceive it.[28]

In his stimulating essay on the place of religions in US–South Asian relations during the early Cold War, Andrew Rotter also states that in recent years, "diplomatic historians found they could not completely ignore developments outside their field, especially in anthropology and in social and cultural history."[29] Arguing that the culturalist school in diplomatic history arose with the intention to go beyond the exclusive focus on power, which tends to privilege predominant powers in the field of diplomatic actions, he says that "I take as my definition of culture one that is good enough for Max Weber and Clifford Geertz: the 'web of significance' spun by human beings."[30] Following these renditions, we may conclude that what Geertz was trying to say about the concept of power in a cross-cultural comparative context (comparing conditions in nineteenth-century Bali with those in mid-twentieth-century America) is brought, in the contemporary cultural historical study of Cold War politics, to different aspects of this political form—that is, the Cold War as power politics and the Cold War as an ideological system and construct.

Some of these debates concerning the place of culture or religion in Cold War power politics are certainly relevant for understanding Korea's Cold War experience. For instance, Billy Graham's visit to Korea is surely a small yet meaningful part of a transnational evangelicalism movement of which he was a preeminent and controversial leader. He was a powerful ambassador for the Kingdom of God, yet his diplomatic career involved prolific engagement with the structure and relations of power in the secular, political world. Notice that his first encounter with Korea was not through the religious event of 1973 but in the theater of the Korean War (1950–1953), a supremely political event both for Korea and for the United States, albeit in different ways. If we take into consideration the fact that Korea's Cold War history is inseparable from its experience of a highly destructive, ideologically charged, armed confrontation and generalized social crisis—which goes against the broadly shared meaning of the Cold War as an imaginary war—religion and religious ideas come to take on a political relevance that is much more radical than how they appear in the existing literature on religion and the Cold War.[31] To consider the unique place of religion in Korea's Cold War experience, we need to shift our attention from the American ambassador of the Kingdom of God to his Korean host and counterpart, the Reverend Han Kyung-chik.

Han Kyung-chik (1903–2000) was a principal figure in both the '73 Crusade and the Centenary revival rally in 1984–1985. Beyond these events, he takes a towering place in the history of Korean Protestantism as a whole. Born in the coastal area northwest of Pyongyang, now in North Korea, he was educated in what was one of Korea's most renowned Christian educational establishments: Sungsil Academy. This was in Pyongyang, and in the 1920s when Korea was under Japan's colonial occupation—that is, the background of the story *Portrait of a Shamaness* that we discussed in the Introduction. The shamaness Mohwa's son Uk-i encountered the American Presbyterian mission in Pyongyang during that time. Uk-i's unfulfilled dream was to visit the missionary's homeland; Han Kyung-chik had the opportunity to do so. After studying at Princeton Theological Seminary, he returned home in 1932. Then, following a brief teaching career at Sungsil Academy, he was ordained as a Presbyterian minister in 1935. Subsequently, he carried out church-building and pastoral work in Manchuria (also occupied by Japan) and in Sinŭiju along Korea's border with China. Shortly after the end of the Pacific War in August 1945, Reverend Han escaped to the then US-occupied South, like many other church leaders north of the 38th Parallel, which was then under Soviet occupation.

The partition of Korea "devastated the Christian community," according to Donald Clark, for it trapped a great number of Christians in the Soviet-occupied North.[32] South Korea's church history scholarship describes the exodus to the South by the northern Christians during this period to be a pivotal episode leading to the ensuing rapid growth of Korean Protestantism in the second half of the twentieth century. Korea's northern regions, especially those in the northwest where Pyongyang is located, were the original stronghold of Protestant missions, primarily those from America's northern Presbyterian society, to the extent that before the 1940s the city of Pyongyang used to be referred to as the Jerusalem in the East.[33] Between 1945 and 1953, a large number of these Northwest Christians, as they were called, left their homeland, threatened by the revolutionary campaigns, first during the Soviet occupation and later by the North Korean state.[34] An estimated seven to ten thousand of them, nearly half of the total number of Korean Protestants at that time, joined the exodus to the US-occupied South. Once in the South, Reverend Han opened a small church in central Seoul, consisting of several dozen northern refugees. In less than two years, his church had grown to a ten-thousand-strong establishment, which some observers today consider to be the first megachurch in Korea. Other northern-origin settler or refugee churches appeared also in Incheon, a port to the west of Seoul, where many refugees from the northern Hwanghae and Pyŏngan regions found their first new home before some of them moved on to Seoul and elsewhere. The largest exodus took place during the time of the Korean War, especially amid the chaos at the end of 1950 and at the beginning of 1951. This was when the United Nations forces, having pushed the North Korean People's Army to Korea's frontier with China, had to retreat following the intervention of China in the theater of the Korean War at the end of October 1950. During the war, the displaced Northwest Christians rebuilt their houses of worship in Pusan, Daegu, and in other places that had escaped occupation by the communist forces during the latter's rapid southward advance from June to September 1950. Reverend Han's church, Youngnak Presbyterian Church in Seoul, for instance, established its chapters in Daegu, Pusan, and on the island of Jeju at the time.

The Korean War caused great suffering to the Koreans, and Korea's Christian population was no exception. During the North Korean occupation, and especially their hurried retreat from southern territory from late September to October 1950, the People's Army and their local recruits committed a number of atrocities directed against civilians they believed harbored hostility to their revolutionary agenda and war efforts. Although the victims were primarily people associated with South Korea's state administration and its military (and their families), and those classified as class enemies, in a number of localities the so-called revolutionary violence was also waged against members of local churches.[35] In the southwestern region of the peninsula, the advancing South Korean forces met fierce resistance from the remaining North Korean troops and their local recruits, some of whom had by then transformed into partisan groups entrenched in the surrounding hills. In the village of Gurim, the communist partisans set fire to the local school and the village's ancestral assembly hall and Protestant church. On October 7, 1950, according to the local annals prepared by the villagers in 2006:

> Part of the remaining forces of the [North Korean] People's Army, together with some elements of the communist partisan forces who had operated during the period of the People's Republic [the occupation regime] and who had lost their sense of reason, arrested the remaining families of the [South Korean] army and police, people who had been wrongly accused of being reactionaries under the rule of the People's Republic, and the followers of the Christian god.[36]

The annals continue that the arrested were subsequently locked up in a private home, which was then set on fire, not knowing "what crimes they had committed to deserve such a cruelty."[37] Some of the places where civilian massacres took place are now sites of pilgrimage, recognized as historic sites of religious martyrdom.

Institutionally, however, the war also provided a great momentum for vitality and growth to Korea's Protestant movement. In her 2005 book, *The Korean War and Protestantism*, the church historian Yoon Jeongran delves into this milieu of religious revival amid the destruction of war, asking why, in some church circles of South Korea, the experience of the Korean War is propagated as the revelation of Grace, a gift from God.[38] The way in which the 1950–1953 war becomes an event of Grace has many facets to it—most notably, the mystical understanding that the suffering and destruction caused by the war were part of a divine plan to realize a Kingdom of God in Asia—that is, to turn Korea into a Christian nation. As a graduate of Sungsil University, which Reverend Han helped to establish in Seoul to replace the defunct Sungsil Academy of Pyongyang, Yoon is familiar with the history of the Christian movement in the Northwest region that was strong, in the early twentieth century, not only with Presbyterian missions but also with the modernizing elite. These two factors, cultural and economic, speak closely to how Max Weber explained the relationship between the Protestant ethic and the logic of capitalism. Seen in a different angle, they also resonate with Webb Keane's incisive observation, in a colonial Indonesian context involving the diffusion of Dutch Calvinism, on the entanglement between modernist ideals and Christian identity, both of which sublimate, according to him, the purification of the human subject from encumbering forces—whether the preexisting ideology of social hierarchy or the traditional culture of fetishism.[39] Yoon Jeongran depicts how the god-fearing, educated, politically moderate, and entrepreneurial Christians, who were also the economic elite and opinion leaders in Pyongyang and its environs, on encountering and suffering the heavy-handed revolutionary politics in their northern home, especially the sweeping land reform that shattered not only their own but also their churches' economic basis, transformed into some of the most fervent and militant anti-communist warriors in the postcolonial era. The experience of the Korean War further radicalized their politically charged religious commitment. The war was a radical existential crisis for the Christian refugees from northern Korea, understood as a possible permanent loss of a secure home after the loss of their original homes in the North.

This existential status, both religious and political, however, was also hugely advantageous on the south side of the 38th Parallel in the early Cold War. According to Sebastian Kim and Kirsteen Kim:

[The] influx from the north energised churches in the south and encouraged them to grow. [In] the Presbyterian Church, which made up 70 per cent of Korean Protestants in 1954, refugees from the north-west had taken over the church structure, purged what they perceived as a liberal church and deeply divided it as a result of disputes which originated in the north. Other Protestant churches also were subject to similar pressures, although not to the same extent. Now the majority of the churches in the south adopted the north-west style of Christianity—conservative, self-supporting, self-propagating, hard-working and vehemently anti-Communist.[40]

The US Military Government saw the Northwest Christian refugees as the natives it could work with. These were people who shared with Americans Christian values and enmity against God-denying communism—in contrast to many other native political leaders they encountered in Korea whom that government regarded as too left-leaning or too nationalistic (meaning, in this context, putting the ideal of national liberation ahead of the imperative of struggle against international communism). Some of these native Christian leaders were educated in America and therefore spoke their language. These included the Princeton-educated nationalist leader and Methodist Elder Rhee Syngman, who became the first President of independent South Korea in August 1948. A vastly disproportionate number of Christian leaders joined Rhee's cabinet, and Rhee kept the Northwest group as a close collaborator (and instrument) for his rule (1948–1960)—as did the US Military Government before him (1945–1948)—although in the later years of his rule, the Northwest Christians came to fall out of Rhee's favor (see below).

It also happened that the establishment of the US Military Government meant the return of the American mission activity to Korea, which had been discontinued during the Pacific War.[41] Some members of the Military Government were children (or grandchildren) of the early American missionaries in Korea, and these people helped provide the Korean church leaders with a privileged access to the Military Government. This connectivity between American missionaries and Korean church leaders was not limited to the sphere of postcolonial Korean society and politics but increasingly took on an international character. Church leaders in nascent South Korea fast resumed and strengthened their ties to their religious counterparts in the United States and, through it, developed access to public opinion and the policy circles. In this regard, Yoon discusses, at length, the international network forged in the 1950s between some of South Korea's church leaders and groups, on the one hand, and, on the other, Carl McIntire and his strongly anti-communist, religiously fundamentalist movement (whose frequent street-march slogan was: "God-Yes, Communism-No")—a political religious movement whose legacies continue to reverberate in both the United States and South Korea today.[42]

Reverend Han Kyung-chik and his close associates interacted with McIntire's fundamentalist group, which is known to have cleared the ground for the rise of the New Christian Right in the United States, as well as with Billy Graham and his neo-evangelical network.[43] Although these two American clerics are depicted to be have had many disagreements in the history of American evangelicalism, their differences are relatively less evident in the history of Korean Protestantism. In the latter, both of them are depicted as voices against the so-called liberalism, a stand typically associated with the prominent post–World War II international ecumenical organization, the World Council of Churches. The shades of difference among these postwar streams of the international evangelical movement are complex; here, suffice it to mention that they all had formative impacts on post–Korean War South Korean society and politics.[44] It is known that the Northwest Presbyterian circles had long been under the strong influence of the biblicism and anti-liberal theology of John Gresham Machen, a noted American fundamentalist cleric and theologian in the early twentieth century. The influence of McIntire-style militantly anti-communist positionality was felt most strongly during the Korean War and in the immediate postwar years, mostly at the time of Rhee's rule. Graham-style neo-evangelicalism became increasingly forceful in the ensuing era of rapid industrialization and urbanization under Park Chung-hee. When Park's authoritarian political rule subsequently met fierce societal resistance in the 1970s, the country's liberal church leaders and groups emerged as important actors in the resistance movement (for political democracy and for workers' rights). Then the voice of the World Council of Churches and especially the support from the National Council of Churches in the United States became increasingly familiar in South Korean society and politics, primarily via their Korean counterpart, the Korean National Council of Churches.

In view of these developments, we may then conclude that the entrenchment of American power in Korea, after 1945, was much more than political and military but also had a strong religious character. This process involved the partitioning of the decolonizing nation into two separate state entities and the subsequent outbreak of civil war between these entities, which brought a radical existential crisis to Christian communities. Under these conditions, the struggle against communism as a holy war against the God-deniers was more a reality in this Asian outpost of the Cold War than the way this idea is discussed in the literature on the religious dimension of post-WWII American politics. Moreover, even today the legacies of the struggle are far from being a thing of the past.

In October 2013 the World Council of Churches (WCC) held its tenth world congress, this time in Korea's southern port town of Pusan. The keywords for this meeting were peace and reconciliation, addressing, in the Korean context, the hopeful rapprochement between the two Koreas. In the run-up to the meeting, South Korea's Protestant communities and their leaders were embroiled in vicious disputes as to the propriety of this meeting being hosted in Korea. The disputes were particularly acute between the country's two separate Presbyterian groupings, a schism that dates back to the late 1950s, involving conflicting views of the Korean church's relationship with the WCC.[45] These disputes between the ecumenicals (or liberals) and evangelicals (or fundamentalists) had a complex background; for our purpose, it suffices to mention that some in the evangelical grouping accused the WCC of being an appeaser of communism (as well as a propagator of liberal theology), so the idea of the Korean Presbyterian Church joining the WCC was regarded as an act of appeasement. Some of these issues of the old postwar period were rekindled in 2013 in relation to the Pusan congress. Rallies and church meetings were held to denounce the "communist" WCC, and protests were staged throughout the week-long congress meeting outside the venue. New issues were added to the protest in 2013. Most critical was the accusation that the WCC tolerates non-heterosexual love relations. There were also other issues, such as the organization's commitment to interreligious dialogue, the related critical approach to militant proselytizing activity, and encouragement for interchurch dialogue between the two Koreas, which were understood by some opponents of the WCC as proofs of the organization's overtly liberal and pluralist orientation.

These troubles in Pusan did not attract much attention from the general public in South Korea, as they concerned the relatively narrow circles of Korean Presbyterians. The following event was different, however. In 2016, amid the public and political crisis that eventually led to the impeachment of the then head of state, Park Geun-hye, the eldest daughter of Park Chung-hee, a large crowd gathered daily in Seoul's city center to protest against the Parliament's impeachment move. Prominent in the protest group were elderly churchgoers carrying three flags: South Korea's national flag *taegŭk-ki*, the Stars and Stripes, and the Star of David. Referred to as the Taegŭk-ki Army, their rallies have since become an integral part of Seoul's cityscape and of what observers call South Korea's "public square politics." It is not clear what the blue Star of David was meant to represent—whether the modern state of Israel (as is the case in the prophetic vision of today's Christian Zionism) or the biblical episode about the freedom-seeking Israelites (as McAlister explains in relation to situations in the mid-twentieth-century American South). We spoke to a fair number of regular Taegŭk-ki rally participants and failed to get a clear answer on this. The same goes for the Stars and Stripes, whose meaning in the rally was never clear to us; whether it addressed the world's most powerful nation or a nation that became the most powerful in the world in the Grace of God. The same was the case with the *taegŭk-ki*, which features symbols of ancient oracles (which originate from Korea's ancient indigenous religiosity as well as, in part, from Daoism). Was this meant to be the emblem of the state of South Korea or was it, instead, a sign and call for God's Grace and power—the power that will one day actualize a reunified Korea as a Christian nation? A year later, in August 2017, the well-known Texas cleric Robert Jeffress, one of President Donald Trump's evangelical advisers who delivered prayers on Trump's inauguration day, issued a statement in which he professed: "God has given Trump authority to take out Kim Jong Un." This was the day after Trump made fierce warnings to Pyongyang on August 8 that its nuclear challenge to the United States would be met "with fire and fury like the world has never seen." Jeffress explained that "when it comes to how we should deal with evil doers, the Bible, in the Book of Romans, is very clear: God has endowed rulers full power to use whatever means necessary—including war—to stop evil."[46] Throughout that summer month, the same verse from the Book of Romans was often heard from the Taegŭk-ki Army loudspeakers.

FIGHT COMMUNISM, FIGHT IDOLATRY

We have discussed the bold claims of some scholars that United States foreign policy in the early Cold War era was, in part yet in a significant way, a product of religious thinking or what William Inboden calls the "diplomatic theology of containment."[47] We do not question that for the United States the Cold War confrontation had an element of religious crusade—against "the devil we knew" and with "atomic bomb in one hand and the cross in the other."[48] Nor do we doubt that such formative ideas in the ideological battle as freedom (as in Eisenhower's "freedom in the world") would make more sense if seen as a "translation of religious language and symbols" into secular politics.[49] As critics mention, however, it is important to remember that the inception of religious language and ideas in secular power politics occurred within the environment of modern constitutional politics that takes the separation of politics from religion and state from church as one of their cardinal rules. This entails that religion was within and without politics, at one and the same time, and that it is this duplicity in the relationship between politics and religion, rather than the primacy of one over the other, that should be the focus of Cold War culture studies.

The last point applies to the historical context of partitioned Korea. South Korea's first state leader, Rhee Syngman, was clearly a Christian leader, not merely in the sense that he was a believer but also in that his vision for an independent Korea had a strong evangelical element.[50] Rhee's early state-building activity was radically and disproportionately affirmative of Christian social leaders and forces; his stand against the communist North during the Korean War was more radical than a rollback strategy and had a strong crusade element. However, he was also a shrewd and calculating political actor in relation to the United States as well as to his domestic opponents and competitors. It is argued that this explains why, in the last years of his rule, Rhee fell out with the radical Northwest anti-communist Christian group, as he believed it was becoming too influential.[51] Kim Il-sung, the founding leader of North Korea, had an eminent Christian family background, on both maternal and paternal sides, and was sympathetic to church communities in the early days of state-building in the northern half. When the northern Protestants began to challenge the communists and the Soviet occupying power that supported them, however, he had no issue with waging aggressive, often violent power struggles against the church.[52] Unlike Rhee or Kim, Park Chung-hee was no Christian and had no credentials as a Christian leader. If anything, he embodied the particular vision of modernization that takes the military institution and the militarization of society as the paramount driving force for it.[53] For Carter Eckert, this vision originates from Park's intimate experience of Japan's expansionist militarism in Manchuria.[54] When he executed a successful coup in May 1961 against the short-lived democratic rule following Rhee's 1948–1960 authoritarian regime, Han Kyung-chik and some other church leaders quickly declared their support for Park and ran a public diplomacy campaign with their contacts in the United States accordingly.[55] John F. Kennedy's administration initially had some doubts about Park, not least because he had a background in Korea's communist movement. The endorsement from South Korea's most trusted and strongly anti-communist church leaders helped soften and eventually deflect these doubts. By the time Kennedy was sworn in as president in 1961, moreover, America's Cold War politics in Asia had come to concentrate more on what Michael Latham calls "the right kind of revolution": economic modernization of the Third World as the key bulwark against international communism, turning away from the relatively more military-focused containment strategy of the previous Truman and Eisenhower administrations.[56] The Kennedy administration believed that it was time for South Korea to have a strong leader who could fight against communism by means of economic takeoff and growth, not an authoritarian politician such as Rhee, under whom postwar South Korea had shown a miserable economic performance. Park indeed subsequently launched an aggressive economic modernization campaign starting in the second half of the 1960s, and he kept the supportive Christian leaders close to himself, in part, to maintain friendly relations with the United States. South Korea's Christian community, in turn, thrived under Park's rule (1961–1979), as Billy Graham stated during his 1973 visit; Park's rule saw one of the highest growth rates in the history of world Christianity, in both the number of converts and churches.

In view of what is said above, we may conclude that political interests in religion were relatively more radically political than religious in the Cold War's peripheral outposts such as in post–civil war Korea—irrespective of whether the same can be said of the metropolitan center of the global conflict such as the post–World War II United States. In his important 1963 essay "Christians and Anti-communism," Reverend Han asserted:

> Christianity and communism cannot coexist. Some may think that democratic countries and communist countries can coexist as they do now. However, Christianity and communism cannot coexist within an individual. In other words, a Christian who is pro-communist is an impossibility. . . . Hence, we need to be resolute. Only we Christians can fight against the Red Dragon of Communism. Non-believers may carry on living, following the Red Wind and changing accordingly. However, this is not possible for us Christians.[57]

The above point about the primacy of politics resonates somewhat with Rotter's conclusion on the US–South Asian relations from the late 1940s to the early 1960s—that early leaders of postcolonial India and Pakistan had much more programmatic attitudes to international affairs compared with the leadership in the United States at the time, such as that of Truman, who allegedly had a religious mindset and held a religiously defined view to America's Cold War enemies.[58] Alternatively, we may consider the issue of religion and politics in a broader view and conclude that in modern politics, political interests necessarily involve concerns about the place of religion in politics, whether in the geopolitical center or in the peripheries, or in nominally secularist societies or otherwise. What makes Korea's early Cold War experience distinct, compared with that of the United States and even those of postcolonial South Asian nations, however, is that this experience involved occupations by two powerful and mutually hostile state actors, the United States and the Soviet Union, which eventually led to a vicious civil war, whose brutality was akin to that of a religious war.

The last is cruelly illustrated in the hidden, tragic history of the displaced Northwest Christian community before and during the Korean War. In April 1992, Reverend Han Kyung-chik received the Templeton Prize in Berlin. This is a prestigious award, given to public figures who contributed to "progress in religion" or "discovery of spiritual realities."[59] The award on this occasion was in recognition of Reverend Han's lifelong commitment to reconciliation between the two Koreas, as well as to charity and social-welfare activities. In announcing the award, the Templeton Foundation highlighted also Rev Han's contribution to the remarkable growth of church communities in South Korea and to these communities' reaching out to Asia, Africa, Europe, and the Americas with their own missionaries. The praise included the mention of Rev. Han's church in Seoul as "the largest Presbyterian church" in the country, as well as his dedication to improving the lives of the displaced and the poor.[60] The timing of this award was significant—marking the end of the Cold War shortly after the disintegration of the Soviet Union, and taking place in the formerly partitioned, now reunited city of Berlin, whose recent history was emblematic of the rise and fall of the bipolarized world order. Given to one of Korea's most prominent religious leaders who had a northern-Korean origin, the award conveyed the hopeful message that what had happened in Berlin might soon be witnessed in Korea. In his award-receiving speech, Reverend Han ended his discourse with a story that spoke of his vision for peace:[61]

Far down in the southern tip of Korea there is a small town called Yosu. A small Presbyterian church and a hospital for lepers were located there. In 1948 a band of communists revolted and ruled the town for two days. During that riot, pastor Sohn Yang-Won was away and his son, a high school boy, was alone in his house. The communist band invaded, found him to be the pastor's son, and killed him right away. The communist revolt was stopped in a day or two and order was restored. Those students who had helped with the communist uprising were also arrested and tried in court for their crimes. Pastor Sohn, having heard the story, felt very sorry so he went to the court and pleaded to pardon one particular student. But the court would not. The final settlement was that the pastor promised that he would adopt the convicted student as his own son and also promised to raise him and educate him. Two years later the communists in North Korea invaded the South and, at one time, occupied the most part of the South. They also occupied the small town Yosu where pastor Sohn lived. They arrested him as well as his adopted son. The story goes that pastor Sohn appealed to the Communists, telling his own story of love. But the communists did not listen and finally killed him and his adopted son, the former communist boy. So we have three graves beside that small Yosu church even now. Pastor Sohn is an example of the kind of love the world needs,—that kind of love which can forgive even enemies. That is the kind of love which can help bring world peace.

During a prayer meeting organized in his honor back in Seoul, Rev. Han reflected on a time long before the Cold War and made a confessional remark about his life during the colonial era. He said he had sinned—like many other church leaders of the time, he had given in to the colonial power's idolatry, the imperial state-Shinto worship that was imposed on colonial Korea. The news about Han's confession shocked church communities across South Korea. The struggle of Korean Christians against Japan's colonial political religion takes a prominent place in the history of the Korean church; it has also been a vexing and explosive issue in the postcolonial era, a major source of disputes and divisions between different denominations and other groupings as to who remained faithful and who did not, as citizens of the Kingdom of God in relation to the "idolatry" of the Japanese empire. These disputes continue to this day, as does the broader issue of political collaboration with colonialism in South Korea's public realm. We will have a chance to briefly look into these disputes later in this book; for now, it suffices to mention two critical questions relating to the conception of colonialism as the coerced worship of an idol and, therefore, an assault on a Christian's fundamental ethical integrity.

Both of these questions broadly relate to issues that are discussed in the literature of Cold War history today, especially that on decolonization and the Cold War—that is, the complications caused in the political process of decolonization by the bipolarization of global politics. They also speak of the particularity of the Korea question in global Cold War history. First, the defeat of Japan in the Pacific War was a liberating event for Koreans, as it was for the people in China, Vietnam, and many other countries in Asia and the Pacific that were under Japanese military occupation. For the Christian Koreans, the event was even more liberating and celebratory because the defeat was achieved by the United States, a Christian nation. Korea's Protestantism was, in origin, an American Protestantism, initiated mostly by American missionaries at the turn of the twentieth century.[62] For Korean Christians, therefore, the end of the Pacific War meant not only freedom from colonial rule but also, equally important, liberation from the idolatry of imperial Japan to which they had been subjected before 1945. The last constitutes Korea's distinct historical experience in comparison with other decolonizing nations in Asia and Africa. In the latter, the colonial power was typically a European or Western power whose politics of civilizing mission involved the diffusion and imposition of Christianity on the indigenous population and society. For Korea's Christians, in contrast, colonialism meant the opposite—namely, a crisis in their religious freedom and the imposition of an alien political-religious ideology that went head-on against their religious morality. For those in the southern half of the partitioned Korea, where American military rule replaced Japan's colonial rule, the change was a liberating experience—the return of the light of the Gospel after many years in darkness. For those in the northern half, however, the end of the dark era was the beginning of another era of darkness—initially the militant atheism of the Soviet-style communism which soon came to involve a different form of idolatry, the cult of personality.

The militarization of the Cold War standoff, and the violent manifestation of this condition in the years leading to the outbreak of the Korean War in 1950, profoundly affected the communities of displaced Christians from the North. During a series of crises in South Korea in the late 1940s, many different actors, especially the youth groups who called themselves the Northwest Youth, were brought into the terror and counterinsurgency activities in southern Korea, first by the US Military Government and later by the South Korean state, after the Military Government handed power over to the latter in August 1948.[63] Most infamous was the youth group deployed to the island of Jeju, near Korea's southern maritime border, amid the crisis of popular protest against the Military Government beginning in March 1947. The crisis escalated to full-scale counterinsurgency warfare after the island's small group of poorly armed communist partisans initiated a concerted assault against several police outposts in April 1948—a state of exception that lasted well into the end of the Korean War in 1953. The 1948 crisis in Yosu (Yŏsu), mentioned by Rev. Han in his speech cited above, was closely connected to the uprising in Jeju—having been triggered by the mutiny of a South Korean army unit that refused to be deployed to Jeju for counterinsurgency operations. The Northwest Youth joined the counterinsurgency war in Jeju as paramilitaries and waged exceptionally brutal terror campaigns against the local population. The core group of the organization originated from a youth group at Reverend Han's refugee church in Seoul.

Another broadly related incident took place in October 1950 in Sinchŏn in Korea's northern Hwanghae region, the former home of some of the Northwest Youth. At that time the United States' approach to the Korean War was changing from containment to a rollback strategy and the war was transforming into a full-blown confrontation between the United States and China, following the intervention of China in the conflict. The last was China's reaction to the crossing of the 38th Parallel by the United Nations forces in the beginning of October 1950, following the amphibious assault against the enemy-occupied Incheon led by Douglas MacArthur (see Chapter 2). The tragedy of Sinchŏn occurred during the brief occupation of northern Korean territory by UN forces, and especially during their chaotic retreat in the face of the Chinese forces. Although this incident, which is known to have killed more than thirty thousand civilians, had a complex background, it was, to a significant extent, a vengeful act by the Northwest Christian youth militants against their former neighbors and other locals whom they believed were responsible for the sufferings that their families and other Christians of the region had endured under the communist repression.

South Korean novelist Hwang Sok-yong wrote a fictional account of the massacre in Sinchŏn. Titled *The Guest* (Son'nim), it renders the tragedy as a result of two imported, foreign-origin ideologies (Communism and Christianity—thus, the idea of "guests") in lethal confrontation.[64] Consisting of twelve chapters corresponding to a typical organization of *kut*, Korea's traditional shamanic rite, the story's title also refers to a particular type of shamanic rite that used to be popular especially in Korea's northern regions, the *son'nim kut*, which was meant to protect people from infectious diseases such as smallpox. In this context, *son'nim* (guest) is a deliberately respectful address to the alien disease-spreading spirit, intended to soften this malicious spirit's ferocious destructive power by making it feel as though it were an honorable and respectable entity. Hwang's composition of the story in accordance with the structure and esthetics of shamanism, which he regards as Korea's ancient and indigenous religious form, is deliberate in that it intends to contrast the "alien" ideology and religion with the authenticity of Korea's traditional popular religious culture (or even possibly to contain their power and influence in the latter's cultural force). Seen from a different angle, the esthetics of shamanism takes up a prominent place in the social history of Jeju, in the aftermath of the political violence of 1948–1953 that devastated numerous communities. For the islanders, as we will see in the next chapter, shamanism has long been a vital means, throughout the postwar years, with which they could grieve for lives lost and somehow live on with the wounds of the vicious violence that penetrated deep into their everyday lives. This violence was waged in the name of a righteous struggle against communism and, for some, also as a vengeful act against the violence to which they were subjected in a radically different context and in a place far away from the island.

We may ask whether a locally confined cultural form such as shamanism can be a meaningful subject for deliberation on religion and the Cold War. The following chapters demonstrate that it indeed can be, as meaningfully and legitimately as global Christian evangelicalism. This accords with the idea of religion (as a system of symbols) that Geertz put forward in his collection of essays mentioned earlier, which, among others, seeks to transcend, as Jane Monnig Atkinson rightly observes, "a conventional distinction between world religions and traditional religions."[65] The inclusion of shamanism in the story of the global Cold War, moreover, can bring Cold War history to have a deeper historical trajectory than is often assumed—not merely to the post–World War II period, when the alliance between the United States and the Soviet Union began to be fractured, but also to the much earlier era at the end of the nineteenth century that William Appleman Williams defined as the onset of the American Century.[66] The deeper time frame is also evident in the recent initiative in anthropology to engage with Cold War history, which introduces reports on Hawaii, Puerto Rico, and the Philippines in parallel with the effects and "affects" of American power on societies in the Asia-Pacific region and Latin America during the second half of the twentieth century (that is, in the historical horizon of the Cold War according to the common, conventional understanding).[67] Moreover, this pioneering initiative throws light on aspects of contemporary global history that have been scarcely touched upon by historians of the Cold War—such as the displacement of indigenous Americans in the United States and Canada during the Cold war and, indeed, the work of "the mission" in the double sense of this term noted earlier, incorporating both the secular-geopolitical and the religious-cultural expansion. In the Korean historical context, the end of the nineteenth century is when American missionaries first came ashore at the Incheon harbor to subsequently launch a powerful diffusion of the Good News. Their effort was part of the larger wave to spread "'universal' faiths through much of a 'pagan' world," and, as such, involved a militant struggle against what they saw as the idolatry and superstition of traditional Korea.[68]

2

THE AMERICAN SPIRIT

Of the refugees who left their homes in the western coastal region of what is now North Korea during the 1950–1953 war, many settled in the harbor town of Incheon, west of Seoul. The city was a principal gateway for people arriving in fishing boats through the sea routes around the small islands found in the peninsula's West Sea, the area known also as Hwanghae or the Yellow Sea.[1] Before the partition of Korea into two separate states in 1948, the city and islands had historically been part of a larger common coastal region, including the coastal communities of the Hwanghae (Yellow Sea) province, now in North Korea. Many of the displaced northerners were members of the Presbyterian movement, a tradition strong in Korea's northwest regions (which include Pyongyang, North Korea's political center) since Protestantism first arrived in Korea at the end of the nineteenth century—again primarily through the gateway of Incheon.[2] However, many other refugees were "secular," having no specific institutional religious affiliation, of either Eastern or Western origin, although their secular status did not mean that their everyday lives were without aspects of religiosity. Unlike the Presbyterians, who were primarily urbanites, including the Pyongyang-based cultural elite acquainted with Western knowledge, these secular refugees were mostly from rural and coastal communities where religiosity was inseparable from their mundane world of kinship and locality (see Chapter 6). In contrast to the Presbyterian exiles and refugees, who quickly reestablished their church communities in Incheon and Seoul, for these non-Christian refugees, displacement meant not only the loss of their homes but also a deracination from their familiar traditional village world where a multitude of spirits existed alongside the human residents. Shamanism had long been integral to this secular yet spirited landscape; in Incheon, it continued to play a part in the lives of the people from Hwanghae and elsewhere in the northwest region.

We saw in Chapter 1 how the experience of the Korean War and related displacement from home affected the northern Presbyterian community and, more broadly, Korea's Protestant movement as a whole. The Korean War involved the forceful military intervention of the United States, and the city of Incheon maintains a number of monumental sites relating to this history. Featuring prominently in this story is General Douglas MacArthur, who commanded the United Nations forces in the Korean conflict during the war's initial, critical period. Since the war was an existential struggle for South Korea and MacArthur made a formative contribution to this struggle, this American general has a prominent place in the story of the Korean War as told in South Korea. The war was an even more critical struggle for survival for Korea's Christian communities—in the face of forces that denied their very *raison d'être*. We saw an illustration of this in Reverend Han Kyung-chik's recollection of the communist violence and Christian martyrdom (see Chapter 1). Against this background, in certain circles of South Korea's Protestant community, MacArthur's place in Korea's modern history is particularly crucial, and even assumes a manifestly religious character. He is akin to a modern crusader in this account; a defender of the Kingdom of God against the menace of the god-denying and church-destroying forces. A publication titled *MacArthur Who Triumphed with Prayer* (2014), for instance, defines MacArthur as a puritan fighter who defended freedom and Christian values with the power of faith—a true Christian "who understood that it was his vocation as a puritan to defend against communism and to protect Christian beliefs."[3] In the foreword to this book, a prominent cleric of one of Seoul's megachurches reflects on the relevance of MacArthur's prayers today. He says emphatically that "South Korea is built on prayers. It is a country that was saved by prayers in most critical times. We need to rediscover the greatness of Prayer and hold tight to it. Prayer is our nation's great wealth."[4]

It is interesting to discover, however, that the legacy of the "puritan" American general has found its way into another religious domain that apparently has nothing to do with the puritan tradition. This domain is the displaced shamanism tradition of the northern coastal Hwanghae region, on which we concentrate in this chapter. We ask: If MacArthur is an embodiment of American power in relation to the history of the Korean War, and this power has both secular and religious connotations in contemporary public discourse in South Korea, then how can we explain the General's place in the displaced northern shamanism now established in Incheon? How should we make sense of the assimilation of the symbol of American power in what observers believe is Korea's ancient religious tradition? As we will see, attention to this incorporative process will raise searching questions, on the one hand, about the place of religion in Korea's Cold War modernity and, on the other, about the very idea of foreign power in its popular religious sensibility.

FIVE-COLOR FLAGS

Obangki is a familiar object in the material culture of contemporary Korean shamanism. Consisting of five hand-held flags, each a different color, it is an important instrument of the *kut*, shamanic rites, especially in the ritual fortune-telling. Each color signifies a specific cardinal direction and a set of divinatory meanings as related to the conditions of human well-being. It also represents a certain type of spirits and the specific supernatural power associated with these spirits. For instance, the yellow flag, which stands for the center, symbolizes the vitality of ancestral spirits, whereas the red flag, associated with the southern orientation, usually represents the power of mountain deities. In a typical *obangki* divination, the shaman interprets the meanings of one or more flags blind-picked by the client. The chosen colors are supposed to help map the client family's health and business prospects by showing which spirits might respond to the family's specific wishes and how strongly they would do so. It is not surprising, therefore, that most people who solicit a *kut* usually show acute interest in the five-flag divination. One can even argue that these clients are willing to endure the long and costly ritual for the sake of those moments in which they can test their luck and fortune with the bundle of the red, white, yellow, blue, and green spirit flags. *Obangki* is a compass for the spirit world, reaching out in all directions to all classes of the animate entities within it; within the act of ritual divination, it is an important means of communication between humans and spirits.

Similar objects exist in the secular domain of traditional Korea: For instance, the instrument of military pomp in the Chosun dynasty era is also called *obangki* or *daeobangki* (great five-direction flags). These traditional military artifacts may feature different animal symbols as well as the five colors, which together make up the four cardinal directions plus the middle position. For instance, the turtle is associated with the north, and speaks of the condition and need to prepare for fortified defense in the image of its shell. The five-direction flags in this secular military form are still found today. We saw one version in August 2016, in the southern coastal town of Tongyoung, during the reenactment of a Chosun-era military procession held in memory of Yi Sun-shin, the celebrated sixteenth-century naval commander. Another example would be the opening ceremony for the 2018 Winter Olympics in Pyeongchang, during which a puppet show of the five-directional animal symbols attracted considerable interest.

It is not clear how these two material forms, ritual-magical and secular-military, are historically interconnected. Some practitioners believe that the five-color, five-direction ritual instrument of today's form (not to be confused with the five-color scheme itself, which goes a long way back in the cultural and religious history of East Asia and even further back in that of North or Inner Asia, particularly in today's Tibet and Mongolia) is relatively new to Korea's shamanism tradition, tracing the origin of this object to the turn of the twentieth century.[5] According to this interpretation, the appearance of *obangki* as a ritual device coincided with the weakening of the relevance of *obangki* as a military instrument amid the crumbling of the traditional political order within which the latter object found its meaning. The crux of the argument is that *obangki* shifted the sphere of its symbolic life from historical reality to a ritual world during an epochal change in the constitution of Korea's sovereign order from the long-held traditional dynastic form to the uncertainties of the modern era involving the advent of colonial politics. Although more historical evidence is needed to prove this interpretation, it is safe to conclude that in exploring the symbolic property of *obangki* as a specific ritual instrument, one may consider not merely questions of supernatural power and ritual efficacy, but also issues of political sovereignty and secular authority. This was demonstrated forcefully by the extraordinary initiative of Queen Min (1851–1885), one of old Korea's last queens, who, before being brutally slain by Japanese mercenaries shortly after Japan's victory over China in the first Sino-Japanese War, sought to bring shamanism squarely into defending Chosun's crumbling sovereignty—by building shrine houses in four cardinal locations (as well as in the middle) of old Seoul. She did this in defiance of Chosun's old Sino-centric neo-Confucian elites as well as of its emerging new elite groups pursuing a Meiji-style political reform, some in alliance with the Japanese power.[6] According to Charles Allen Clark, one of the early American missionaries to Korea and an acute observer of Korea's traditional religions, this was an astonishing encounter of shamanism (which had long been looked down upon by Chosun's neo-Confucian elite) with secular power politics (concerning the survival of these elites' cherished Confucian polity).[7] The implication of this encounter between shamanism's ritual power and the vital question of political sovereignty is exactly of a substitutive process mentioned earlier—the symbolic property of shamanism as shown in the five-directional ritual instrument for the secular political cosmology represented by the military instrument of *obangki*. Considering the novelty and audacity of this encounter, it is perhaps no surprise that Queen Min is an important helper-spirit persona today in circles of Korean shamanism (as well as a popular figure in the country's art world, such as in the opera) today, especially among those based in Seoul. This way of understanding *obangki*, attending to both secular-political and religious-symbolic historical trajectories, is also broadly in line with the emphasis in the existing scholarship of Korean religion on the merit of historical contextualization in understanding the evolution of the country's popular religious concepts and symbols—as Boudewijn Walraven argues and as also shown in James Grayson's majestic treatise on Korea's religious evolution in deep political history.[8] Similar issues are explored in Caroline Humphrey and Urgunge Onon's now-classic study of shamanism in history that considers the world of Daur shamanism in Manchuria in relation to the region's turbulent, war-torn political landscape of the 1920s and 1930s.[9] Humphrey and Onon's focus is also significantly on the Daur people's struggle for autonomous existence in the chaotic environment of "competing imperialisms on all sides: by the Republic of China and war-lords, by the Russians looming from the north, by the Japanese advancing from the east, and by the Mongolian communists to the west," and on how their ritual order and imagination changed in that struggle.[10]

One may explore the combined issues of ritual power and political sovereignty with regard to the political condition in the Korean peninsula at the turn of the twentieth century, during which time Korea was powerless in the face of escalating tensions of competing imperialisms in broader northeast Asia, involving the Sino-Japanese war of 1894–1895 and the Russo-Japanese war of 1904–1905. A similar question can be explored in the context of another major military and political crisis in Korea's modern history: the experience of the Korean War following the partition of the nation into two separate political entities in the mid-twentieth century. Here, we will focus our inquiry on the field of contemporary Korean shamanism that has assimilated symbols of American power into the vista of its spirit world. This shamanism is practiced by a group of ritual specialists, originally from the Hwanghae region in northern Korea but now based in Incheon. One of them, Chung Hak-bong, has made prolific use of the traditional five-colored flags. She had a wealth of knowledge about the Hwanghae-do shamanic tradition and is known as a "traditionalist" among some of her colleagues and academic experts on Korean popular religion—someone who put great value on preserving this tradition's authentic ritual esthetic forms. However, Madame Chung possesses an object that would be difficult to define as traditional. Kept in her modest domestic spirit shrine along an old railway in central Incheon, this object consists of five flags: the national flag of Korea plus those of four political entities that have had a great impact on the unfolding of Korea's modern history: China, Japan, Russia, and the United States. Kim Kŭm-hwa is another authoritative figure in the cultural tradition of Hwanghae-do *kut*. In her home in Seoul we found the American flag displayed prominently as part of her spirit shrine. One of Chung Hak-bong's former pupils employs in her ritual performance the portrait of arguably the most famous American known to Koreans from the time of the Korean War: Douglas MacArthur. In the *hwan* or spirit portrait of another ritual specialist, the American General is standing alongside General Yi Sun-shin, Korea's national war hero from the sixteenth century mentioned earlier.[11] The two generals are depicted in the same space of the painting; yet, these figures exist independently from (and in *parallel* with) each other against two separate backgrounds of old and modern naval battle scenes. We will come back to this "parallelist" composition later in the chapter (see also Chapter 6). In the *kut* performance of another Hwanghae-do shaman in the greater Incheon area, the spirit of MacArthur likes to give divinations using South Korea's national flag, which has become part of this shaman's *obangki*.

What is the American General doing in the ritual world of Korean shamanism? Might Chung Hak-bong's five-nation flags, including the American flag, be considered a new form of *obangki*? Notable in the background of Madame Chung, and other Hwanghae-origin shamans of her generation, is her experience of the Korean War. These ritual actors were displaced from their homeland in northern Korea because of the war, and Incheon, the place in southern Korea where they made a new home after the war, is the site of an important event in the Korean War. Is it possible, then, to read traces of this war in Chung's unconventional five-flag artifact? What is MacArthur's role in connecting the historical reality of war to the displaced ritual world of Hwanghae-do shamanism?

FREEDOM PARK

The port city of Incheon, located 30 kilometers west of Seoul, is the site of a key tide-turning event in the Korean War. In September 1950, the town's coast and harbor became the theater for a massive amphibious action by the United Nations forces. MacArthur led the operation against the North Korean forces that were then occupying Incheon and Seoul, as well as much of the rest of South Korea. Known as the Incheon Landing, this successful assault broke the strategic order of North Korea's military actions and contributed to transforming their hitherto triumphant march to the southern reaches of the peninsula into a chaotic retreat to the 38th Parallel, and then further to the border with China—before the situation changed yet again, following China's intervention in the Korean War in October 1950. South Korea's official history of the three-year-long Korean War describes the landing as a pivotal event in the conflict. Incheon now has a public museum dedicated to the story of the Incheon Landing, where pictures of MacArthur, the then-Supreme Commander of the United Nations Forces in Korea, are featured prominently, together with his signature corncob pipe and sunglasses. In recent years, the city has turned Wŏlmido, the site of one of the fiercest fights of the Incheon operation, into a heritage site and tourist attraction. The heritage site includes a tree—the single tree, on a hill in the middle of the island, that survived the heavy naval bombardment of the area. Wŏlmido used to be a small island in the West Sea, located off the coastline of Incheon, before it became part of the city through land reclamation. The South Korean navy, together with the Incheon municipality, hosts a public commemorative event in Wŏlmido each year in the presence of a great number of war veterans and other interested visitors. Dubbed

as the Victory Day of the Korean War, the event includes a modest reenactment of the landing. The island is also well known in North Korea, as it is
associated, in their accounts, with a supremely heroic resistance by the
country's coastal defense forces against superior American firepower. The
Wŏlmido battle is one of the five most heroic and victorious episodes in
North Korea's official Korean War narrative; the 1983 war film *Wŏlmido*
remains one of the country's most important cultural productions.

Although the Incheon Landing is sometimes referred to as the "Nor-
mandy of the Korean War" and has been typically associated in the past
with the military savvy of MacArthur, it is interesting to note that, in recent years, the memorial event has become increasingly indigenous in content. South Korea's public media outlets today emphasize the hitherto
forgotten sacrifice of the country's marine troops and special forces in se-
curing Wŏlmido and other locations along the Incheon coastline. This is
the case with the feature film released in 2016, *Incheon Landing*, in which
the struggle over Wŏlmido is central to the plot. In the memorial gathering
held on the Wŏlmido shore in September 2016, MacArthur was celebrated
along with Yi Sun-shin, the powerful naval commander of the Chosun era
who is a figure familiar to every schoolchild in South Korea in relation to
Korea's war against Japan in the sixteenth century. Today, therefore,
Wŏlmido is an important heritage site of the Korean War and of the war-
forged alliance between South Korea and the United States. However, its
popularity had long been overshadowed by another memorable site in
Incheon's old quarter.

This site is on a modest hill called Ŭngbongsan, overlooking Wŏlmido,
that is widely known for Freedom Park, the public recreation space located
on the hilltop. The Freedom Park premises boast several prominent memorials, including an imposing concrete structure built for the centennial celebration of Korea's opening of ties with the United States in 1882. The area
also holds other historic relics relating to the opening of Chosun, the so-
called Hermit Kingdom, to other foreign powers.[12] Ŭngbongsan and its environs were an exclusive residential area for Westerners at the turn of the
twentieth century. The recreation area on the hilltop is known to have been
the first modern public park in Korea, *Man'guk Gongwŏn* (international
park, or literally, "Ten Thousand Nation Park"). The expression "ten thousand nations" was at that time a popular way to refer to international soci-

Statue of General Douglas MacArthur in Freedom Park, Incheon. Photo by
Jun Hwan Park.

ety.[13] The "ten thousand" speaks of multitude and entirety, and the same is
true with *mansin*, meaning literally "ten thousand spirits," in popular reference to the practitioners of shamanism in Korea. The park's name was
changed to Western Park during the Japanese colonial occupation, and re-
gained its original name briefly after the end of the Pacific War in 1945. After
the Korean War was over, the park's name changed once again, this time to
Freedom Park. The last change was part of the general transformation of
the park premises into a memorial space for the Incheon Landing, especially
in recognition of the hero of this important episode of the Korean War,
Douglas MacArthur. The result includes the erection of a prominent bronze
statue of MacArthur in 1957, which overlooks the old theater of the amphibious assault that took place on September 15–19, 1950.

In 1957, the city of Incheon, as elsewhere in Korea, was struggling to recover from the destruction of the 1950–1953 war. At that time, Ŭngbongsan
was, along with the nearby Chinatown, a cherished recreation area for the

war-exhausted townspeople, bustling with cheap eateries and makeshift fortune-teller stalls. Because of its proximity to the maritime border between the two Koreas, Incheon received a large influx of refugees from northern Korea who, immediately after the war, made up about 30 percent of the town's population.[14] The refugees came especially from the Hwanghae and Pyŏngan provinces along the West Sea coast, a region in northern Korea traditionally with a large Protestant population. Referred to as the North-west Christians in Korea's church history (see Chapter 1), the displaced Christians from this region built new bases in Incheon before some moved on to Seoul and elsewhere to build a powerful evangelical movement and the megachurches that South Korea came to be associated with in subsequent decades. Harboring strong anti-communist sentiments, some of these originally Incheon-based, war-displaced faith groups played a pivotal role in South Korea's postwar Protestant communities.[15] However, the northwest region's tradition of shamanism also found a new home in Incheon alongside this powerful Protestant group, before some of the actors in this tradition expanded their sphere of activity to Seoul. Of the most prominent of these actors, Chung Hak-bong settled in Incheon, whereas Kim Kŭm-hwa made her mark in Seoul, establishing a strong network of clients in the metropolis and eventually earning the title of "National Human Cultural Treasure," an official honor bestowed by the government. Kim later became an international celebrity. Among her numerous overseas activities was the 1982 *kut* she performed in Knoxville, Tennessee, held in celebration of the centenary of Korean–US diplomatic relations (see Chapter 3). Both Chung and Kim belong to the Hwanghae shamanism tradition, and the *kut* they perform have many elements in common. However, people who have known them both for many years sometimes remark on stylistic differences in the rituals they perform: Chung's *kut* was traditionalist in the sense that her rituals are faithful in form to the old northern Hwanghae shamanism tradition, whereas Kim's performances were both traditional and creative in that the events she prepared for the public rather than the clients, although structurally authentic, employed creative esthetic paraphernalia that appealed to urban and international audiences. In this chapter, we will draw attention to another interesting difference between these two eminent practitioners of Hwanghae shamanism. Kim Kŭm-hwa did not shy away from the fact that her spirit world included a symbolic element of American power, as illustrated earlier by the presence of the American flag in her shrine room (see Chapter 3). In contrast, Chung Hak-bong's relationship with emblems of American power has been a more discreet and guarded subject, known only to her immediate circles of clients, students, and friends, even though Chung also kept the American flag in her shrine room as part of her cherished collection of five-nation flags. This symbol of American power, which she found difficult to disclose, was connected to Freedom Park and the statue of the American general that dominates that public space.

THE AMERICAN GENERAL

Douglas MacArthur is sometimes referred to as a man of the American Century.[16] Historians have varying opinions as to when this so-called American Century began. Henry Luce famously coined the expression on the eve of the Unites States joining World War II in 1941—the war that the nation, uniquely among the Western powers, was to fight on both the European and Asian fronts by the end of the year.[17] Luce said: "The 20th Century is the American Century. . . . It is not only in the sense that we [Americans] happen to live in it but also ours because it is America's first century as a dominant power in the world."[18] Other observers, especially those focused on transatlantic history, would favor an earlier date—notably, when Woodrow Wilson decided to send his troops to the trenches of northern France in 1917. In *Empire as a Way of Life*, William Appleman Williams goes further to highlight the last decade of the nineteenth century when the United States joined Europe's imperial club, after its victory in the Spanish–American War.[19] In Williams's scheme, the United States' colonization of Hawaii and the Philippines are among the pivotal episodes in the making of the American Century. Douglas MacArthur's life history is compatible with all these different renderings of the American Century. MacArthur was a crucial actor in America's Pacific War. After the war was over, he governed the defeated, US-occupied Japan.[20] His job in Japan included overseeing the dismantling of Japan's imperial sphere, which, for Korea, meant the American military occupation of what is now South Korea. Shortly after war broke out in the Korean peninsula in June 1950, MacArthur took on the role of Supreme Commander of the United Nations forces in Korea. MacArthur's life history is also closely intertwined with the longer versions of the story of the American Century. He was the adviser to the Philippines government before the imperial power of the United States was challenged there by Japan,

Asia's unique regional imperial power. He took part in World War I, which, while being a formative event in modern European history, had broader relevance globally. The era constitutes the beginning of the long process of decolonization in Asia, the Middle East, and Latin America, as well as that of the rise of the United States as a global power.[21] Before World War I, MacArthur toured Japan, China, the Philippines, and elsewhere in Asia, sometimes as an aide to his father, Arthur MacArthur Jr., who served as the military governor-general of the Philippines during the Philippine–American War (1899–1902). These tours were followed by other short tours of duty, including to the Panama Canal in 1912.

Douglas MacArthur's experience in Panama made a mark on the ethnographical literature. The Kuna Indians of Panama are renowned for their powerful figurative art, *nuchukana*. Created for divinatory or healing purposes, Kuna shamanic art includes a multitude of amulets in anthropomorphic and other forms and in various sizes.[22] Some of these amulets feature white colonists, which include a quite sizable wood carving that is supposed to represent Douglas MacArthur. Michael Taussig explores these figurative forms in the logic of negative dialectics.[23] His interpretation focuses on the politics of reproduction: specifically, the political relationship between an image and the substance the image reproduces. Taussig does not see the gringo amulets as syncretic artifacts that bring together indigenous form and foreign identity. The introduction of the foreign into the indigenous form, according to him, should be considered not merely in a formal analysis, but rather with reference to the concrete context within which these objects are made to exist. The context is healing rituals in which the Kuna shamans confront ailments in indigenous bodies resulting from the exposure of these bodies to the white-ruled, exploitative labor regime. The whites are powerful, economically and politically, and the gringo amulets confront their secular power by transforming it, within the healing rite, into a curative power. Taussig's analysis presents two forms of power in confrontation (without a move to synthesis, so the idea of negative dialectics): secular politico-economic power versus magical-ritual power. Their sources are the same—the world of the whites, in this case—and the art of the shamanic rite consists, crucially, in the appropriating of the foreign power to protect the indigenous body from the abuse of that very power. Taussig defines this process as the magical power of mimetic art.[24]

Similar ideas are explored in Danilyn Rutherford's approach to the images of *amber beba* (big foreigners) found among the Biak in Irian Jaya.[25] These images from Indonesia's West Papua include a figurative depiction of MacArthur in relation to his historical foothold on the island and its environs during the final years of the Pacific War. Rutherford asks how the "big white foreigners" became a source of magical power in the Biak eschatology. Another important, broadly relevant example is Seong-nae Kim's work on the images of American power appearing in Jeju shamanic discourses.[26] Her work focuses on the legacies of the political violence experienced in the chaos of the early postcolonial years of 1947–1949 by the people of this beautiful island on Korea's southern maritime border with Japan. Referred to as the April Third incident, the violence against the people of Jeju was committed mainly as part of the counterinsurgency warfare waged initially by the US Military Government that was occupying the southern half of the Korean peninsula at that time, following an insurrection by a small group of local communists in April 1948. Kim highlights an oversized, intimidating image of an American serviceman appearing in the shamanic initiation dream of her key Jeju informant, asking how this dream imagery relates to the shaman's ritual healing power in relation to the many Jeju families whose genealogical pasts hold deep scars from the 1948–1949 violence. Kim's careful analysis of Jeju shamanism's confrontation with the history of postcolonial state violence suggests a point that resonates with Taussig's, relating the image of American power (the political and military power of the American occupation of postcolonial Korea) to the efficacy of Jeju shamanism's ritual healing power. Like Taussig, she emphasizes the politics of alterity found in the process of mimetic representation: the fact that the imperial power actualized in the ritual healing is radically different in character from the secular imperial power that the ritual organization appropriates. The former is life-affirming and life-regenerating, in contrast to the power that is brought into the ritual as part of mimesis, which approaches life as a mere object of power and is thus indifferent to life's inalienable authenticity and sovereignty.

We shall return to the question of sovereignty at the end of this chapter and with reference to Yim Suk-jay and his powerful political theory of Korean shamanism (see also Chapters 5 and 6).[27] For now, it suffices to mention that the above discussions on the inception of American power into indigenous ritual worlds deal with the dynamics of symbolic formation in the contexts of colonial or postcolonial domination: a situation that accompanies a radical hierarchy of power between the indigenous world and the foreign forces. Concerning this chapter's principal subject matter, which relates to the milieu and legacy of a civil war, however, the interpretative strategy may require further deliberation on the relationship between indigenous symbolic forms and the foreign power.

MacArthur takes up a controversial place in Korea's modern history and memory. At one extreme, he is considered a hero of South Korea who, at the outset of the Korean War crisis, rescued the country's political existence from the peril of annihilation. His heroic status is in large measure anchored in the episode of the Incheon Landing and part of the broader public understanding of the history of the war-forged Korean–US alliance. This understanding was strong in South Korea during wartime. An illustration would be a prayer that addresses MacArthur as the savior of the Korean nation, which was popular among some Christian groups in postwar South Korea.[28] On the other hand, MacArthur is considered responsible for some powerfully regrettable episodes and legacies of America's Korean War. These include the indiscriminate aerial bombing campaigns that the United States waged in North Korea (and in parts of South Korea), and the threat of thermonuclear attack against enemies, the legacy of which continues to reverberate in today's Korean peninsula in terms of North Korea's determined pursuit of nuclear armament. They incorporate a broader critical understanding of the United States' place in the unfolding of modern Korean history: notably, its formative role in the partitioning of Korea in the first place. Gregory Henderson observed that "there is no division for which the US government bears so heavy a share of the responsibility as it bears on the division of Korea."[29] The tragedy of Korea started, according to Bruce Cumings, when "Dean Rusk first etched a line at the 38th parallel in August 1945."[30]

These radically diverging understandings of American power's place in modern Korean history are sometimes played out in Freedom Park where, in recent years, competing civic groups have clashed with one another in front of the park's MacArthur statue.[31] Some of these groups consider the statue a stain on Korea's public space and have called for its removal, whereas the opposing groups have protested against this appeal, regarding it as treacherous and benefiting North Korea. The controversy surrounding MacArthur's legacies has resulted in a curious situation—that the American

General's statue in Freedom Park was being guarded round the clock by Incheon's municipal police forces. While this is regarded as regrettable and cumbersome by the locals who frequent the park, the situation probably represents the health and strength of South Korea's political democracy today. Such conflict would have long been unthinkable under a military-led authoritarian rule, during which time criticizing American power was considered synonymous with supporting communism. This also illustrates how different the public understanding is today of US–Korean relations, compared with during the early postwar years. For instance, some of the youth who took part in the student-led democratic uprising in April 1960, which led to the toppling of South Korea's postwar authoritarian regime led by Rhee Syng-man, brought flowers to MacArthur's statue, which was then considered a symbol of liberty, after hearing that Rhee had stepped down.[32] Such an act of tribute would be unthinkable to the majority of South Korean youth today.

The important point is that in the historical context of the Cold War, es-pecially in that of a civil war that took place as part of global political bipo-larization, unlike in the context of colonial domination as in colonial Panama, the symbolism of the empire's power may go beyond the horizon of alterity between the foreign and the indigenous. In Cold War politics, the dominant foreign power did not necessarily cancel out the indigenous so-ciety's formal sovereign existence, but was often exercised through the lat-ter. The relationship of domination, in this political world, was justified by the existence of an external ideological enemy and the imperative of a com-mon existential struggle against that enemy. Accordingly, American pow-er's foreignness had to be negotiated, for a society like South Korea that was at the frontline of the global ideological struggle, with the foreignness of its ideological nemesis—in this case, communist North Korea. In the process of rapprochement between the two Koreas at the beginning of the 2000s, therefore, critical new understandings of the character of American power advanced in the South Korean public world. Likewise, when relations be-tween Seoul and Pyongyang deteriorated in the following decade, the for-eignness of North Korea was once again magnified while the old ties of alliance with the United States were reemphasized. In short, in the Cold War historical context of the Korean peninsula, past and present, the character of American power remains a contentious subject in South Korean society, in sharp contrast to the public's clearly negative and critical view of the legacies of Japan's old colonial rule. Nowhere was this reality manifested more clearly than in the controversies surrounding the memorial for MacArthur in Freedom Park.

Freedom Park is an important site of memory in today's South Korea, involving contrasting views of the country's experience of national partition and civil war as part of the advent of the American Century. Beyond this domain of secular politics and public history, MacArthur's place on the hill in central Incheon is also of considerable importance for the tradition of Hwanghae shamanism that found a new home in Incheon after the Korean War. In this tradition's postwar magico-religious geography, the American General has a much more localized existence (see below), compared with his controversial place in the wider secular public sphere. Moreover, the General's place within this tradition closely relates to the experience, among those who follow the Hwanghae shamanic tradition, of a war-caused, radical displacement from home. It needs to be made clear that displacement in this context refers primarily to the specific process in which a locally grounded spiritual, cosmological form had to adapt to a new landscape, after having been uprooted from its familiar locale. The dislocation may have had a political character; in this case, the fact that shamanism in northern Korea had confronted an existential crisis in the postcolonial years, under North Korea's anti-religion, anti-superstition campaigns. Considering this fact, Hwanghae shamanism's displacement from home may be considered from the angle of religious freedom, an angle that is strongly part of the discourse of northwest Korean Protestantism during and after the Korean War. Seen from this angle, one may be tempted to approach the American symbols found in post–Korean War Hwanghae-origin shamanism primarily as representations of American power in the secular sense—that is, the power that helped defend the southern part of Korea from the menace of communism or the foreign power that has dictated the fate of Korea in recent history.[33] However, this is not what we will do in this chapter. On this issue, we agree with Taussig and Kim that the concept of power in shamanism's ritual world cannot be reduced to the notions of power relations that are familiar in the secular political world.[34] We argue that what appears to be American as part of the spirit world is not the same as the "American" as in the American Century. For an understanding of the unique place of this foreignness in the spirit world, we need to turn to the spirit of MacArthur.

General Im Kyŭong-ŏp in the West Sea, General Yi Sun-shin in the South
Sea, General MacArthur in Incheon's coastal water—let us go to obtain
their agreement!

—Chung Hak-bong

The above is part of Chung Hak-bong's invocation of invitation to the
multitude of spirit-helpers during her *kut*. Variations of this invocation
are used by several other shamans who follow the Hwanghae-do *kut* tradition in the greater Incheon area. Hwanghae shamanism is known to
have a particularly pronounced esthetical form involving warrior helper-
spirits, compared to other regional shamanism traditions in Korea. Some
specialists in Korean popular religion associate this distinct character of
Hwanghae shamanism with the position of Hwanghae and its environs in
traditional Korea as a border region with Korea's northern neighbors, a
region that has historically been vulnerable to the chaos of war. The
Hwanghae region is located along the northeast coast of the West Sea, an area
that has traditionally been active in seasonal croaker fishing; accordingly,
the Hwanghae shamanism tradition is also renowned for its elaborate fish
fertility ceremonies. Im Kyŭong-ŏp, an official of the seventeenth-century
Chosun court, is an established shamanic spirit-helper whose legends
bring together the work of a warrior and that of wealth generation through
fishing.

Legend has it that General Im was on his way to China to help the declining Ming order defend itself against the rising Qing. His men were
hungry, and so were the residents of an island where his ships stopped en
route. In the face of this dire situation, General Im came up with the inge-
nious idea of a fish trap, with which the islanders were able to catch many
nutrition-rich yellow croakers and thereby overcome hunger and depriva-
tion. Croaker fishing and trading then became a vital economic activity for
the islanders and for people in coastal Hwanghae, as well as in other communities on the West Sea coastline that lie along the migration route of the
yellow croakers. In gratitude, people began to erect shrines in honor of
General Im, some of which still exist today on some islands near the maritime border with North Korea. These include Yŏnpyŏng, an island northwest of Incheon and west of North Korea's Hwanghae coast, which keeps a
shrine for General Im on a small hill. Today, the island also has a museum

General Im Kyŭong-ŏp, spirit portrait. Photo by Jun Hwan Park.

that tells the history of the area's once-prosperous croaker fishing industry and commerce.

Some of those who learned their ritual knowledge from Chung Hak-bong make pilgrimages to these shrines. One of them, Incheon resident Lee Jong-ja, routinely renews her spiritual ties to General Im through a visit to Im Kyŭong-ŏp's shrine on Yŏnpyŏng Island. She regularly visits shrines along Korea's South Sea coast dedicated to Yi Sun-shin as well, often with her own disciples. Madame Lee usually begins her shrine tour with a visit to MacArthur's statue in Freedom Park. This is in part because the spirit of MacArthur is her tutelary helper-spirit; however, it is also because the American General is, for her, a locally seated shamanic deity, just as the coastal water of Incheon, with which MacArthur is associated, is more immediate to her spirit world than the relatively distant maritime sphere represented by General Im or General Yi. Lee Jong-ja came across occasional difficulties during her journey, especially with the local authorities who disapproved of activities of religious character at sites they considered to be part of a public historical heritage. These difficulties were particularly pronounced in Freedom Park. MacArthur's statue in the park premises is a modern memorial, whereas the shrines for General Im and General Yi resemble, in form, a traditional ancestral or communal house of worship from the Cho-sun era. The park has recently been the site of disputes between contending civic groups, who gathered on the premises with clashing messages over the significance of the site of memory. For both groups, who were mostly from outside the locality, irrespective of their diverging views, the local shamans' prayer and offering-giving activity at what they considered a war memorial appeared strange and was unwelcome. For Lee and her students, however, Freedom Park was no different from any other sacred site they regularly visited to renew their ties with spirit-helpers. Although she often visited several other places as part of her annual pilgrimage, her engagement with the place of MacArthur and those of the two other generals has been a must in Lee's long career. In her view, an amicable relationship with these spirit generals is vital for her fame and popularity, as it brings luck both to her and to her regular clients.

Korea's traditional popular religious knowledge demonstrates two distinct types of supernatural spatiality in relation to the maritime world. One type concerns the master of the sea, the Dragon King, whose authority in the maritime environment is believed to be universal and all-encompassing (and, at the same time, particular and place-specific; see Chapter 6). In contrast, the second type points to a specific maritime sphere that is defined in terms relative to a marker in the terrestrial world. All the warrior spirits mentioned above belong to this second type. For instance, the spirit of Mac-Arthur is identified with the coastal water of Incheon and, as we will see shortly, with the hill where his statue is located. Moreover, these spatially limited shamanic spirits' places in the maritime world entail a certain movement between the sea and the land. In the case of Im Kyŭong-ŏp, this movement takes on an alimentary and economic character. This spirit persona is referred to as the master of croakers (*jogisin*) in places on the West Sea coast, and his magical power is associated primarily with fishing activity. The differentiation between these two types—the mythical universal deity figures such as the Dragon King, and the historical sphere-specific personae that speak of movements between the sea and the land—is made evident in the Hwanghae fish-fertility rites. These rites present the human relationship with the sea in the terms of generosity (the sea deity's gifts to humans) and reciprocity (offerings made by humans to the generous giver to show their gratitude). The persona of Im Kyŭong-ŏp is introduced to this broadly reciprocal relationship between the sea world and the land-based community in the image of *homo faber*, as it were—the inventor of the technology used to exploit the sea's resources. Referred to as a spirit entity that is anchored in the maritime world of the West Sea, General Im's actual existential sphere is, nevertheless, firmly placed in the land-based community of the human world. For this reason, in part, in communities that commemorate Im's power and efficacy such as on the island of Yŏnpyŏng, the General's spirit is worshipped as part of the community's ritual for mountain deities. The same is true in Sŏsan along the West Sea coastline, where the spirit of General Im shares with the coastal community's existing mountain deity the honor of receiving ceremonial offerings during its *sansin-je* (ritual for the mountain deity).

The legendary history of Yi Sun-shin is relatively weak in the symbolism of economic disposition. This history is anchored in the territorial defense against foreign invasion and in the related idea of sovereignty. The sea-to-land movement here consists of *hwa* (disaster), rather than *bok* (fortune), as was the case with General Im's legends—in other words, the flow of life-threatening and life-destructive forces against which the spirit general must wield his spirit sword and spear to help the community protect their lives. General Yi's close figurative association with the imperative of territorial sovereignty is far from being a property of shamanism alone. In the heart of South Korea's capital, Seoul, a statue of Yi Sun-shin stands imposingly on the city's most prominent boulevard, with Korea's old palatial complex behind his back. General Yi is a much more recognized and publicly prominent historical figure than General Im in South Korea today. In the popular religious realm, however, Im has deeper roots and a relatively more established status than Yi. General Yi's sphere of supernatural influence is identified primarily with the peninsula's southern coastal world. This is in line with the fact that his historical legacy as a heroic defender of Korea against Japan's invasion is concentrated in Korea's South Sea. In contrast, the realm of Im's spiritual power covers nearly the entirety of Korea's long West Sea coastline, which corresponds with the migration routes of the yellow croaker and the related, seasonally shifting, fishing locations. The existence of the MacArthur spirit, as noted in the song of spirit invitation cited above, is much more localized, being restricted to Incheon's coastal water. This way of imagining his realm is grounded in the historical event of the Incheon Landing and in the broader history of the Korean War, within which this military event finds its meanings. The amphibious action involved a movement from the sea to the land, an important element in the legend of General Im. There might be another possible point of correspondence between the two warrior spirits. Earlier we mentioned Im's status as being one that is anchored in a local mountain, as well as a spiritual entity whose magical power is identified with the maritime sphere. Interestingly, it may be possible to see MacArthur's statue on Incheon's Ŭngbongsan in the light of the hilltop shrine for General Im, as a place for a principal local spirit in Incheon that is equivalent to the place of General Im in the historical context of Hwanghae. This is far from speculation if observed in relation to the way Lee Jong-ja and her students perform their pilgrimage. The analogical relationship between the religious topography of Im and that of MacArthur opens an interesting question as to the rise of the American General as a shamanic helper-spirit in the first place. To explore this question, however, it is first necessary to come to terms with the war-caused displacement of the Hwanghae-do shamanism tradition from its familiar landscape in the northern coastal region.

It is not clear exactly when MacArthur's spirit was first introduced into Incheon's Hwanghae-origin shamanism. According to Chung Hak-bong and others, it was sometime in the 1960s, most definitely after the statue was completed in 1957 and probably following MacArthur's death on April 5, 1964 (in Washington, DC). Chung belongs to the first generation of Hwanghae-origin shamans in South Korea; however, she considers herself to be part of a second generation, because her teacher and spirit mother, Woo Ok-ju, also left her homeland to settle in Incheon at the very beginning of the 1950 war. Woo Ok-ju taught others, and Chung, in turn, has tutored many trainees during the postwar years. Today, the genealogy of Hwanghae shamanism in South Korea has extended to a fourth generation. Evidence suggests that by the third generation—that is, the generation after Chung Hak-bong's—the spirit of MacArthur had become an established element in Incheon's Hwanghae shamanic world. Several of Chung's spirit daughters had by then come to take the spirit of MacArthur as their tutelary and/or initiatory spirit. Such connectivity has intensified in the subsequent generation. Conditions were different in the time of Chung Hak-bong, to whom MacArthur, although being part of her ritual world, remained so as one of a multitude of spirit-helpers. How things were in the first generation remains largely unknown. Chung Hak-bong argued that her teacher Woo Ok-ju and other older generation Hwanghae shamans in Incheon had not meaningfully related to "the General in Freedom Park," as she often referred to MacArthur. However, we find that even in the first generation, practitioners of shamanism in Incheon were obliged to relate to traces of American power, though this was not necessarily by means of MacArthur's spirit.

The organization of a Hwanghae-do *kut*, especially that familiar to Woo Ok-ju and her line of descent in terms of ritual knowledge, is known to contain a particularly vigorous performance involving warrior spirits, compared to other regional traditions of Korean shamanism.[35] A typical Korean *kut* introduces a multitude of spirits, moving from one distinct category of spirits to another. The idea is that for a successful *kut*, one has to entertain all the spirits of different cosmological dispositions, even though the specific purpose of the *kut* may highlight a particular class of helper-spirits and their functional prominence. For instance, warrior spirits may take on a relatively higher relevance than other spirit entities in a curative rite (as these spirits are believed to be effective in fighting against illness-causing spirits), whereas in a ritual intended mainly to augment the client family's business prospects, the performance with spirits associated with the generation of wealth, typically referred to as *daegam*, can be relatively more pronounced.[36] The performance with spirits that belong to the category of *jang'gun* (warriors or generals) is, therefore, only a small part of the complex and long ritual procedure. However, in the Hwanghae-do tradition, as already noted, the place of these warrior spirits goes beyond a functionally specific, structurally partial existence within the ritual process, to the extent that the efficacy of the entire ritual is sometimes measured in terms of the *jang'gun* spirit's power and its realization.

The Hwanghae shamanic ritual tradition is, however, also known for its particularly vigorous performance involving the *kun'ung* spirits. Coming typically at a later phase of a *kut*, this performance invites the crowd of anonymous spirits and provides offerings to these hungry, unremembered spirits that have not had the privilege of being entertained in the previous phases of the ritual. The *kun'ung* signifies spiritual existences that are other than the shaman's established kindred spirits or spirits that are not an integral part of the client's kinship identity. For this reason, the *kun'ung* performance usually takes place outside the space in which the shaman and her clients interact with their invited kindred spirits. The anonymous spirits may include some illness-causing or misfortune-causing spirits, which are, although related to the client family in ties of kinship, not so in the family's understanding. These spiritual entities can be categorically ancestral in the sense that they are related to the client family in ties of kinship. However, they are non-ancestral spirits in the practical sense that their historical existence is not remembered by the family. Despite these specificities, the most typical image of the *kun'ung* is as spirits of nameless soldiers fallen in battlefields.[37] The Hwanghae shamanic rituals for *kun'ung* spirits display a powerfully vivid and vigorous scene in which the performer, under the influence of these hungry spirits, devours the bloody raw meat offered to her. While this is underway, the glimpse of a look of satisfaction on the shaman's face can be a haunting experience for onlookers. The look delivers the pleasurable sensation, on the part of the anonymous spirits, that their marginal existence in the spirit world is recognized by the living.

Our interlocutors in Incheon broadly share the view that rituals for *kun'ung* spirits are a particularly challenging task in that locale. On several occasions, Chung Hak-bong told us about her daunting experience taking up the *kun'ung* phase of a *kut* that she performed with her teacher Woo Ok-ju when she was a relatively novice shaman. The *kut* took place in Wŏlmido, the site of a fierce battle during the Incheon Landing. She vividly described her awe in confronting the immensity of the spirit crowd that day, the intensity of this crowd's collective interest in what she was doing, and in the offerings prepared for the occasion. Since then, in her career, she performed *kut* on many other occasions on this former coastal battlefield, in the capacity of presiding shaman and together with other younger shamans under her tutelage. According to Chung, in the transmission of ritual knowledge from Woo Ok-ju, one of the most difficult and most necessary skills for her as a novice shaman was to manage effectively the consolation rite for the crowd of hungry spirits. A similar observation is made by later followers of Incheon's Hwanghae ritual tradition. As noted earlier, some of these actors relate to the spirit of MacArthur as their tutelary helper-spirit and, accordingly, regard the MacArthur statue in Freedom Park as a focal point of spiritual power within Incheon's local religious geography. They developed a host of highly inventive iconography relating to the power and eminence of this novel local spirit-persona. In the *kut* performed by these actors today, the spirit of MacArthur appears in a dazzling array of demonstrative forms: American-brand cigarettes and liquor, a smoking pipe, sunglasses, and a portrait. These forms also include a US Army uniform bought on the black market, and the dance of a shaman wearing this uniform. In parallel with these demonstrative forms associated with the hero of the Incheon Landing, the ritual world of Incheon's Hwanghae shamanism holds other traces of the Korean War. Notable among them is the intensity of the hungry spirits of the anonymous sea dead, demonstrated through the shaman's heavy breathing and trembling body while under the influence of these desperate souls, and the messages of appreciation and gratitude from these nameless beings that the exhausted shaman later delivers.

Jang'gun and *kun'ung* are coextensive categories that are both related to a history of war, although they are dealt with separately within the ritual order. Moreover, some *kun'ung* spirits are considered a type of *jang'gun* spirit, as testified by identities referred to as *kun'ung jang'gun*. What distinguishes these two categories is the dynamics of individuation. All *jang'gun* spirits possess some specific historical characteristics and related individual personalities, which are demonstrated during the *kut* by particular items

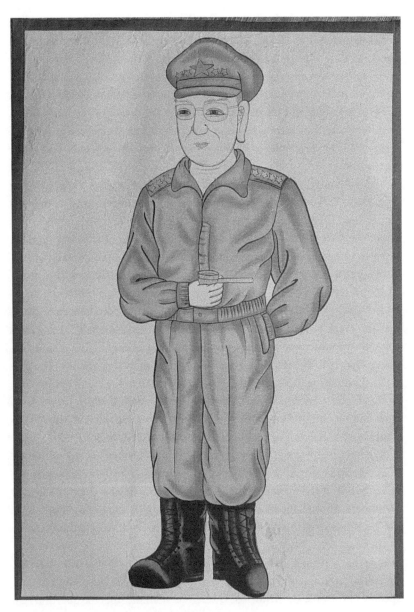

General MacArthur, spirit portrait. Photo by Jun Hwan Park.

of clothing and other material objects—for instance, offerings of foreign whisky or cigarettes are associated exclusively with MacArthur. These esthetic qualities of individuation are absent from the world of *kun'ung*. The ritual for the lost and unremembered souls presents no such personable artifacts or individuated offerings as seen in the ritual phase conducted with the eminent general's spirit. The *kun'ung* are the *demos* of the spirit world, as it were, and their strong presence in the ritual world has been an integral element in the development of Hwanghae shamanism since the end of the Korean War.

One of our principal interlocutors in Incheon, Lee Jong-ja, once told us that "the spirits are history. No spirits exist without history, and we may not understand them without history." She said this while we were conversing about the background in which the spirit of General MacArthur came to settle in her ritual world as a principal helper-spirit. Our conversation is ongoing, and we note that the following is a tentative conclusion. The idea of history referred to here is not in opposition to myth. It is a subtle and open-ended notion about temporal depth that is attentive to both historical events and the preexisting scheme of ideas—akin to what Marshall Sahlins calls the dialectics of event and structure in making history.[38] The idea is that history has both event-focused and structurally shaped properties, and that an understanding of this history requires attention to the contingent events, as well as the existent scheme of ideas and values within which these events turn into meaningful episodes. If we conclude that the spirit of MacArthur is a history, following Lee, what kind of history is this *history*?

We have proposed an understanding of this "history" as a conjuncture of two analytically separate historical trajectories. One of these trajectories is anchored in the events of the Korean War, including the war's locally prominent episode, the MacArthur-led Incheon Landing in September 1950. The prominence of this episode in local history is manifested in the cityscape of Incheon, most notably, in the form of Freedom Park and the statue of MacArthur within it. Related to this locally specific monumental, material-historical heritage of the Korean War, there are other questions that are specific to the postwar history of Hwanghae shamanism. One question that is central to understanding this historical trajectory relates to the experience of displacement and the related imperative to find a home in a foreign environment. We have explored this question in terms of an analogical relationship between two spirit identities: General Im in the old home of

Hwanghae and General MacArthur in the new home of Incheon. We proposed that seen within this historical trajectory in which the subject of historical experience is the tradition of Hwanghae shamanism, it is possible to consider the novice spirit of MacArthur as an extension (or invention) of a traditional shamanic entity, especially that of General Im.

These two historical paths are distinct from each other in a way that is akin to the analytical differentiation between event and structure mentioned earlier, although we believe that they are inseparable in the making of the MacArthur spirit. Another distinction between the two is worth mentioning. In the event-focused, secular historical trajectory, MacArthur's legacies are today a controversial subject, as explained earlier, signifying the merit of the South Korean–US alliance, on the one hand, and, on the other, the hierarchical, negative aspects of this international relationship. Either way, MacArthur is principally an embodiment of American power in this sphere. Along the mythic, structure-focused trajectory, in contrast, MacArthur's place finds its relevance primarily in the context of the local landscape of postwar Incheon and in the extension of Hwanghae shamanism's traditional local pattern of spirited topography. This observation is in line with Carlo Severi's exposition of the carved images of the white people found among the Kuna, including his objections to Taussig's interpretation.[39] Although Severi also finds that the life of these ritual objects is grounded in the Kuna's turbulent historical experience of contact with foreign powers, it is, according to him, equally anchored in traditional Kuna perceptions—notably, that of the forest world which is a space of spirit-caused dangers as well as a vital source of healing power. This world is also where balsa wood, the material for shamanic carvings, originates. Hence, Severi defines the images these carvings display, which he calls "paradoxical images," as *Kuna's* white spirits.[40] We may approach MacArthur in today's Hwanghae shamanism in a similar light. Seen in this way, it is not certain whether MacArthur is an *American* general, an identity that is paramount in the secular historical discourse. MacArthur in the mythic narrative rather has a *Hwanghae* identity of northern Korean origin that happens to have been brought to the new locality in coastal southern Korea.

If the spirit of MacArthur has both secular-international and localized, mythic structural properties, a similar idea can perhaps be extended to the constitution of the material object we introduced at the beginning of this chapter. The object consists of the five national flags in a row that Chung Hak-bong keeps in her domestic spirit shrine in central Incheon. Korea (its traditional flag now representing South Korea) stands in the middle, together with the flags of the four powers that have had great impact on the unfolding of Korea's modern history. On its right are the United States and Japan, and China and Russia are on its left. Like the traditional military object *obangki*, the four foreign territorial entities represented by Chung's five-nation flags encompass four directions: to China across the West Sea, the United States on the other side of the Pacific, Japan across the South Sea and Russia in the north. Hence, the artifact may be considered a representation of the geopolitical relations that have shaped Korea's fate in modern history: in recent times, with China and Russia on one political side, and Japan and the United States on the other. All these political entities have a history of waging war with one another in and around the Korean peninsula since the end of the nineteenth century, and their powers continue to affect the unfolding of events in the region. The city of Incheon, as the gateway for Western and other foreign powers to Korea, keeps the traces of these powers in terms of numerous material heritage sites, especially in and around the Ten Thousand Nations Park, today's Freedom Park. This is a story of brute power politics, a history of the pursuit of power, and of violent wars that were unleashed as part of the contest for power.

On a closing note, we take another look at this artifact and ask whether we can see in it a geopolitical property that is distinct from the secular geopolitical history noted above. In a conversation held shortly before she retired to a care home, Madame Chung returned to her experience of performing *kut* at the Incheon seashore. The occasion was a public event hosted by the Incheon municipal authority, aimed at praying for peace in the West Sea and on the Korean peninsula more broadly. Chung vividly recalled the confusion and fear she felt while confronting the powerful collective of *kun'ung* spirits from the West Sea. She said that these spirits were all hungry and desperate individuals, and that they appeared to be of different national groupings. The collective of these spirits included, according to her, some Japanese *kun'ung* and Russian *kun'ung*, which we understood related to the incidents of the Sino-Japanese War (1894–1895) and the Russo-Japanese War (1904–1905) that took place in the West Sea at the turn of the twentieth century. In the light of this conversation, we speculate whether one may approach the relevance of her five-nation flags from the perspective of the world of nameless spirits, as objects that represent the ruins and living traces of modern history in the maritime world of the West Sea. If such an approach is justified, we note that the world represented by the five-nation flags departs radically from the historical space of geopolitics that is familiar to us. For this world is not one that is formed by modern sovereignty-claiming political entities, imperial or otherwise, but is rather a world of those whose lives were broken by these entities' relentless pursuit of power and whose afterlives in the spirit world constitute a *sovereign* existence, meaningful and powerful in its own right.

Although this observation remains a speculative point, the idea of sovereignty behind it is not. According to Yim Suk-jay, the legendary scholar of the culture of Korean shamanism, Korea's shamanism tradition demonstrates a distinct political theory that he calls parallelism—a theory that postulates subjectively sovereign and mutually parallel existences in all types of spirits and in all the ten thousand spirits.[41] He observes that deities in Korean shamanism have each a unique and specific functional qualification and much more, and that, seen together, they are all equal to and independent from each other (see Chapter 5 for more).[42] Following Yim's insights, for now we may conclude that the symbolic presence of American power is possible in Korean shamanism only to the extent that this power coexists with other powers and respects the unique sovereign existence of each of them. According to Yim, this radically pluralist and equalitarian worldview is embedded in Korean shamanism. A related question is raised by Bhrigupai Singh, who asks in his investigation of roadside spirit sites in the Shahbad district of Rajasthan: "How might a god or a spirit (existing in a pluralistic, polytheistic religious context) inspire us to think differently about sovereignty, or life (that is, from that discussed in political theology that rests on Abrahamic monotheistic heritage)?"[43] Brian Goldstone also asks: "How is it that this single figure [Hobbes's Leviathan] has managed so thoroughly to capture our political and philosophical imagination? . . . How is it, in a word, that sovereignty has become so damn sovereign?"[44] Citing and referring to what the Catholic philosopher Jacques Maritain said during the last days of the 1914–1918 war, Goldstone writes: "[The] concept of sovereignty [which is but one with the concept of Absolutism] must definitely be abandoned. It was no longer appropriate, he contended, to the political spirit of the times. He went on to say that of course we are free to conceive of sovereignty in horizontal, democratic, or in non-absolutist terms."[45] Broadly similar views and aspirations are found in the idea of the international world that prevailed in Korea and East Asia in general at the turn of the twentieth century, as demonstrated by the Freedom Park area's original reference to "ten thousand nations," which celebrates not only the reality of multitude but also the principle of equality among all the constituent units of world society (see Chapter 6 for more). The same idea may apply to the process in which the spirit of MacArthur has become part of the world of Hwanghae shamanism's "ten thousand spirits" after the Korean War. If this is indeed the case, we can add that the point raised by Kim and Taussig on the critical property of power in shamanism is pertinent: The power of the American General in the ritual world is distinct from the General's power as a representative historical figure of the American Century and is quite *un-American*.

3

VOYAGE TO KNOXVILLE, 1982

Today, Douglas MacArthur is an established spirit actor in Incheon, playing a preeminent role in the ritual performance of the local shamanism
tradition that was displaced from the northern Korean region of Hwanghae. In Chapter 2 we investigated this phenomenon in terms of an inter-
play between the historical event of the Korean War, which caused the
displacement, and Hwanghae shamanism's traditional ritual structure
and cosmological form. We argued that the spirit of MacArthur can be
considered an extension of (and substitution for) an old established spirit
figure in Hwanghae shamanism's original habitat in the northern Korean
region. We proposed that, seen in this light, MacArthur is far from being
merely a representation of American power, as some observers see him.
Instead, the spirit general's symbolic property incorporates both a secular political-historical trajectory of a national and global proportion, and
a locally specific, ritual structural condition. It demonstrates a duplex disposition in this regard, and the spirit-helper thrives on this entwinement
of secular historicity and magical formality in its continued historical existence today.

Two further issues arise from this investigation. One concerns the concept of the foreign and the process in which a stranger to the indigenous
world is brought forward as a meaningful symbolic entity in this world.
Korea's popular religious tradition abounds with stories of such transformation. Hwanghae-do shamanism itself involves a plethora of variously
named warrior spirits from ancient China. Another example would be the
cult of Gwan-u (Guan Yu in Chinese), an iconic war hero from China's Three

Kingdom era of the third century. Extremely popular in Taiwan and in Chinese communities elsewhere, including among Incheon's ethnic Chinese residents, the Guan Yu cult is associated with the diffusion of Daoism into the traditional Sino-centered political and cultural world of East Asia. The cult practices are known to have been introduced to Korea during the Imjin War, the Great East Asian War of the sixteenth century involving Toyotomi Hideyoshi's Japan, Yi-dynasty Korea, and late Ming China.[1] The war constitutes the background of the story of Korea's naval hero Yi Sun-shin (who fought against Toyotomi's naval forces), and, seen in a broader perspective of the era that includes the decline of the Ming and the rise of the Qing dynasty, in part as a result of the war, also that of Im Kyŏng-ŏp (whose legend in the West Sea involves his naval expedition to China to help the Ming defend themselves against the Manchus)—that is, both of the two traditional warrior spirits with which the spirit of MacArthur associates in the ritual world of contemporary Hwanghae shamanism. We may thus consider the introduction of MacArthur into this ritual world in relation to the given tradition of openness to foreigner spirits within Korea's shamanism and its popular religiosity more broadly—that is, in complement to the historical perspective that focuses on the specificity of Hwanghae-do shamanism's localized religious landscape before and after its displacement to Incheon.

Before moving to the concept of the foreign existing within a longuedurée history of Korea's popular religiosity, however, it is necessary to first review the spectrum of MacArthur's foreignness in a secular and contemporary historical sense. As we saw in Chapter 2, in Incheon's material culture, MacArthur is closely identified with the history of the Korean War and the role of the United States in it. American power continued to be a formative element in the evolution of South Korean politics and society after the Korean War was over. The same is true, in fact, in the very making of South Korea as an independent political entity since the end of the Pacific War in 1945. The question of what to do with the traditionality of shamanism has been a critically integral element in this political evolution, which in turn has had considerable impact on the everyday life of the ritual actors we met earlier. The idea of *superstition* appears as a powerful and powerfully politicized concept in this historical trajectory, shaping the lifeworld of these actors and changing the moral and cultural landscape of post–Korean War South Korea as a whole.

Incheon's Freedom Park has a host of historic relics. Many relate to the history of Korea's opening its doors to Western and other foreign powers—notably, British, French, German, American, Russian, Japanese, and Chinese—at the end of the nineteenth century.[2] The city is where several eminent American Protestant missionaries first landed in Korea in 1885 and it has several monuments and museums that celebrate the origin of Korea's Protestantism. Freedom Park keeps several other memorials that originate from more recent times. One of them is the statue of Douglas MacArthur, erected in 1957 in memory of this hero of the Incheon Landing by United Nations forces in September 1950, a pivotal episode in the Korean War. A short distance from the statue, the visitors find an imposing monument, erected in 1982 to celebrate the centenary of Korea's opening of ties with the United States in 1882. We saw in Chapter 2 how the emergence of MacArthur's statue into the postwar cityscape of Incheon developed into a significant event in the constitution of Hwanghae shamanism's symbolic vista in its new home in this coastal city. The erection of the centennial Tower for Korean–American Friendship and the broader circumstances in which this memorial came into being were also of considerable significance for Hwanghae shamanism. This is especially the case for Kim Kŭm-hwa, a prominent Hwanghae-do shaman who passed away in 2019. In her memoirs, Kim speaks of 1982 as a decisive turning point in her long career. In the summer of that year, she became one of the first Korean shamans to take *kut* to an international stage.[3]

The occasion was the World's Fair held in Knoxville, Tennessee, where the headquarters of the Tennessee Valley Authority have long been located. Known popularly among the townspeople as Jake's Fair, in reference to Jake Butcher, a banker and local notable who played a key role in bringing the international fair to the town, the event was of great significance for the town's leaders, who hoped the fair would provide a springboard for the recovery of the town and the broader Tennessee Valley from the economic recession of the late 1970s.[4] For South Korea, this event coincided with the centennial celebration of the ties between Korea and the United States, with a treaty on trade and commerce signed in Incheon (which was then called Jemulpo) on May 22, 1882. The centennial celebration involved a

Korean-American Centennial Friendship Tower, Incheon. Photo by
Jun Hwan Park.

number of other events, including the erection of the Centennial Friendship Tower in Incheon's city center, and an equivalent gesture in San Francisco, where emissaries of the king of Chosun had first landed in 1883, before heading on to the East Coast. The Knoxville event was one of multiple events of considerable significance for South Korea; as for the town's notables, the event's significance was primarily economic, as they wanted to demonstrate their ability to be a major producer of nuclear energy, a new energy source that was emerging then. South Korea's participation in the 1982 World Fair was therefore a meeting of Korea's national interest in forging stronger ties with the United States than in the previous era (see below) with the commercial interests of a particular US community. Kim Kŭm-hwa's role in the six-month-long festivity was as a cultural emissary, introducing the American public to an "authentic traditional culture and art from Korea."[5] Madame Kim recalled her time in Knoxville very fondly; she especially remembered one occasion in which the six-hundred-strong audience responded to her performative art with more enthusiasm than she had ever encountered before. She was clearly aware of the significance of taking her *kut* to a foreign country, and of the fact that this was part of an important cultural diplomatic initiative on the part of South Korea. So were her spirit-helpers, according to her, who responded to her invitation at the fair with exceptional vigor and enthusiasm. She was proud to be chosen for the occasion; however, the experience meant a great deal more to her. After Knoxville, she went on to Washington, DC, where she had the opportunity to perform at the country's preeminent cultural establishment, the Smithsonian Institution. She recalled her two-month-long trip to the United States as an exhausting and yet rare liberating experience. In her memoir, Kim writes of her complex feelings about the experience, especially concerning how a tradition, which is regarded in her home country as a backward custom and a superstition to be expunged from society, is disseminated overseas as Korea's proud traditional art, attracting so much attention from foreigners.[6] The trip was a time of freedom for her, she adds—liberation from the social stigma to which she had long been subject. In the end, her voyage to Knoxville was a deeply contradictory experience for Madame Kim, in that she was specially selected to demonstrate an art form overseas as an authentic and worthy Korean culture, which was condemned back home as a tradition with no place in modernizing and industrializing Korea.

Chung Hak-bong, another prominent figure in Hwanghae shamanism who lives in Incheon, reported similar contradictions. In her 2013 media interview, Chung contrasted her past experience of social stigma and discrimination as a performer of shamanism to "the changed world today" in which, in her words, "*kut* activities are even exported to foreign countries."[7] The folklore specialist who interviewed her adds:

> As *musok* [culture of shamanism] began to be recognized as culture and art since the 1980s, [Chung's] *man'gudaetak kut* [a brand of Hwanghae-do *kut*, meaning "the *kut* that protects ten thousand humans from ten thousand misfortunes"] came to be known and performed inside and outside the country. When the *man'gudaetak kut* was nominated [by the South Korean government] as Hwanghae-do's number one intangible heritage in 2006, Chung Hak-bong became the guardian of this heritage.[8]

Many other reports take note of the transition of Korean shamanism from the category of "superstition" to that of "traditional culture and art." Notably, Laurel Kendall makes a trenchant criticism of the concept of superstition as applied to shamanism and its many closely associated local traditions and customary domestic practices.[9] Interestingly, her critical gaze extends to the idea of cultural heritage, which, as is the case in the interview with Chung Hak-bong cited above, is often presented as a more enlightened way to define the existence of traditional popular spirituality in modern industrialized society than the term *misin* (superstition; literally, "false belief").

Kendall's criticism points to several directions. First are South Korea's political campaigns in the 1970s to cleanse what it considered to be the remains of backwardness from social space. In the countryside, the heavy-handed, mass-mobilized political campaign was called the New Village Movement. Kendall's criticism also points to the combatant polemics against superstition or idolatry emanating from some of the then-increasingly powerful evangelical sectors, the growth of which was intertwined with the country's rapid economic growth during the era (see Chapter 1). The militant polemic against superstition (as regards shamanism and other forms of popular religiosity, and by the church as well as by the state) also closely interacted with the era's other powerful militancy—against communist North Korea, which was regarded as a religion-denying and idol-worshipping society—the latter referring to the personality cult of Kim Il-sung, the country's founding leader. For Kendall, critical review is also necessary against some of the moralizing traditionalist discourse that prevailed in the 1960s and 1970s—such as the argument that assigns shamanism to women while placing this allegedly feminized popular religious sphere in contrast to the neo-Confucian tradition that some traditionalists claimed as Korea's true moral tradition. In the conservative interpretation of neo-Confucianism, as explained by Lee Nŭng-hwa, a legendary scholar of Korea's popular religion during the colonial era, shamanism is relegated to the status of "shadowy rituals (ŭmsa)," to place it outside the confines of the public moral sphere and into the domestic interiority in a gendered domestic–public divide and hierarchy (see Conclusion to this volume).[10]

Kendall's insights into the politics of superstition are derived from her long-term observation of changes taking place in a rural village on the outskirts of Seoul, especially those in the life of Youngsu's mother, her key informant and the village shaman.[11] Today the place is no longer a rural backwater as it has been integrated into the urban sprawl of the megacity Seoul. Youngsu's mother is no longer an aspiring novice shaman in a village struggling with poverty, but enjoys economic comfort and considerable fame among her clients. The main thrust of Kendall's account of Youngsu's mother and her village, past and present, is that there is no radical break from the traditional to the modern in it. Youngsu's mother now responds to her urban middle-class clients' aspirations and anxieties over economic security and social mobility, just as she did a generation ago to the village women's myriad concerns and predicaments in an economically struggling, socially conservative (patriarchal) community. Now, as in the past, an amicable relationship with family ancestors appears, both in the kut Youngsu's mother performs and in the ritual production of luck and fortune she oversees, to be of great importance for human well-being. This leads her to refute an overtly rigid separation between shamanism and neo-Confucianism, too, as harmony between the living and the dead also constitutes a supreme value in the Confucian moral education and is displayed prominently in the ritualized act of ancestral remembrance that is central to this moral religious tradition.[12] Kendall does not deny the fact that some formidable changes have taken place in her informant's village over the past generation, and that these socioeconomic changes can generate a particular sense of past and present. However, she warns against interpreting these changes in a one-way-street perspective that encapsulates popular religiosity either in the ideology of cultural modernization or in a traditionalist, gendered moralizing discourse. For Kendall, shamanism is a living culture and a culture in the present in grassroots Korea, historically rooted yet also capable of reinventing itself in changing times. Her conception of tradition and modernity is at odds with both of the prevailing ideologies of the 1970s that have weighed on Korea's shamanism—the state ideology of modernization free from the burden of the backward past, and the equally preponderant sublimation of past heritage exclusive of subaltern religious interests.

Of the era's cultural politics against superstition, the explicitly political dimension calls for some further attention. The life history of Youngsu's mother, as depicted by Kendall, consists not only of a transition from rural poverty to urban economic prosperity but also, as it is for most other people in the profession, it involves confrontation with state power as part of that transition. "There is no more shocking event in the history of Korea's folklore studies (in the post–Korean War era) than the New Village Movement (*saemaŭl undong*) of the 1970s," writes a veteran South Korean scholar in this field.[13] Following the so-called New Life Movement of the late 1960s, the New Village Movement had a complex background in the rapidly changing domestic and international situations of the time. The initiative was principally a rural economic reform program in the context of sweeping industrialization, which involved a mass migration of labor forces from rural to urban areas. It also had elements of an agricultural revolution, which in this context refers to the introduction of biochemically engineered, high-yielding rice crops as well as the infrastructural intervention in rural spaces in terms of road-building, modernization of the hygienic order, and new housing construction—elements that are widely observed in the construction of economic modernity elsewhere in Asia.[14] The way this drive of rural reform became a concern for scholars of folklore such as the observer cited above, however, relates to the fact that the drive purported to radically transform the mentality and spirituality of rural Korea, not merely its material conditions.

It is reported that amid the New Village Movement of 1971–1981, more than two thirds of the hitherto existing, communal popular religious sites and built objects were systematically obliterated from rural Korea. This wanton destruction of the cultural heritage was orchestrated by the state hierarchy. However, it also involved zealous local administrative bodies that competed with one another to show their efficacy in this policy domain, as well as the mobilized village youth and other grassroots organizations that the state instituted locally as part of the national campaign. A news report from 1973 depicts a situation typical of the time. Titled "300-year-old Rotten Customs Are Blown Away by the Warm Wind of Saemaŭl Undong," the article tells of the heroism of a lone local activist in a seaside village. The man singlehandedly succeeded in bringing the enlightening spirit of the New Village Movement to the villagers, who had "long lived in terror of superstition, believing that should they anger Yongwang [Dragon King, master of the maritime world in traditional thought], lightning would strike them from the heaven."[15] In an admirable leap of faith, the article claims, this conservative village, which annually held about twenty community rites on behalf of various guardian spirits, decided to part with their shameful past by discontinuing these rites. The village assembly also decided that, in the future, the communal fund that the village had kept for hosting its annual fishing fertility rite should be invested in New Village activities instead. The report notes that when the residents met to discuss these matters, their assembly had an air of solemnity. No one raised objections, and the decision to end the tradition of the fishing rite was endorsed unanimously. It is not difficult to imagine why this was so, taking into consideration the fact that, by 1973, the New Village campaigns were not merely a rural development scheme but had also became a powerful instrument of societal control under the rule of a political dictatorship.[16]

This wave of destruction did not spare urban space, although here it is sometimes difficult to tease out the destructive force of the state's coercive spiritual enlightenment campaigns from the effects of urbanization and urban development. For instance, the veteran folklorist Yang Jong-sung writes of *Sasin-dang* (the Shrine for Envoys) in Seoul. Having been one of the four prominent sites of popular pilgrimage and shamanic religiosity in old Seoul, the shrine came to be thoroughly uprooted from the lives of townspeople starting in the early 1970s.[17] In bustling central Seoul, it is not difficult today to find old residents eager to tell the history of their neighborhood. During our research in Jong-ro and its environs, we heard many stories about the anti-superstition drive in the 1970s. One story was about the felling of *jangsŭng*, the traditional guardian figures of a community, by a group of local church activists. Another story concerned our interlocutor's grandmother, who, having long had a close relationship with a neighborhood fortune-teller, was forced to travel to a far peripheral corner of the city to meet and consult with her. The fortune-teller left the neighborhood in 1970, after running into trouble with some neighbors who disapproved of her practice and eventually reported her to the police. Kim Kŭm-hwa reported a similar experience. The *kut* was held mostly in the client's home in the past, unlike today, where it can be hosted only in a specially designated place way away from residential areas. On one occasion, in Seoul's increasingly hostile environment to her trade in the early 1970s, Kim had to halt her *byung-kut* (curative rite) and make a quick dash from her client's home, though the back windows, when the police raided the place after being informed of the event by her client's neighbor. Against this background, one can sometimes hear during a *kut* event today statements such as "Saemaŭl Ghost, I command you to step aside!," declared as part of the calls against misfortune-causing spirit entities. This command is sometimes paired with "IMF Ghost, step aside!" (IMF here refers to the Asian financial crisis in 1997–1998 that hit South Korea's social economy hard).

Kim Kŭm-hwa recalled the era of the Saemaŭl campaign as the greatest test of her long career, as it resulted in social exclusion and related feelings of indignation on her part against unjust treatment. She makes it clear that Saemaŭl was unlike other similar campaigns she had undergone earlier in her career (see below), for it was based on a bottom-up mass mobilization, not merely the abusive power of the state, which closed in on her from all corners of her everyday life. Her memories involved troubles with state authorities but also with some church groups—such as the incident of a small ritual she held on a hill (not to attract the attention of the police) being surrounded by a group of protesters from a local church, reciting aloud the part of Matthew on Satan-chasing (Matt 12:28). There were other challenging times, however. Notable was her confrontation with another state authority—the revolutionary power in northern Korea during the 1950–1953 war. Encounter with this power and the difficulties it caused were shared broadly by nearly all the first-generation Hwanghae-origin shamans in Incheon; it was also one of the main reasons for their leaving their homes in northern Korea. Many other townspeople of Incheon, originally from western areas of northern Korea, where Christianity had a strong foothold during the first half of the twentieth century, had similar experiences. North

Korea waged an aggressive assault against religion and religious communities during the war and its postwar reconstruction era, especially against those communities that challenged their political mandate.[18] In the early postcolonial era, the North Korean revolution initially did have elements of pragmatism, seeking to bring these communities into a united front for state-building. The Soviet power that supported this process also applied a more conciliatory approach to Christian communities in Korea than it did in the East European or Baltic regions, not to mention in its own society. According to Charles Armstrong, this was because the Soviets realized that the Protestants, despite their relatively small numbers, had a considerable voice in the northern society and tremendous organizational capacity in the space of decolonization.[19] After the Korean War, however, the North Korean revolution began to define religious questions increasingly in a dogmatically Soviet way—ignoring the immense difference between pre-revolutionary Russia, where the Orthodox Church exerted enormous political influence, and postcolonial situations in Korea, which traditionally is a predominantly secular and religiously pluralist society having no such state–church collusion. The civil war of 1950–1953 radicalized the fault line between the revolutionary state and what it regarded as counter-revolutionary religions, in part because of the intervention in the war by a "Protestant" country, the United States, that frustrated North Korea's ambition for national unification. Added to the northern state's association of Korean Protestantism with America's imperial power (and hence, as the enemy of the Korean revolution) was the historical fact that Protestantism was introduced to Korea, at the turn of the twentieth century, primarily by American missionaries.[20] In this story of American power in Korean religion involving northern Presbyterian communities and their displacement to the South, the struggle against superstition had multiple aspects and fronts.

Kim Kŭm-hwa's memoirs highlight two historical periods as times of great hardship. One was during the Korean War, especially during the early days of the war, when her home region of Hwanghae, like other places of North Korea, was briefly occupied by the South Korean and United Nations forces. By October 1950, North Korea's People's Army was in disarray and in hurried retreat to north of the 38th Parallel and then on to the country's border with China. This followed the army's swift and triumphant takeover of nearly the whole of South Korea, from July to September 1950. This change was facilitated by the successful amphibious landing of US and South Korean forces in Incheon harbor in mid-September 1950. Evidence suggests that during this brief and turbulent time, which led to a reversal of the tide following China's intervention in the Korean conflict at the end of October 1950, the retreating northern military and political forces conducted a clean-up action against people whose loyalty to the revolutionary regime and war efforts they doubted. These allegedly subversive elements included people who held religious beliefs or practiced "superstitions." By that time, Kim Kŭm-hwa was an established *mansin* in her village area on the western coast, having been chosen by the village to conduct the important *dong-je*, a community-wide ritual on behalf of the village's guardian spirits. Facing the prospect of being publicly labeled as a believer in superstition, and trying to escape persecution, Kim volunteered to join the local revolutionary Women's League. In another episode, Kim underwent an intense ordeal of interrogation (including sessions of self-criticism) in the hands of the local party cell, after a modest healing rite she held in a neighbor's house had been caught by the party's security network and its webs of neighborhood self-surveillance system called *inminban*.[21] Fortunately for her, a longtime client intervened and rescued her from captivity. The woman's son was in a position of considerable authority in the local Workers' Party, and she and her family had benefited from Kim's curative ritual before.

Political repression against shamanism did not only come from North Korea's revolutionary state authorities, however. Kim's testimony makes it clear that the brief occupation of her northern homeland by the southern paramilitary forces during the Korean War, at the end of 1950, was an equally terrifying time, and the intimidation she underwent during this time was in some ways more menacing than any she had experienced earlier in the hands of the northern revolutionary vanguard and youth groups. In her memoirs, she recalls a life-threatening moment during the occupation, in the presence of a South Korean state security officer (whom she calls a CID officer), to whom communism and shamanism were indistinguishable and belonged in the same pit of abominable superstitions.[22] The CID stands for the "criminal investigation department," plainclothes personnel in the British police forces. In the American system, it refers to the United States Army Criminal Investigation Command, whereas in South Korea, during the Korean War, the same acronym was used for the special branch of the military specializing in anti-communist surveillance and counterinsurgency combat activities. The organization carried out sweeping arrests and summary killings against alleged communist suspects during the very early days of the Korean War in areas of South Korea that were at risk of being run over by the rapidly advancing northern communist army. It is known that about 200,000 civilians, who were citizens of South Korea, fell victim to this generalized state terror against society, whose rationale was to prevent these individuals from aiding and collaborating with the enemy.[23] The assault against civilian lives continued throughout the war, later changing in character to a punitive action, directed against those who were suspected of having collaborated with the northern communist forces during their occupation of the South. It is no surprise then that the so-called CID was an object of great fear for numerous families and communities in South Korea during the war. What we learn from Kim's memoirs—she is not alone in testifying to the brutality of South Korea's CID—is that this organization's terror against society also extended to places in northern Korea. We also learn that the state violence such as that committed by the South Korean CID was not merely against ideological and political suspects but also could be against any individuals and social groups that the state machinery regarded as not conforming to the specific form of political modernity that it aspired to realize.

Shamanism was under pressure from the state-driven anti-superstition politics on the other side of the Cold War border, too, and during the time of state-building in the southern part of Korea, although this does not appear in Kim's testimony as it was not part of her life experience. In his report "The US Military Government's Religion Policy," the historian of religion Kang Don-ku explores the strong institutional favoritism shown toward Christian leaders and groups by the US Military Government in Korea (1945–1948), and again under South Korea's first postcolonial government headed by Rhee Syngman, who the military government helped bring to power.[24] This favoritism was manifested in a number of ways, including the introduction of a disproportionate number of Christian leaders to key state administrative positions, legislation about the so-called recognized public religions (thus excluding other social religious sectors), and the empowerment of northern-refugee Protestant leaders and youth groups as part of the militancy against communism. It also involved the introduction of the institution of (Christian-only) chaplaincy into the nascent Republic of Korea army, a measure whose significance in the history of Korean Protestantism was later manifested in the aftermath of the Korean War when the number of church attendees began to explode in South Korea. Proselytizing in the army was extended to the enemy, in the camps for captured Korean and Chinese combatants. When the country's Parliament first opened on May 31, 1948, Rhee asked a parliamentarian and Methodist preacher to open the historic event with a prayer. The prayer lasted for about ten minutes, at the end of which all the parliamentarians stood up and collectively joined it. This extraordinary happening was irrespective of the fact that at that time only about 2 percent of the southern Korean population identified themselves as Protestants. The imposition of this affirmative policy, which privileged the church in such a predominantly secular and religiously diverse society as Korea, evolved in the southern half in parallel with the emergence of a broadly Soviet-style anti-church and anti-religion politics in the northern half. The North's postwar anti-religion politics eventually crushed all religions, as they were all considered opiumate and superstitious beliefs; the South's Christianity-privileging politics might be considered pro-religious freedom, but only in a highly selective sense, thereby creating its own derivative moral hierarchy of what makes the true worldview versus what constitutes a superstition. In 1947, the Seoul Metropolitan Police (of the US Military Government) declared a "war against superstition" with an astonishingly belligerent message:[25]

> Nowadays superstitious deeds such as mudang's *kut*-plays and *pudakgŏri* [derogatory reference to shamanic rituals] are prospering, thereby exerting grave evil influences in the domain of social re-education. This situation cannot be ignored. Acknowledging that it is difficult to obliterate long-inherited customs at a single stroke, the Metropolitan Police has chosen fifteen sites in different parts of the city and issued a stern directive that, from now on, all prayer activities must be held only within these designated places. If, despite our directive, we discover any noisy *pudakgŏri* and *kut*-plays are held in private homes or mudang's own houses within the city boundary, these will be punished severely and we shall thoroughly purge them.

The above demonstrates that popular religions were under considerable political pressure on both sides of partitioned postcolonial Korea. The ensuing Korean War was a life-changing experience for Kim Kŭm-hwa, and other Hwanghae-do shamans, not only with the changing waves of violence it involved, but also because it meant the loss of the communal basis on which her vocational and existential being as a practitioner of indigenous religious form depended. In her memoirs Madame Kim describes the latter as the most painful and irrevocable consequence of her war-induced dislocation from home. As we discussed in Chapter 2, the advent of MacArthur as a shamanic spirit in the postwar years was, in a crucial way, part of the story of dislocation and the concurrent process of making a home in the new environment. We shall return to the displacement, political as well as physical, of Hwanghae shamanism from home. For now, it needs to be remembered that the experience of dislocation in a political sense was far from over with the end of the Korean War in the mid-1950s. On the contrary, an even more radical and more generalized crisis of deracination was to be forced onto Kim Kŭm-hwa and her colleagues in the following decades, especially in the 1970s.

1982

It is against this background of political and social stigmatization that reached its apex in the 1970s that the transition to the 1980s appears to have had particular significance for Kim Kŭm-hwa and similar guardians of what the above-cited decree refers to as "long-inherited customs." Chung Hak-bong, in her interview introduced earlier, describes this transition in terms of the idea of cultural heritage replacing that of superstition in regard to shamanism and its associated myriad traditional popular customs. In his recent review of South Korea's public and academic discourses on shamanism from the late 1960s to the 1980s, Yoshinobu Shinzato, a historian of religion, similarly notes the rise of the concept of cultural heritage as a key aspect of the era's changing policies toward traditional religious forms.[26] He highlights efforts made by the country's prominent folklorists (including Yim Suk-jay, introduced in Chapter 2) and the growing interest in the 1970s in traditional art and culture among students and intellectuals, who advanced this interest as part of their political activism against Park Chung-hee's political dictatorship. Shinzato also makes some critical observations on collusions between some folklore studies groups and the Park regime's cultural politics. His observations concentrate on the fact that the centuries-old popular religious culture was under threat by the authoritarian state's heavy-handed developmentalism, whereas folklore studies concentrated on recording and compiling these cultural relics before they disappeared (assuming this was inevitable). Kendall similarly writes critically about the idea of national heritage, observing that with the advent of this idea, sympathetic engagement with grassroots religiosity as a living and continuously transforming culture here and now had gone missing.[27]

The New Village Movement was a powerful mass politics, combining a top-down administrative system that penetrated deep into local lives with a bottom-up mass mobilization, in large part, by means of what Benedict Anderson calls "print capitalism"—referring to the role of universal literacy, schooling, and mass media in the construction of national identity.[28] The Song of Saemaŭl, for instance, is still fondly and nostalgically recalled by many.[29] Considering its vertical command structure, it is not surprising that the movement abruptly ran out of steam when the central figure of the authoritarian political system, President Park, who had been in power for nearly two decades after seizing it with the military coup in May 1961, disappeared from the political stage in December 1979 (he was assassinated by his security chief). Even though the preponderance of the power of the military elite continued in the subsequent decade, Park's death in 1979 nevertheless opened up an important space in the sphere of South Korean cultural politics.

The military leaders of South Korea's so-called Fifth Republic (1981–1988) inherited many elements from the Park era, but also sought to free themselves from the burdens of his legacies. They also seized power through a coup, but in doing so they sparked off a strong wave of civil resistance, notably in the city of Kwangju, to which the coup leaders responded violently and brutally, using the army and paratrooper units under their command. Two years after the massacre of civilians in Kwangju in May 1980, another defining incident took place, this time in Pusan. Called the Arson of the US Information Center (in Pusan) and staged by a handful of college students led by a theology student in Pusan's renowned Presbyterian university, this incident in March 1982 followed an earlier arson attempt at the US Information Center in Kwangju in December 1980. The two incidents together are considered by many observers of modern Korea to signal the beginning of a decisive change in the public perception of American power in South Korea—notably, the growing public awareness that the successive military-led authoritarian regimes in South Korea were not Korea's problem (e.g., a political underdevelopment) but were made possible by the complicity of the United States. There was a broad awakening in South Korean society as to the contradictions inherent in the presence of American power in the Korean peninsula—between the United States' leadership in the liberal international world and its illiberal foreign policies in relation to its allied states in Asia and elsewhere. In consequence, the 1980s became the time when South Koreans began to question the meaning of American power in their modern history and, accordingly, to soul-search the place of their polity and society within the broader world and beyond the American hegemon.

The military leaders of the Fifth Republic were acutely aware of these changing vistas in South Korea's political society as well as the fact that their power-grabbing was stained with blood. It is under these circumstances that they came to take great interest in the centennial anniversary of the opening of diplomatic ties between Korea and the United States in 1982. There was also an attempt to turn away from the Park era in the cultural sphere: the era that Youngju Ryu calls the Winter Republic, characterized by a depressive (and repressive) political atmosphere, yet vibrant (and resistant) activism in literature and art.[30] As a result, the post-Park regime pursued a relatively more liberal policy in cultural production and consumption, encouraging entertainment and sport (the last eventually led to the hosting of the Asian Games in 1985 and then to the Summer Olympics in 1988). At the same time, they sought to counter the growing interest among students and intellectuals in elements of Korea's traditional popular culture by presenting the state as the guardian and promoter of this cultural heritage. The tradition of shamanism especially was fast becoming an important battleground in this milieu. The growing resistance movement to the military rule took shamanism as a key part of its cultural (or countercultural) activity, increasingly seeing it as an authentic spirituality of the repressed and resisting masses. One of this book's authors had a direct experience of this change: Arriving in Seoul in 1981 as a new college student, he was stunned to hear from several senior members of the college that what he needed to study and understand first in order to be a properly politically conscious person was shamanism. As the veteran South Korean anthropologist Kim Kwang-ok observed, shamanism (or the idea of shamanism) was rapidly becoming central to the culture of resistance during this era.[31] The state's culture-policy pundits took careful note of this development and countered with their own politics of authenticity—notably, by bestowing titles of intangible heritage to various regional forms of shamanic rites and their notable practitioners, as well as by introducing these rites into the realm of public art and entertainment performance. All these were happening while the government was cracking down on dissenting politicians as well as a broad swath of student and civic protesters. The Fifth Republic also reinvigorated the politics of the Red Scare—by inventing a series of allegedly seditious groupings, including some family-run communist spy ring cases, which were disseminated widely in the news media and through the then newly available color television.[32]

The era's new cultural policy is well illustrated by the festivity of National Wind (*kukpung*, "the wind of new national culture") in May 1981, held in Yŏŭido Square. The timing was deliberate—to mark the anniversary of the Kwangju tragedy, mobilizations for protest were under way in university campuses. The week-long festivity was hailed as the largest public feast in Korea's history thus far, "a great youth festival."[33] The event is reported to have attracted around ten million attendees, some of whom were later discovered to be conscript soldiers disguised as students. In content, the national feast combined a "modern pop festival," including youth song contests, with the performance of traditional themes. The latter included the reenactment of the *sonoli-kut* (Play-the-ox *kut*) from Yangju county, Kyung-gi Province. *Sonoli-kut* was a popular communal festivity in pre-1945 Korea, having an element of agricultural fertility rite and being structurally similar to a *kut* proper. Although village shamans did take part in the communal procession (and when they did, the feast did have a real ritual, religious character), Play-the-ox *kut* was also a carnivalesque event (in the Russian critic Mikhail Bakhtin's sense) or an art of communitas (à la the anthropologist Victor Turner), in which mockeries of the anachronism of existing class and gender hierarchies can generate a feast of laughter and a sense of surreal liminality.[34] The introduction of this local ritual form to the national feast of 1981 followed the nomination of Yangju *sonoli-kut* in 1980 as an intangible national heritage. The heritization initiative was extended to other regional traditions in the following years. Hwanghae's fishing rite (*baeyŏnsin-kut*) and community *kut* (*daedong-kut*) entered the honored list of intangible cultural heritages in 1985, with Kim Kŭm-hwa being elected as the guardian of this local cultural tradition.

FREEDOM

It was amid this momentum of shamanism (or *musok* as it is referred to in contemporary Korea) changing from "deplorable superstition" to "notable cultural heritage" that Kim Kŭm-hwa made her trip to Knoxville in 1982 as part of the Korean cultural-diplomatic envoy to the United States to celebrate the centenary of the two countries' friendship. After that, she continued to be a prolific actor in South Korea's diplomatic and cultural exchange events, until she passed away in February 2019. These events included a performance in 1995 on the third anniversary of the normalization of diplomatic ties between China and South Korea. After the tragedy in New York and Washington, DC, in September 2011, Kim was invited back to the United States—this time, to perform a spirit-consolation rite for the victims of 9/11. Although her visit to Knoxville was part of a greater sociopolitical change that had already been set in motion, Kim did not see it in this way and instead considered the experience to be a defining moment. In Knoxville, she said that she had witnessed a world where she could be free from social stigma and be proud to be a performer and guardian of traditional culture.

The world of freedom she encountered is perhaps best illustrated by the constitutive order of the international organization that specializes in questions of cultural heritage, the United Nations Education, Science and Cultural Organization. The organization's headquarters in Paris, the UNESCO House, is not merely a place for intergovernmental meetings for educational, scientific, and cultural policy-making. Completed in 1958, it also purports to be a "universal museum" where diverse art objects and cultural artifacts from all corners of the world are kept and displayed. This is in line with UNESCO's pursuit of "tolerance" (of differences) and celebration of "diversity" (in unity) since its inception after the destruction of World War II. One can marvel at an indigenous artifact from the Northwest Coast of Canada in one of the house's main conference halls. Elsewhere in the building are many other objects, including a painting from Korea, each of which is supposed to best represent the cultural and artistic heritage of the place from which it originates. The artifacts are displayed within UNESCO House, together with some of the great modernist works of art— for instance, those of Miro, Picasso, and Le Corbusier. The house itself is of a striking modernist shape of a brutalist orientation, standing out sharply from the surrounding neighborhood, which consists primarily of imposing eighteenth- or nineteenth-century buildings. The idea is to preserve the treasures of the world's diverse artistic traditions within an esthetically modernist space without privileging any particular traditional form (see Conclusion to this volume).

The artifact chosen to represent Korea's traditional culture, found in the corridor that connects two main conference halls, is especially interesting in this regard—the integration of diverse past traditions and common pursuit of modern knowledge and sensibility. The painting depicts a shamaness engaged in her *kut* performance—what appears to be the ritual stage involving *kun'ung*, the displaced spirits. The ritual performer is holding a bundle of copper bells in one hand and a handheld fan in the other—two of a Korean shaman's principal ritual instruments. On a low table in a corner lies the offering of a pig's head for spirit guests. The painting has a distinct ritual esthetic form which, if seen as part of UNESCO House and the principle of cultural diversity celebrated in it, delivers the message that this ritual form represents Korea's unique and authentic cultural tradition. In terms of composition, however, the *kut* painting is far removed from "traditional" forms. Korea's shamanism tradition has developed many artistic forms of its own, including a type of portrait art. Called *hwan*, these portraits represent specific helper-spirit identities, or it may be even said that these portraits actually are the spirits. The painting illustrating Korean shamanism in UNESCO House makes no connection with Korean shamanism's own artistic heritage. On the contrary, the painting's composition is deliberately modern, and even cubist—the contours of the shaman's face remind the visitors of Pablo Picasso's *Les demoiselles d'Avignon* (1907). The person whose ritual actions are depicted in this quaint painting is none other than Kim Kŭm-hwa.

In her memoirs, Kim speaks at length of her liberating experience in Knoxville. Because of this experience, she kept the souvenir she had brought from this trip, an American flag, at the center of her spirit shrine in her central-Seoul residence. Madame Kim movingly tells of her encounters with a few visitors to her Knoxville performance as the most memorable episode of her 1982 trip. These visitors were members of America's First Nations, who, according to Kim, showed particularly acute interest in what she was doing in the fair. This encounter made her sad as well, as it forced her to realize that earthly spirituality was looked down upon, not merely in her homeland but also in the land she was visiting. Moving on from this recol-

Kim Kŭm-hwa's home shrine. Photo by Jun Hwan Park.

lection, Kim later reflects on the entirety of her life trajectory from a village in Hwanghae to a position of considerable fame, as a beholder of an intangible national heritage and, as often mentioned in the media, even as a "national shaman" (*nara mansin*). In this reflection, she no longer shows any bitterness about the political culture of anti-superstition, or any particular enthusiasm about her heritage entitlement and the related politics of cultural conservation and recognition. One gets the impression from her mildly spoken narrative that, in her experience, the transition from one domain to the other of cultural politics is more of a continuation of alienation than necessarily a betterment or decisive progression. Her fondest memories, rather, remain with the time in her birthplace, now in North Korea. The vitality of these memories is not because of her being young then, or due to the fact that this was the place where she was born and raised. Rather, it is because then and there, she was a shaman with a place to belong to and act in, not one who was perpetually in search of a place where she could meaningfully dwell. She calls this place her Home World—a home for many familiar spirits and a world of many places which are these spirits' homes.

4

SEEKING GOOD LUCK

Douglas MacArthur landed in Kanagawa on August 30, 1945, to take up his job as the Supreme Commander of US-occupied Japan. He spent three days at Hotel New Grand in nearby Yokohama, one of the few buildings still standing after the city was flattened by American bombardment. This was before he headed on to Tokyo to start work in his GHQ office at Japan's Dai-ichi Mutual building, from which he could look down at the Imperial Palace. In that hotel room, he prepared the address that he would deliver on September 2—the speech to mark the surrender of Japan that would set the tone of the US occupation of Japan. The landing was a highly symbolic gesture. The area is where the Parry Convention that ended Japan's century-long seclusion, also known as the Treaty of Kanagawa, was signed between Japan and the United States in 1854.

Five years later, in September 1950, MacArthur landed on the western seashore of Korea, after successfully completing the assault against the North Korean positions in Incheon—an acclaimed military episode that followed another amphibious action in his career: the landing on Red Beach of Leyte Gulf in October 1944 as part of his campaign to recover the Philippines from Japanese occupation. MacArthur's life history connects Yokohama to Incheon, closely following the way in which the character of the larger history he was part of changed from the time of the Pacific War to that of the early Cold War. We can connect Incheon and Yokohama in yet another way.[1] The story of the port of Incheon from the nineteenth century is strikingly akin to that of Kanagawa-Yokohama (Kanagawa is now part of Yokohama), although the former has a notable difference from the latter, and this difference is crucial to continuing the investigation into the concept of superstition that we started in Chapter 3. Looming large in this story are the unfolding of the Korean War and related opposition to the religion-negating ideology of communism. However, communism is not the only -ism that appears in this story; vexing questions on what constitutes superstition and what to do with its supposedly preeminent manifestation, shamanism, are also part and parcel of the evolution of South Korean politics in the post–Korean War era. The controversy involves the idea of *gibok sinang* (literally, "pray-for-luck religion"), of which shamanism is considered a towering example—a controversy that continues today.

THE CENTENARY, 1885–1985

While the centennial festivities of Korean–American relations were in full swing in May 1982 (see Chapter 3), preparations for another important centennial anniversary were underway—to celebrate the introduction of Protestantism in Korea at the end of the nineteenth century. Beginning in December 1980, the preparations brought together various church groups and denominations existing in South Korea. The resulting collective was headed by the prominent preacher and the founder of one of South Korea's great megachurches, Reverend Han Kyung-chik. Declaring its broad objective "to look back upon the legacies of faith for the past one-hundred years and transmit them [to the future] in more correct ways," the occasion celebrated the remarkable growth of Korean Protestant churches. The number of Protestants multiplied more than ten times in South Korea from the 1950s to the early 1980s (from roughly half a million in 1950 to more than six million in 1985), while the number of churches increased from about three thousand to more than twenty thousand during the same period. Another aim of these centennial celebrations was to repent the history of division and conflict existing within the church community as a whole and to set the direction for the Korean church in its second century. The vision statement was principally "to transform from a church that receives to a church that gives"—a transformation that was realized in the following decade when the Korean church became increasingly prominent in the sphere of international mission activities, both across Asia and Africa, but also in the Americas and eastern Europe. Incheon was an important site for the centennial commemoration of Korean Protestantism. The city's harbor is where Horace G. Underwood and Henry G. Appenzeller, two of the most famous Protestant missionaries in Korea's church history, landed on Easter Sunday 1885, representing the American Presbyterian and the Methodist missions respectively.[2] The mass services by Billy Graham, held in Yŏŭido in August 1984, attracted a million and a half attendees. Following a number of other smaller rallies and events, the centennial prayer took place in Han Kyung-chik's Youngnak Presbyterian Church in central Seoul. In November 1986, an imposing memorial was erected in Incheon harbor, dedicated to the memory of three founders of Korea's Protestant Church: Underwood, Appenzeller, and his wife, Ella.

The arrival of these three American missionaries in Incheon constitutes a foundational episode in the history of Korean Protestantism, and it was made possible by the political event that the 1982 centenary event celebrated: the Treaty of Peace, Amity, Commerce, and Navigation.[3] Also known as the Shufeldt Treaty, it was signed in Incheon on May 22, 1882, by Admiral Robert W. Shufeldt and his Korean counterparts, King Gojong's two representatives Sin Hŏn and Kim Hong-jip. Although this was Korea's first treaty of amity with a Western power, it was not, however, the first modern treaty that the crumbling old Korea had made with a foreign power. By 1882, Incheon was, together with two other major ports, Pusan on the southern coast and Wonsan in the northeast, under the strong influence of Japan. Japan had gained access to Korea through a typical (and mimetic of Western imperial practices) gunboat diplomacy, leading to the treaty of Ganghwa, an island off Incheon, in 1876. Japan's advance to Korea alarmed China, which regarded Korea as an ancient vassal state. Korea was then turning into a space of a bitter power struggle between the two Asian empires: one new and rapidly rising while the other was fast declining and losing its long-held traditional centrality in the wider region. This struggle exploded into the full-blown military conflict of 1894–1895: the first Sino-Japanese war.

When the three American missionaries landed in Incheon, via Japan, in 1885, Japan and China already had established a strong presence in the port town. In 1883, a modern customs house was introduced in Incheon, closely modeled on China's customs service.[4] As various foreign trade posts (American, Russian, and British, as well as Japanese and Chinese) were established, the originally obscure fishing village of Jemulpo (Incheon's old name) grew rapidly in size and population. Relics of this time still remain in central Incheon today. These include the original Freedom Park, which was located inside the foreign concessions, and the Jemulpo Club, a recreational gathering place for residents from the West. Incheon's municipal authority today is keen on appropriating these historical relics for tourism, while promoting the town as "the gateway of modern culture" and "where the transition from an agricultural society to a modern capitalist society began."[5] According to the city's tourism office, Incheon has so many firsts: the first railroad (in Korea), telegraph lines, minting, post office, and lighthouses, and so on. The city also has several public museums in the former foreign settlement area and its environs. They include the Opening of Incheon Museum and the Museum of Modern Architecture in Incheon. There is also a Museum of the History of Emigration that concentrates on, among other things, the first contact between Korea and the United States in terms of mass population movement—the export of Korean laborers to Hawaii's sugar plantations, beginning in 1902.

A great proportion of these early emigrants to the United States were initially recruited from Incheon and its environs, especially from the town's church communities, then led by American missionaries.[6] Accordingly, Incheon keeps a number of historic sites relating to Korea's early evangelical history. These include the centenary memorial of the evangel, mentioned earlier, and the prominent International Bible Museum that keeps thousands of Bible exemplars collected from all corners of the world. Keeping also a number of rare materials relating to Korea's church history, the Bible Museum opened in 1995 when South Korea's Protestant groupings were extremely active in overseas evangelical missions, as proclaimed by the centennial declaration a decade earlier. Other notable sites include Korea's first Methodist church, Naeri Church, and Incheon's first Presbyterian establishment, Jeil Church. Located within the premises of Freedom Park, the latter prides itself on the fact that it follows in the steps of Reverend Underwood, who is regarded as the father of Korean Presbyterianism. Meanwhile, the Methodist Naeri Church is sometimes called, even more proudly, "Korea's mother church." Although this may be disputed by some church groups, Naeri Church's heritage has a towering presence in Korea's Methodist movement as a whole, as well as within Incheon, where the movement historically has had a predominant presence.

Presbyterianism took root in Incheon much later than Methodism and through a unique historical detour. The origin of Incheon's first Presbyterian Church (Jeil Church) traces back to 1946, shortly after the end of the Pacific War and the ensuing partition of Korea into two separate zones of military occupation. The founders of this church were all exiles from the part of Korea that was then occupied by the Soviet army and from the western region of today's North Korea, which is often referred to as *Sŏbuk* (the "northwest" region). This northwest region, which includes Pyongyang, North Korea's capital city today, had a strong Presbyterian presence before 1945, to the extent that Pyongyang used to be referred to as the Jerusalem of the Orient. One significant effect of evangelization in this region was particularly in the educational sector, as education was one of the principal arenas of mission activity of the early Protestant missionaries, together with the introduction of modern medicine. This led to the establishment of one of the most renowned mission schools in Korea's church history, Sungsil Academy, by the Presbyterian missionary William M. Baird from Indiana. Baird began with an informal school modeled on *sarangbang* (a room in a traditional Korean house where men held conversations about the Confucian texts and other matters) in Pyongyang. This was in 1897, and his *sarangbang* quickly grew and become a formal school in 1899, attracting the town's youth who were hungry for modern ideas. It continued to grow to the extent that, in 1906, this led to the opening of Sungsil Academy, one of the first modern higher education establishments in Korea.[7] A number of eminent literary and public historical figures were alumni of Sungsil Academy, including the musician Anh Ik-tae, who composed Korea's national anthem (originally in the style of a gospel song); the renowned poet Yun Dong-ju, whose life was cut short in a Japanese prison; and the scholar of Korean literature, Yang Ju-dong. They also include Cho Man-sik, a prominent figure in the Christian Youth movement and anti-colonial and later anti-communist activist, and Kim Hyung-chik, a church leader and father of North Korea's founding leader, Kim Il-sung. Reverend Han Kyung-chik, one of the most formative figures in South Korea's post–Korean War church history, was also a graduate of the powerful Presbyterian mission educational establishment in Pyongyang. It was through him and other exiled church elders and leaders from Pyongyang and the broader Northwest that the Presbyterian mission came to Incheon in the mid-twentieth century—many years after the London-born American Presbyterian missionary, Horace Underwood, came ashore at Incheon harbor in 1885.

The journals of these early American missionaries to Korea make a fascinating read. Notable among their numerous observations and judgments on lives in late-Chosun-era Korea is the question of religion in traditional

Korea. Nearly all the early Western missionaries regarded Korea's existing religious environment (as of the late nineteenth century) as an eclectic, sometimes chaotic, mixture of Confucianism, Buddhism, and shamanism. Some missionaries even saw Korea as a religion-less place. This was because Buddhism, which had been thriving before the fifteenth century, had been marginalized and weakened under the Chosun's long and strongly neo-Confucian rule. Those who regarded Korea as a religion-free society questioned whether Confucianism was a religion or rather a body of secular moral principles—a debate that, in fact, continues today. Horace N. Allen, a pioneering medical missionary from Ohio, thought that Koreans did not have a religion of their own and that Confucianism was only a system of ethics (i.e., having no gods in it). Some recognized that Confucianism and shamanism shared a belief in the afterlife and that the practice of ancestral veneration was found in both domains. They noted that belief in ancestors was principally family-centered and therefore lacked the idea of transcendence, the hallmark of the concept of religion proper that they held. Like Buddhism, moreover, shamanism was looked down upon by the Confucian elite and marginalized within the social order. As Korea was considered to be a religion-less place, it was an "ideal mission field," a tabula rasa awaiting the arrival of the Gospel.[8]

However, other missionaries advanced different interpretations of Korea's spirituality, especially with regard to shamanism. They argued that Koreans had a belief system with the fear of spirits at its core. These fear-generating spirits were everywhere: Some were animistic spirits associated with trees, rocks, rivers, and the sea, whereas others were domestic—such as those anchored in the garden or in the kitchen. Of particular interest was the moral ambiguity of ancestral spirits and the way in which these intimate entities could also be feared. Among those who advanced the view that the fear of spirits constituted the basis of the traditional Korean worldview, some oversimplified this idea to a sweeping generalization. For instance, in his travelogue of Korea at the end of the nineteenth century, the London-born, Princeton-educated missionary George Gilmore defined Confucianism and Buddhism as the two pillars of religion in Korea:

The real worship of Coreans is before the ancestral tables and at the graves. It is simple in character. It consists merely of setting out on small tables offerings, particularly rice with various condiments, before which prostrations are made and prayers offered. The spirit is supposed to be present, and to partake of the gifts thus presented. But subsidiary to these two religions [Confucianism and Buddhism], which are the prominent religious features, is a belief in a multiplicity of spirits and demons of different powers and various characters. The gates of the cities, palaces, temples, and often of private houses, are surmounted by grotesque shapes of animals and contorted figures of men. These are to frighten off the various spirits of evil and the demons, which otherwise might enter the city to disturb its peace and destroy its prosperity.[9]

Gilmore termed the "grotesque" objects that he saw widely distributed in Korea, from the domestic space to the royal residence, "idols," and assigned the related "belief in a multiplicity of spirits and demons" to "superstitions."[10] There were also less impressionistic reports that were based on a more engaged observation and contact. Robert Oppenheim has provided a fascinating report in this light on Allen, who, despite being a medical missionary, took great interest in the material culture of Korean shamanism and collected "mootang" artifacts for the United States National Museum.[11] Also notable is the report on their tour of Korea in 1911 by two German priests of the Benedictine order, Andreas Eckardt and Norbert Weber.[12] Fluent in Korean, Eckardt skillfully guided his visiting superior Weber around diverse popular religious sites and events in early colonial Korea. The result is a careful portrait of Korea's traditional spirituality. Weber witnessed people making offerings to their community's spirit-tree and marveled at the intensity of human sincerity emanating from these actions. He portrayed the morality of filial piety emphasized in Korea's neo-Confucian tradition as an indigenous ethical disposition that could be conducive, if properly harnessed, to mission activity.

Even in this sympathetic rendering, however, the limit of sympathy and tolerance was clearly drawn against shamanism-related customs. In 1925, a priest named D. d'Avernas reported to the Benedictine Congregation of Saint Ottilien in Jakobsberg about a *kut* that he said was intended to chase away malignant spirits. In it, he wrote, "The spirits returned despite the mudang's best efforts." Another Benedictine priest reported in 1927 that he had sought to persuade people (of Chungjin on the northeast coast, where he was based) "to throw away their *sinju danji* [an object in the traditional domestic space where ancestral spirits are believed to rest] and the demons held within them." In December 1930, the missionary F. Damm, from Won-san, warned that whereas the old generations held on to ancestor worship stubbornly, the young ones were prone to contamination by Bolshevik ide-ology. In 1933, another German missionary reported that controversies about Japanese Shinto shrines were becoming a problem for the Far Eastern Cath-olic church. Around the same time, a priest named G. Steger conveyed the news about the colonial authority's new measures against objects of super-stition in Korea: "The Japanese police are removing *sinju danji* [from homes] and [from the village] *sansin-je* [rites for mountain deities], which are held four times a year. This will be helpful for our future mission activities."[13]

By the time Steger sent these reports from colonial Korea, Japan's impe-rial politics were fast expanding into China and becoming more militarized, leading to the outbreak of the second Sino-Japanese war in 1937. The colo-nial experience, and the ensuing war experience of 1937–1945, had a profound impact on Korea's religious landscape. Japan's colonial politics had many similarities with those advanced by the European powers. This was the case in the cultural and ideological spheres, as well as in the political and infra-structural realms. Compared with other, better-known colonial conditions involving European expansion, however, Japan's colonization of Korea had a profoundly unique dimension. Most notable and prolifically discussed is the element of anti-Westernism (or even anti-imperialism) in Japan's impe-rial adventure, which justified its territorial expansion in Asia as a defense of Asia from the West's colonial conquest.[14] Another distinct element of Japanese colonialism has not attracted due attention, however, despite its obvious close relation to its claimed Asianism. Nowhere is this distinctive-ness better expressed than in the history of Korean Christianity. It is an es-tablished cliché that when colonialism starts, it starts not only with the arrival of merchants and mercenaries, but also with that of Christian mis-sionaries (and sometimes anthropologists, too). For this reason, when Ghana declared independence in 1958, Kwame Nkrumah, the founding leader of independent Ghana, commissioned a painting and proudly displayed it in his presidential office. The painting depicts the leader himself breaking off the chains of colonialism with a background of thunder and lightning. It also depicts small human figures, three white men on the run: "One of them is the capitalist, he carries a briefcase. Another is a priest or missionary, he car-ries the Bible" (and the last, of an even lesser figure, is the anthropologist).[15] The colonial history of Korea diverges considerably from this classical portrait of what comes with and after colonialism. The missionaries who arrived in Korea at the dawn of Korea's colonial history were, like elsewhere in the colonial world, from the West and predominantly from the New World part of the West. The colonial order that these missionaries and their followers confronted was not created by Westerners, but by Japan, Korea's neighboring state in Asia which was far from a Christian civilization. In other words, the full colonial occupation of Korea came with the capitalist carrying a briefcase (and a few anthropologists as well, as we will see later), but not together with the Bible-holding missionary—that is, "at the hands of a non-Christian, non-Western power," as Kenneth Wells writes.[16] The diversion of Korea's colonial experience from modern colonial history proper, as it were—the dominant form of colonial experience in global history anchored in the indigenous society's contact with the Christian West— drove Korea's evangelical history along a unique pathway, especially in the postcolonial time and space after 1945, when Christian brethren, people of the land from which the Gospel to Korea originated, returned to Korea to liberate Korean Christians from the idolatry that Asia's colonialism had forced upon them.

DIVERGENCE

Some of the issues raised above are far from unfamiliar in the tradition of modern anthropology. Early anthropological literature of the late nineteenth century abounds with notes on a plethora of spirit-belief phenomena from all corners of the non-Western world. This drew considerably on reports made by Christian missionaries around the world during the so-called Great Century of modern religious mission, the nineteenth century. This was the case with Edward B. Tylor, a founding figure of modern anthropology in Britain, who delved into animism, the set of ideas and practices in which animals and natural objects are endowed with the distinctly human-only property in traditional Western religious thought—the soul.[17] Tylor saw animism as a religious form that should be distinguished from institutional religions such as Buddhism, Christianity, Hinduism, and Judaism. The demarcation line was morality. According to Tylor, all the great institutional religions that human civilization has known have an elaborate system of moral principles; in contrast, animistic beliefs are an *un*-moral and *natural* religion, wherein questions of right or wrong, and just or unjust, are irrelevant.

The great Scottish anthropologist James G. Frazer engaged with the high-brow culture of the late Victorian era in which the educated public were increasingly fascinated by mysterious human customs existing in faraway places. He introduced to them a dazzling variety of magical ideas and practices from Oceania, Asia, and Africa—that is, broadly within the realm of the British empire—while also trying to awaken his readers to the fact that these are not merely properties of the primitive world but that similar phenomena also existed once in the Western world in a forgotten time.[18] In doing so, Frazer benefited greatly, as did Tylor, from the studies of indigenous cultures prepared by learned missionaries. Missionaries and anthropologists had other mutual overlaps. The work of good missionaries typically involves a long training in the indigenous world—their language, law, social organization, and material culture—only through which they can deliver the Gospel in an effective and impactful way. Similarly, for students of modern anthropology, the set of practices referred to as participant observation—a long-term process of language learning, living together, and experiencing what the natives experience—remains something akin to the first commandment, which also has long distinguished the discipline of anthropology from other social science fields and thereby gives the former a distinct identity. Partly due to this similarity in the method of knowing, many missionaries were also good anthropologists. Some produced great ethnographic reports—as was the case with Léopold Cadière, a French Jesuit missionary to Indochina, whose works on the Vietnamese language, customs, and religions continue to be an important source of reference for students of Vietnamese studies today.[19]

The analogy probably stops here, though. While sharing the methodical emphasis on understanding based on an immersion in the indigenous world, anthropology's participatory observation, as the name suggests, is purely for observation and its purpose is for the advancement of scientific knowledge (of the human world) through careful and disciplined empirical observation. There is no space in this realm of participation for the explicit purpose of spiritual transformation, as found in modern missionary participation.[20] Many anthropologists study religious phenomena; however, they do so because they believe an understanding of these phenomena is vital for an understanding of an indigenous world as a whole of which these religious ideas and practices are part. Since this world is a sovereign entity in a linguistic and cultural sense, it is extremely difficult, if not impossible, in fact, to see these ideas and practices in the prism of religion versus superstition, or "real" religion versus "fake" religion (*yusa-jong'gyo* in Korean, literally "religion-looking religion that is actually not a religion")—the conceptual contrast that was integral to Japan's colonial politics in Korea.

Seen in this way, we might say that Tylor's "natural" religion (as in contrast to moral religion) and Frazer's "magic" (as distinct from religion) were both linguistic devices employed to engage with human affairs that might otherwise fall easily into the conceptual realm of superstition in the context of late-Victorian Britain. In the subsequent era, scholars of British anthropological circles came to freely use the concept of religion (as well as that of magic) to describe tribal religious customs, thereby departing more decisively than their late-nineteenth-century predecessors from the ordering of moral hierarchy as found in the religion versus superstition scheme. The term "custom" was also brought in, intended to convey the sense that even though these practices may appear supernatural and magical, the point is that they are real, with historical depth, and that they are meaningful, in the sense of fulfilling certain important functions in the present time—such as holding the social group together or acting as a kind of law in societies without the institution of the state and related legal structure.[21] On the other side of the Atlantic, during the same era at the turn of the century, the key conceptual device that played this role of parting with the past was "culture." Closely associated with the ideas of the German-born, Berlin-trained American anthropologist Franz Boas, the concept of culture was closely akin to that of language. All languages existing in human history are a complete system on their own (not to be confused with a closed system, as a language is a product of long-standing contact with other languages and language groups), all unique and each of them sovereign. In a powerful analogical logic, each cultural system, like each language system, is complete in its own (again not closed off), and in this sense, it is impossible to think of culture in terms of higher- or lower-level cultures (unlike the concept of civilization). The same logic applied to the idea of "race" and the ideology of racial difference.[22] In fact, Boas and his students shared the belief that cultural anthropology was a powerful political project in that the substitution of the idea of cultural diversity for that of racial difference was vital for the construction of liberal, tolerant, pluralist, and internationalist modern citizens—an ideal that we briefly discussed in Chapter 3 with reference to UNESCO and the ideal of global citizenship that this organization promotes (see also Conclusion to this volume).

The most radical conceptual revolution in this sphere was undertaken, however, by the French sociological school, especially by Emile Durkheim. In his now-classic thesis in the sociology of religion, first published in 1912, *The Elementary Forms of Religious Life*, Durkheim strongly refutes Tylor's natural religion versus moral religion contrast, arguing instead that all religious forms, even those found in the supposedly most archaic societies, are moral systems.[23] Advancing this argument, he turned his attention from the phenomenon of animism, on which Tylor concentrated, to that of totemism—a religious and social form that was fairly widely talked about in the learned circles of Europe at that time (thus, Sigmund Freud's important work *Totem and Taboo*). If, in animism, what is distinctly human (in the Western religious tradition), the soul, is extended to natural objects, the reverse is true with totemism, which is the phenomenon of expressing differences in the human world through differences found in the natural world. Hence, an indigenous group in Australia claims that they are Kangaroo people, in distinction to their neighboring groups that take on different natural symbols. Reports from early missionaries and travelers who encountered this phenomenon questioned how humans could believe that they shared substance with animal or other natural species. According to Durkheim, this was the wrong way to approach totemism. He argued that a totem is a symbol of society and a representation of collective existence, not a result of a category mistake on the boundary between nature and humanity. The idea of totem also involves the associated notion of taboo; hence, it is a fundamentally moral and legal concept.[24]

In the subsequent development of modern anthropology, especially after the end of World War II, both Durkheim's legacy (the religious is at once moral and social) and the Boasian legacy (the religious has many culturally specific and variant expressions) have together become the discipline's guiding principles—a creed, if you like. There was no space for the idea of superstition within this developmental trajectory, although the concept of magic and magical religion, in contrast, continued to be in currency. Notable exceptions were found in research dealing with the historical contexts of colonial conquest (e.g., the conquest of America), in which the investigators were bound to confront the conceptual moral hierarchy of religion versus superstition at work as part of the politics of conquest. The moral hierarchy is far from confined to a context of culture contact but, instead, often becomes an integral element in the indigenous worldview and language. In a growing number of cases, the idea of superstition can even incorporate elements of the self-claimed "true" beliefs—for instance, when a new revivalist mission arrives in an indigenous society and tries to distinguish itself from the version of Christianity to which the society had long been faithful. This is evidently the case in parts of today's Oceania and Africa where anthropological research on indigenous religious culture is taking on a strong identity as an anthropological study of Christianity.[25] In this context, the idea of *kastom* (the popular expression in New Guinea addressing customary tradition) departs considerably from the idea of traditional indigenous culture in the nineteenth- and twentieth-century sense. Despite these exceptions, however, the decoupling of religion from the old moral hierarchy of religion versus superstition still constitutes the disciplinary ethos of modern anthropology. Putting this more bluntly, we might even say that the anthropology of religion is a discipline born in a struggle against the idea of superstition or against the idea of religion that propagates its position against superstition.

We introduce this highly skeletal history of the anthropology of religion, in part, in order to clarify our position in relation to the language of superstition in Korea's modern political history. This position is not necessarily against the language. On the contrary, it involves a critical reflection on the history of the discipline within which the idea of superstition has been long expunged from its descriptive and analytical sphere, despite the fact that the idea proliferated in historical milieus and continues to be influential in the constitution of contemporary social reality. It is one thing to steer away from the value-laden notion of superstition (and various other similar expressions) in descriptive projects. However, in certain historical contexts the notion is so profusely integral to the prevailing public moral discourse that it has almost become an ordinary language. The idea of superstition has a long and complex etymological background. For the intellectuals of ancient Greece, the concept was used to describe popular religious practices the Greeks disapproved of.[26] For the Romans, *superstitio* pointed, among other things, to the rise of early Christian power. The term took on different meanings for the followers of Hippocrates and, for a long time, evolved alongside the development of modern medical knowledge. Scholarly clerics in late medieval Europe imagined the world outside the wall of theological integrity as the realm of superstition or as what scholars in a later era called "popular mentality." Some militant Enlightenment thinkers imagined an ideal rational society on the basis of a war against the persistent popular mentality, "the madness of the crowd" as Charles MacKay called it.[27]

During the Reformation, polemicists relegated the Roman Catholic Church as a whole to a system of superstitions, and some eminent Enlightenment writers assigned the entirety of the Christian tradition to the category of superstition, making it incompatible with the Age of Reason.[28] The last was greatly empowered in the state-driven social revolutions of the twentieth century in Soviet Russia and elsewhere, where religions were categorized as preeminent expressions of false consciousness. For the revivalist preachers in Oceania and elsewhere today, the entire history of Christian conversion prior to their arrival is akin to a sorry history of superstition-worship.[29] So the concept of superstition has a long and multifaceted history—as long as the history of Western civilization. It has roots in ancient times, and has an extraordinarily enduring life, continuing to find new niches in changing circumstances to the present moment.

If the idea of superstition is deeply rooted in human history, it is also the case that it takes on new meanings and relevance in specific historical milieus and contexts. In the history of Korea's Christianity, the transition from colonialism to the Cold War calls for special attention in this respect. As noted earlier, Korea's colonial experience is a uniquely interesting case in the global history of colonialism, for the reason that, in this case, the politics of colonial conquest advanced, not in the hands of a Western power but in those of a late-coming Asian empire, and that they involved, rather than the diffusion of Western Christian beliefs, that of a political religion that was invented as a reaction to Western dominance. For the Christian elite of colonial Korea, the culture of Japan's colonial politics was, therefore, much more than cultural imperialism disguised as a civilizing mission, as was the case in other colonial contexts. It was also an imposition of idolatry—an intolerable situation that brought a profound existential crisis to Korea's church communities. This explains how Japan's surrender in 1945 was a liberating experience for these communities in a double sense of the term—as both a national liberation from colonial misery and a liberation from coerced idol-worshipping. This duality constitutes a crucial and distinct aspect of Korea's cultural experience of colonialism, which we may call an inverted moral hierarchy in the sense that, in this case, the colonized regarded the colonizer as the follower of a false belief. Japan's colonial culture in Korea advanced its own moral hierarchy and civilizing discourse, especially with regard to

Korea's eclectic customary religious culture involving elements of shaman-ism—as shown in a report by the Benedictine priest Steger about the colonial authority's assault against household spirit pots, which he hailed as a laud-able action conducive for the church's anti-superstition, anti-idolatry ef-forts.[30] Japan's colonial power enforced on Korea punitive rules against "any claims to dare to generate luck and prevent misfortune" as early as in 1912.[31] In this way, the politics of anti-superstition became part of both the colonial cultural ruling and the resistance against it.

IDOLATRY

The hilltop area of central Incheon, where the statue of MacArthur is lo-cated today, has had several different names. At the turn of the twentieth century, the area was a recreational space exclusively for the use of foreign residents and called Ten Thousand Nations Park (*manguk gongwŏn*) or All Nations Park (*gakguk gongwŏn*). It became Freedom Park after the end of the Pacific War in 1945, along with the ensuing military occupation of what is now South Korea by the United States. In between these two eras was the colonial occupation of Korea by Imperial Japan, which began with Japan's victory in the Russo-Japanese War in 1905 (where Incheon Harbor was one of the key sites), and ended with its defeat in the Pacific War. During this colonial era, the name of the hilltop and its environs changed to Western Park, in distinction to Eastern Park—the town's residential cluster of Japa-nese settlers. The "eastern" of Eastern Park was not a geographical reference (Eastern Park was south of Western Park) but a political notion, which spoke of the ideology of anti-Westernism in Japan's imperial politics mentioned earlier—the unique aspect of Japanese imperialism that justified its imperial expansion into Asia as an act of defending Asia from the malheur of Western imperialism.

The Eastern Park area was also a religious and cultural space, associated with the prominent built object within it—the "great shrine of Incheon"— where the Japanese settlers worshipped their Sun Goddess and other Shinto spirits, as well as interacting with memories of their deceased relatives. The settlers crowded the park premises, especially during the spring cherry blos-som festival and the Shinto temple ceremony in the autumn. When it was first established in 1890, the shrine was more of a communal worship place. After Korea was annexed into Japan's imperial realm, however, the Japanese shrine in Incheon underwent a major expansion, financed and controlled by the colonial office, and it increasingly became a site of political religion in which traditional popular worship and the worship of the Emperor and his lineage were closely intertwined.[32] As Masaaki Aono shows, the transformation of Shintoism into an imperial religious ideology affected, in turn, the fabric of Shintoism as practiced within Japan's domestic sphere.[33] As in other places under its influence, such as Taiwan and later in the Pacific islands, Japan's imperial power sought to assert its authority, not only with the ideology of anti-Westernism and the related rhetoric of Asia for Asians (the so-called Great Asian Co-prosperity idea) but also with the imposition of its political religion upon colonial subjects. In hindsight, the religious colonization was pitifully unsuccessful—there are no remnants of Shinto worship in the former Japanese imperial territory today. However, it was imposed on Koreans with a ferocious force, especially in the 1930s after the outbreak of the second Sino-Japanese war, as part of the drive toward a totalizing war mobilization, both in Japan and in its colonies.

In this environment, the worship at Shinto shrines and of the divine political spirit of *kokutai* (national/imperial essence) associated with these shrines became a vital imperial-civic duty for the colonized subjects, as well as for the Japanese. By that time, Shinto shrines had penetrated deep into colonial Korea—in every rural county and all educational establishments. Attempts were even made to penetrate into the domestic ritual space and to turn this space (where, traditionally, ancestors and other household deities were cared for) into a *kokutai*-worshipping space, as illustrated by the report made by the Benedictine priest Steger in the 1930s about the destruction of household spirit pots by the colonial authority. These were part of the broader colonial project of "mental reform" initiated at the start of the 1930s, under the somewhat mind-boggling slogan of "mind cultivation reform movement."[34] Evidence suggests that most Koreans responded to this drive of religious colonialism with apathy and through tacit resistance such as foot-dragging. Shinto's sun worship was a strange idea to Koreans, and the idea of remembering ancestors in a temple, rather than through the traditional household rituals, was especially alien and offensive to Korean society, in which the ancestor ritual of *jesa* was equal in relevance and meaning to the integrity of kinship relations themselves. The imposition of this alien religion came as an especially critical challenge, however, to Korea's Christian communities, to whom the policy meant the imposition of idolatry.

The year 1938 is regarded as a threshold in this matter—the time known as the Year of Great Shame in Korea's church history when many leaders of Korean Protestant movements capitulated to the colonial power's politics of religion. This followed the acquiescence of the Catholic church to the colonial power's demand for Shinto worship in mission schools and even in church meetings. There was strong resistance, too. Sungsil Academy, the prominent mission school and modern educational institute in Pyongyang mentioned earlier, chose to close the school in protest against this colonial policy. Elsewhere, the imposition of Shinto worship provoked conflicts among church leaders and missionaries. Many understood the policy as an assault against the church and an intrusion of secular politics into the sacred space of religious worship. Some missionaries disputed with their regional mission office in Japan that they were capitulating to blasphemy and were disappointed with the US administration's indifference to the crisis, despite their repeated appeal for diplomatic intervention. The American missions in Korea had placed a strong emphasis on educational and medical activities from their very early days. As testified by the New Haven–born American medical missionary to Korea, William B. Scranton, and his mother, Mary F. Scranton, who founded Ehwa school (today South Korea's prominent women's higher educational institution), the mission's modern educational activity involved the preaching of ideas of natural rights. These ideas were initially explosive, under the class and gender inequalities of old Korea, but, in the deepening colonial situation, they also influenced young minds to question the unequal relations between states and nations.[35] Therefore, it was not a surprise that Christian leaders and students of mission schools played prominent roles in anti-colonial mobilization, such as the peaceful popular uprising against the colonial order in the March First Movement of 1919; the foundational episode of Korea's modern constitutional history. In contrast to this proud chapter of Korea's church history, the shame of "giving in to idolatry" in 1938 became a hugely controversial issue among Korea's Protestant movement in the postcolonial era.

FURTHER DIVERGENCE

Japan's imperial expansion diverged considerably in the cultural sphere from the like political forms associated with the Western powers. This was in part because of the ideological imperative of anti-Westernism and the related advent of the political religion of Shintoism as part of their empire-building. The divergence is also linked to the fact that Japan's imperial process involved not only the colonial domination of neighboring territories but also armed confrontation with other contending powers, which radicalized the ferocity of their political religiosity. These crucial differences in imperial politics were manifested in colonial Korea, among other places, through confrontation between evangelism and Shintoism.[36] In mentioning these differences, however, we do not mean to ignore the fact that modern imperial formations, both European and Asian, have considerable similarities. Observers argue that *all* modern colonial forms suffer from inherent internal contradictions. Notable among them is the disparity between the rhetoric of inclusion and the reality of exclusion.[37] Modern empires maintain that all imperial subjects are citizens of the imperial polity; in all modern empires, however, civil rights are ordered hierarchically along racial, ethnic, or cultural grounds. Japan's imperial history in Korea is not an exception on this front, and, here, the tradition of shamanism in Korea was exploited to play a key role in building the hierarchical order of culture and spirituality between the metropolis and the colony.

Korea's shamanism tradition attracted intense interest from Japan's early scholars trained in sociology and ethnology. Notable among them was Murayama Chijun, who produced several notable works on Korea's traditional religiosity, such as *Spirits in Korea* (1929), *Korean Shamanism* (1932), and *Village Rituals in Korea* (1937), all commissioned by the Japanese colonial government in Korea. In his preface to *Spirits in Korea*, Murayama clarifies the purpose of his multivolume study of Korea's popular religions: "We ought to understand Korean thought in order to correctly understand their culture. In order to understand Korean thought, it is natural to start with their popular beliefs."[38] His stated objective was to get to the most authentic of Korean popular beliefs that were allegedly free of foreign cultural influences. Murayama highlighted Confucianism and Buddhism as preeminent examples of non-authentic, foreign-origin religious systems. He made numerous references to new critical challenges of his time—namely, Western material and cultural influence in Asia. Presenting a plethora of local customs, this Japanese scholar's view of spirit beliefs in colonial Korea shows a quaint similarity with those expressed by the early American missionaries to Korea. The similarity takes on several aspects. Murayama argues that spirits are an object of fear for Koreans. This is followed by the argument that traditional communal life in rural Korea constitutes an island of precarious security, surrounded by a multitude of threatening spirit entities that are omnipresent in their immediate environment. His notion of "spirits" is a generalized category close in meaning to evil spirits, whether these are animistic entities or ancestral spirits, although in his renderings of customs in a concrete locale, he also introduces many observations that contradict this generalization. Based on this generalization, he concludes that popular rituals in the colony—shamanic, domestic, or communal—are all an instrument of appeasement in the sense that they are intended to dissuade evil spirits from exerting negative influences on society. In other words, according to him, the telos of popular religious practices in Korea is to augment luck for the individual and the family (for Murayama, a Korean village is a family writ large), whereas this pursuit of luck is grounded in the generalized thought-culture at the core of which lies the fear of spirits. Murayama warns the reader not to apply too hastily the idea of superstition to this culture and thought phenomenon. However, he also carefully builds up a moral hierarchy between the thought culture of the colony and the thought tradition in the metropolis. This is done in two ways. On the one hand, he makes repeated remarks on the correspondence between the living religious life in Korea and the religious tradition in ancient Japan. On the other hand, he also writes of the absence of transcendental religious conception in grassroots Korea, where spirits are very much like humans and, therefore, lack supernatural, beyond-humanity qualities. In other words, according to him, Korea's religiosity appears to constitute a pre-religion spirituality that is as yet unaware of universal and transcendent ideas—such as what the Sun God of Shintoism represents.

Scholars in South Korea specializing in colonial-era religious discourses share the view that Murayama conducted his research on popular beliefs in Korea in close communication with the colonial office. The question is, then, why the colonial power, from its very early days, took an especially strong interest in grassroots spirit beliefs, rather than in more institutionalized religious forms, such as Buddhism or Confucianism. Murayama explains that this is because popular religions are the backbone of "the thought" of the colonial subjects, their collective mentality.

Kim Seong-nae, South Korea's prominent expert on shamanism, proposes a different explanation: Confucianism and Buddhism were both part of East Asia's high religious and moral civilization, and Shintoism had many syncretic elements adopted from the tradition of Buddhism.[39] Therefore, identifying Korea's cultural tradition with Buddhism and Confucianism would have caused problems in the construction of civilizational hierarchy between Japan and Korea. According to her, shamanism worked well in building this hierarchy. If Korea's true religion was spirit beliefs, it was possible to project a distance, within the scheme of social evolution, between the Japanese "thought" familiar with the transcendental religion of Shinto, on the one hand, and, on the other, the Korean "thought" that remained on a lower mental ladder of non-transcendental worldliness. For the colonial office, Kim explains that Buddhism was a foreign religion to Koreans in origin, and Confucianism was merely an ideology of their ruling elite. The colonial office's interest in indigenous shamanism was therefore a carefully crafted extension of the Western imperial powers' scheme of civilizational hierarchy in regard to non-European cultures.[40] Japan modified this scheme to suit its own colonial project on a nation with which the colonizer had long had close cultural exchanges. The high religion of Shintoism versus the low collective "thought" of spirit beliefs fitted the bill, and, in this sense, the research on Korea's "evil spirits" (*gwisin*) by Murayama and his colleagues was a political project with a foregone conclusion.

Kim Seong-nae proceeds to compare the colonial office's interest in Korea's spirit beliefs with similar interests advanced by some of Korea's early nationalist scholars—such as Choi Nam-son and Shin Chae-ho. These scholars also advocated shamanism as the foundation of Korea's spirituality, yet with an aim that was contrary to that of the colonial administration—not in terms of grassroots culture but rather in a deep historical, social evolutionary narrative that traced Korea's national cultural origin to ancient polities where shamans were both priests and political leaders. This narrative related Korea's claimed ancient shamanism-centered civilization to the northern Siberian and Eurasian route of cultural diffusion and transhumance, thereby seeking a trajectory of cultural identity separate from the Sino-centric world and, more importantly, from the southern maritime route of cultural diffusion involving ancient Japan. Reviewing these nationalist projects of cultural identity and sovereignty-making in relation to the colonial project of creating civilizational hierarchy, Kim argues further that these two projects, despite the fact that their political objectives were opposed to each other, had much in common—for instance, locating sha-manism as Korea's archaic ideology. Other observers advance an even harsher criticism, questioning whether cultural nationalism was, in the end, even complicit with cultural imperialism. They justify this argument partly with reference to the fact that in the harsh climate of the 1930s, when Japan pro-voked crises of war in China and eventually in wider Asia and the Pacific, some of these cultural nationalists lost their will to resist and entered into a collaboration with the then-heavily militarized, increasingly violent im-perial power.

We have no intention here to join the tortuous debates on the politics of collaboration in relation to Japan's imperial history. These debates consti-tute an important domain of historical scholarship in China and Korea, and continue to fire up heated public reactions in both countries. We saw earlier how related issues continue to haunt Korea's church history scholarship even today, many years after the end of World War II. As Timothy Brooks shows, collaboration addresses a complex historical milieu where human action (and inaction) confronted a brutally coercive power—not a place for the moralizing language of purity and betrayal.[41] Our concern is rather with the invention of shamanism's cultural authenticity within the turbulent, com-plex milieu of colonial domination. Kim argues that the colonial era was when shamanism became Korea's principal superstition. This is the case, yet only partially so, since the colonial period was also, as she explains, when efforts were also made to enthrone shamanism as Korea's most authentic, most indigenous religious tradition. The distance between the label of su-perstition and the entitlement of authentic culture is so large that it can be an almost impossible task to bridge the two modes of identification. More-over, as we saw in Chapter 3, a struggle between the two opposing identifi-cations has continued in Korea in much more recent times, not merely in the now-distant colonial era. The bifurcating moral identity of shamanism remains entrenched even today, thereby continuing to be the source of ex-istential predicament for the practitioners of this popular art. The condi-tion has been even more critical for the Hwanghae shamans in Incheon who are associated with spirits such as that of MacArthur—an unauthorized his-torical persona and a foreigner, which, as we will see in the ensuing discus-sion, has long been considered a proof of an improper spirituality in Korea's history of religion. The question is: How can you justify the introduction of a foreign identity to a domain, if this domain is supposed to embody an authentic national spirituality? Why can't a foreigner spirit play a role in the augmentation of human welfare in the form of luck-making? Furthermore, what is wrong with seeking good luck? Don't we all do it—from the foragers in a remote hunting society to the customary well-wishes in electronic communication today? Why do modern sovereign powers, imperial or otherwise, fear the pursuit of luck by humans and the power of spirits that is brought into this act of world-making?

5

ORIGINAL POLITICAL SOCIETY

MacArthur was at a meeting. Together with many other spirits, he was seated around a large round table. Wearing his usual army uniform, he stood out and looked full of confidence. He showed some humility, too—out of respect for the old ones. This is how Lee Jong-ja opened her account of a dream she recently had of her tutelary spirit-helper, General MacArthur. Madame Lee encounters the General in her dreamworld regularly—mostly ahead of a new *kut* event. She usually took his appearance to be an auspicious sign, signaling to her that the upcoming ritual event would be a success. On other occasions when, for instance, Lee was troubled by personal and domestic problems such as conflicts among her follower novice-shamans, a dreamtime meeting with the General could also be a warning.

Like other Korean shamans, Lee communicates with her guardian spirits on an everyday basis—through early morning prayer and meditation, as well as divinatory sessions with clients. These include occasional visits to Freedom Park, where the statue of MacArthur is located. Dreaming is also an important means of communication. Details matter greatly in the interpretation of a dream—for example, the spirit's facial expression, how he is dressed, and in what circumstances he appears. The round-table scenery was powerfully auspicious in this sense and in its minute details: that he was dressed in a freshly ironed outfit and, moreover, in the presence of a large number of dignitaries—such images are an extremely positive sign in Korea's traditional dream interpretations.

The round table is particularly noteworthy in this story. During our conversation, Lee returned to this image repeatedly, presenting it as proof that MacArthur had become a fully legitimate and integral member of the collective of the spirit-helpers, many of which, unlike the American General, have long been part of Korea's shamanism and popular spirituality. She took great satisfaction in the fact that her tutelary spirit, a foreigner in origin and extremely young in terms of historical depth, was now a member of the eminent council of spirits, together with other much older historical figures and much more established mythical powers—such as the spirit entities that represent the heavenly authority or those considered masters of the mountain realm or in the production of wealth. We may approach the round-table imagery from yet another perspective. Being a purposeful assembly of individual entities or actors, the imagery may speak of a particular political character and composition of this assembly—that its participants are equal to one another rather than structured according to a hierarchical order as in the typical image of the other world, akin to that of a feudal imperial court, in China and in China-influenced traditional East Asia.

Indeed, the existing scholarship of Korea's shamanic tradition includes an interesting debate on the political structure of supernature found in this tradition. Some observers view that Korean shamanism's pantheon of spirits takes on a vast hierarchical order, from the *chŏnsin* (heavenly deities) on the top layer to the *japsin* ("miscellaneous spirits") on the lowest rungs of the ladder. This view resonates with the idea of "the original political society" in recent anthropological conversation, as we will see shortly.[1] For now, it needs to be mentioned that this view is more than a factual assertion. It also relates to a conceptual issue of a political character that speaks closely to the turbulent political history involving the place of shamanism in Korean culture, especially that of the colonial era, as discussed earlier. Crudely put, the hierarchical thesis is, in a significant sense, an extension of the cultural-nationalist resistance against Japan's colonial cultural politics, which, as we saw in the preceding chapter, reduced shamanism in Korea to an archaic, animistic spirit belief—that is, as part of an effort to present shamanism, in contradistinction to the colonialist projection, as a sophisticated "religion" in the sense of an institutional religion, entertaining an elaborate structure of authority and power in the image of a feudal or ancient kingdom. It is debatable whether and to what extent such an antianimism rendering of shamanism was effective in rescuing shamanism from the encapsulating logic of colonial politics or in being a genuine challenge to the latter in the first place (for the reason, among others, that both arguments, colonialist and nationalist, share the fundamental assumption that a hierarchical structure is a superior civilizational formation). The important point is that there were scholars who advanced an opposite view of shamanism's supernatural order and who, in so doing, we believe, expressed doubts about the cultural-nationalist claim for shamanism being a (high) religion, not only the empirical grounding of this claim but also its effectiveness as a resistance discourse. According to this view, the composition of supernature in Korean shamanism departs radically from the equivalents familiar in major world religions, in that spirit entities featured in it are all vigorously independent of one another. The vigor entails stubborn adherence to the principle of autonomy or self-determination among these entities, irrespective of any difference in their origin and spheres of influence. The most prominent advocate of this anti-hierarchy perspective was Yim Suk-jay, whom we briefly encountered in Chapter 2.

YIM SUK-JAY

Yim Suk-jay (1903–1998) was one of the most prominent anthropologists in South Korea in the post–Korean War era. He was also an eminent folklorist who devoted his entire career to the recording and compiling of Korea's traditional popular religious customs, notably the diverse regional traditions of shamanism, including those now in North Korea. Yim studied psychology at Kyungsung University, Japan's higher education institute in colonial Korea. He began his career as a folklorist in 1927, first as a research assistant to two Japanese researchers into Korean culture and religion, Akiba Takashi and Akamatsu Jizo. This was followed by his independent research into *minsok*, meaning broadly popular culture in Korean, while teaching at a secondary school in northern Pyŏngan province (now in North Korea) in 1931–1942. After Korea's liberation from Japan's colonial occupation, he worked as a professor of psychology in the College of Education at Seoul National University (what was Kyungsung University before), until his retirement in 1967. While teaching psychology, his research interests focused very much on shamanism and its related diverse popular cultural relics. He founded the Korean Cultural Anthropological Association in 1958 and also played a formative role in establishing the Korean Folkloric Society. He left a large corpus of work, ranging from earlier reports on popular religion and art in northern Korean regions, to his later encyclopedic treatise on Korean shamanism. He also wrote a number of children's books, introducing local legends that he had collected from different parts of Korea. Here, we concentrate on his two-piece journal article, published in 1970–1971, in which he proposed the theory of shamanic deities and their organizational form that he named parallelism.[2]

Yim's theoretical intervention was the culmination of his lifelong engagement with the subject. It was also a critical response to the prevailing political atmosphere of the time in South Korea regarding traditional cultures, including shamanic tradition. As illustrated earlier (see Chapter 3), the late 1960s and early 1970s was a dark time for this religious form and the myriad of local heritages associated with it. This era witnessed a strong state-driven, mass-mobilized economic modernization and social reform campaign. The campaign involved a generalized anti-superstition drive and heavy-handed assault on existing local material cultures and customary practices that are broadly referred to, in the literature, as popular religions. This was the time when all that was "traditional" (other than what the state regarded to be worthy of conservation and promotion) risked being expunged from society under the labels of irrationality, inefficacy, and counter-modernization. Shamanism in particular—including a broad swath of popular beliefs and practices associated with it—was considered a paramount social evil and the principal target of this coercive disenchantment campaign. The campaign was effective, as it employed both a top-down approach, based on a strong state bureaucracy resembling a military command structure, and a ground-up mass mobilization involving prolific grassroots organization and the propagation of the ideology of modernization. In this milieu, shamanism stood out as a principal object of containment in the cultural sphere and public enemy to the nation's march to future economic growth—toward the destination that some historians call "the right kind of revolution" in the Cold War.[3]

Yim Suk-jay's treatise on Korea's shamanism demonstrates that he was critically aware of the prevailing atmosphere of the time. It responded to the state-instituted disenchantment drive in carefully crafted and subtly argued prose, opposing the rendering of shamanism in the language of superstition and as the key object of culture reform. He did this along several steps. First, he challenged the way in which shamanism was singled out as a distinct and independently standing religious form, separate from the myriad of customary ideas and everyday practice, arguing that his concerns were with the shamanism-related cultural habitat (i.e., *musok*), not shamanism as such, which referred to a specific ritualism and related ritual expertise.[4] He argued that if shamanism was taken out of these everyday customary practices, the very notion of traditional Korean culture becomes vacuous and indefinable. Following from this, it then becomes apparent that some of the most mundane practices (such as offering a hand of prayer in the morning to the site of a kitchen god in a discreet corner of the household cooking arena) become as shamanic as the extraordinary act of a ritual expert during a *kut*, stepping on a pair of razor-sharp blades as a way of demonstrating the spirit power. Conversely, the very term *shamanism* loses much of its esoteric relevance because the art and aesthetics referred to as such are part and parcel of ordinary life—rather than the extraordinary spiritual phenomena they are usually presented as being in the existing literature on shamanism. As a result, ordinary actions are an enactment of shamanism, as effective and meaningful as any ritualized acts referred to as shamanic. The idea is that the *kut* is merely a particular manifestation of *musok* (meaning in this context, the habitat [*sok*] of shamanism [*mu*]), whose horizon is far broader and much more embedded in everyday life. The reference to shamans in Korean, *mudang*, in fact, does not merely mean a person who has expertise in the performance of the particular ritual called *kut*, as popular knowledge has it today. Rather, it signifies the shamanism of *mu* that is attached to a *dang*, a communal house of worship. As such, the reference invokes a public status and related condition of attachment to a community; this is how Kim Kŭm-hwa writes of her life in her natal village in Hwanghae before she was displaced by war (see Chapter 3), fondly recalling her place in the village as a locally grounded shaman proudly in charge of the community's annual and seasonal ritual calendar. This condition of local grounding is linked closely to what, for Kim, was the village's spirited landscape, consisting of shrine houses, spirit trees, and a host of other sacred or auspicious sites. Such sites were a primary target of the aggressive culture reform movement in the 1970s, which waged a concerted campaign for the removal of these sites from the local milieu as a necessary condition for the nation's march toward economic and social modernity. The destruction was also to be proof of the "spiritual armament" of the local population for the desired forward march. In order to be rightful citizens of the national community in this political atmosphere, it was necessary to disembed shamanism from their lives and lived environment—as Yim remarks, "to put and keep shamanism in the air-tight earthenware pot."[5]

Against this background, Yim makes the emphatic statement that "the study of *musok* is in a sense a study of [Korean] culture."[6] In parallel with this comment on the spatiality of shamanism, which, according to him, is much broader than the sphere of esoteric ritualism commonly referred to as shamanism, and much more deeply embedded in popular culture than imagined, Yim proceeds to make an observation on shamanism's historicity. He reiterates the point made in earlier works on Korea's shamanism tradition—namely, that this tradition traces back to ancient and archaic times, and is rooted in archaic tribal lives and ancient chiefly tribal polities. He introduces the ideas of *mana* (magical force) and *anima* (soul or vitality)—concepts that were once central to the anthropology of religion, especially with regard to animism and what E. B. Tylor called "natural religion." He does so, however, as part of his specific effort to make a break from a field that was long dominated by Japan's colonial-era ethnohistorical studies. We will come back to this issue of an analytical break with the property of social evolutionism; for now, suffice it to mention that the question he is most concerned with, as regards shamanism's historicity, is how this cultural form has had such extraordinary longevity and survived across numerous epochs, from ancient to modern times.

While confronting this question, also raised by many other observers of Korean shamanism, Yim distinguishes himself from most of the rest, among whom the explanation typically falls into a vague, ahistorical notion of popular mentality or authentic Korean mental culture. The argument is a simple tautology: If a seemingly archaic-origin cultural form survives in modern times, the resilience must be an expression of the fact that the aesthetic form constitutes the core property of Korea's collective personality. Such rendering of shamanism's historical resilience is in tune with the theory of cultural personality, a notable paradigm in the mid-twentieth century (see Conclusion to this volume). The theory postulates that each defined cultural entity can be considered an extension of the human individual, believed to entertain unique psychological dispositions, while relegating the aspect of communication and mutual influence to the concept of diffusion. As will be discussed, this conceptual rendering of human diversity was closely associated with the prevailing political condition of the era on the global scale, notably the process of decolonization. The postcolonial political process was principally about achieving the right to self-govern and self-determine and, relatedly, obtaining an equal status in the international society consisting of a multitude of these rights-claiming sovereign units. The politics of decolonization also involved the construction of a supposedly unique national culture and cultural heritage, a phenomenon that is referred to as the invention of tradition in the scholarship of cultural history.[7]

Seen from another perspective, the point about cultural survival, when this relates to such an arguably archaic religious form as shamanism, also relates closely to the widely made critique of the Weberian picture of religion and society. Max Weber explained the advent of modernity with the idea of disenchantment—that "with the rise of secularization the world becomes disenchanted, leaving behind the image of an expressive world replete with multiple signs from God"—although he was far from believing that this process necessarily meant the further flowering of human freedom.[8] Many studies of contemporary Asian religions cast doubt on this thesis, highlighting a variety of conditions in the region that involve the persistence of magical customs in modern life and/or recurrent revivals of popular religious passions.[9] Other observers such as Simon Coleman and Rosaline Hackett, leading scholars in the growing field of the anthropology of world Christianity, take note of the crucial fact that Christianity has been globally Southernized—that a vast majority of the world's two billion Christians today practice their beliefs in Africa, Latin America, and Asia, no longer in Europe and North America as was broadly the case before the 1950s.[10] Relatedly, some critics advance the view that Weber's perspective on this matter was overly Europe-centered, oblivious of different significances that religion may have in non-Western societies and non-Christian civilizations.[11] This broadly postcolonial criticism of the disenchantment thesis, which often involves debates on secularization, however, tends to circumvent one crucial fact—that even in the history of Western modernity, there have been recurrent arguments about the process of re-enchantment arising as part of the rationalization of the sociopolitical order—as forcefully argued by the scholarship of German critical philosophy. Interestingly, sociologist Mark Schneider writes of the discipline of anthropology as part of the re-enchantment dynamics in modern society—a discipline that began to explore, exactly at the time that a disenchanted society became an established notion in the Western world, a multitude of magical customs in the wider world.[12]

The theory of cultural personality, and the related idea of a culturally diverse world consisting of various entities entertaining unique collective characters, represented the prevailing atmosphere of the mid-twentieth century. It was also instrumental in the making of the era's global order, consisting of a growing number of sovereignty-claiming political entities.[13] While perhaps making certain sense in the international terrain, seen within the interiority of a postcolonial nation-state, however, the theoretical posture ran into a host of vexing problems. Notable among these is the question of how to decouple the concept of cultural authenticity from the characterization of the primitive or the superstitious inherited from colonial politics. As Yim's career testifies, the colonial power in Korea also had a strong interest in this cultural domain, especially in the idea that at the core of Korean "mental ideology" lurked the archaic and primitive religiosity represented by shamanism (see Chapter 4). This made the colonized nation stand on the lower tier of civilizational maturity and cultural evolution, thereby justifying the politics of colonization—according to the logic of *mission civilisatrice*.

The identification of Korea's collective character with shamanism was part and parcel of colonial political reasoning. This is illustrated by the fact that early research into Korean shamanism was directed and commissioned by Japan's colonial office in Korea, whose results were published by that office as part of its policy papers. The relegation of Korea's core national cultural property to shamanism was, therefore, a great challenge to Korea's nationalist intellectuals, who struggled to decouple the idea of authenticity, with regard to shamanism, from the colonial ideology of primitivism. It continued to challenge Korean folklore studies in the subsequent eras, as these delved into the body of religious cultural customs and relics that were regarded, by the political authority and in the broader public world, as remnants of a backward past to be overcome for the nation's forward march toward socioeconomic modernity. As one former student of Yim Suk-jay recalls, it was difficult to reconcile what he was learning from the anthropologist (in the 1970s) with what he heard from his family elders: "Those who like stories of old days live in poverty."[14]

It is against these complex backgrounds, with which Yim was familiar (as he lived through the times), that the anthropologist moves on to his thoughts on shamanism's constitutive political order in his 1970 essay. Implicit in his exposition are the three critical questions: (1) What is needed to free the concept of authenticity from the politics of primitivism? (2) How can we make sense of shamanism's resilience over time? (3) To what extent is shamanism embedded in everyday lives? Yim argues that any attempt to confront these questions must start with shamanism's own distinct world order. And, according to him, this calls for nothing less than imagining an original political society.

METAPERSONS

Does the society of immortals, or the social organization of gods, mirror the society of mortals? Or does this organization have its own authentic structural order oblivious of and wildly different from the structure of existence among the living? The eminent American cultural anthropologist Marshall Sahlins explores these hugely ambitious questions in his 2017 essay, evocatively titled "The Original Political Society."[15]

Sahlins's take on the question of cosmic proportion has two parts. The first one is relatively simple and argues that many peoples and cultures the world over do not imagine the world order of supernature as a mirror image of their own worldly order. In support of this conclusion, Sahlins introduces a large variety of ethnographic reports on indigenous cosmology and religious ideology. Important for his argument are reports on egalitarian societies. These small-scale societies in the Malaysian rainforest, Oceania, Amazonia, and the Arctic may possess no discernible class or status system. Despite the absence or relative lack of hierarchical relations, according to Sahlins, the cultures of these societies typically project a stratified and hierarchical relationship between the human society and the world of spirits, gods, and deities, which they typically portray in the image of human beings—"metapersons," as Sahlins calls them. Hence, his simple answer to the above questions is anti-mimetic—supernature is not a mirror image of society, even though supernatural beings may be in the image of human beings. These egalitarian societies observe rules that discourage human individuals from being overtly privileged over the others, whereas concerning other-than-human metapersons, beings in supernature, these rules fall apart and the world order takes on a non-equal, hierarchical formation. Thus, the Inuit in the extreme north of North America may harbor a fervent egalitarian ideology among themselves, whereas their lives, as a whole, are at the mercy of the Supreme Deity who holds "supreme sway over the destinies of mankind," as Sahlins argues, citing Franz Boas.[16] As for the Chewong of the Malaysian rainforests, studied by Signe Howell, Sahlins argues that "although Chewong society is described as classically 'egalitarian,' it is in practice coercively ruled by a host of cosmic authorities, themselves of human character and metahuman powers."[17]

Sahlins's main assertion is that there is a radical disparity between the order of human society and that of supernatural society. His principal concern is with the phenomenon that "there are kingly beings in heaven even where there are no chiefs on earth."[18] Regarding chief-less or egalitarian societies, this observation entails a type of an inversion of order between socius and cosmos, the collective of human persons and the political order constituted by a multitude of metapersons. Sahlins has a more complex assertion in mind, however, while making this generalization about the duplexity of human culture. Referring to the Araweté in Brazilian rainforest studied by Eduardo Viveiros de Castro, he summarizes his argument:

> [Araweté society] is not complete on earth: the living are part of the global social structure founded on the alliance between heaven and earth [according to Viveiros de Castro]. We need something like a Copernican revolution in anthropological perspective: from human society as the center of a universe onto which it projects its own forms—that is to say, from the Durkheimian or structural functional wisdom—to the ethnographic realities of people's dependence on the encompassing life-giving and death-dealing powers, themselves of human attributes, which rule earthly order, welfare, and existence. For, Hobbes notwithstanding, something like the political state is the condition of humanity in the state of nature.[19]

Several things are going on here. First, as we understand it, the "Copernican revolution" he is advocating has, at its core, the act of parting with the foundation of modern social anthropology, and that of modern social science at large, which Sahlins believes is intrinsically androcentric and sociocentric. He picks a bone with Emile Durkheim in this light, among other heroes (or anti-heroes) in the pantheon (or the idolatry) of this allegedly super-androcentric tradition of modern sociology. "Anthropology was founded by freeing itself from the confines of religious authority," Michael Lambek rightly observes, and most memorable in this struggle for freedom was Durkheim's *The Elementary Forms of Religious Life*, which revolutionized how we think about divinity in relation to society.[20] Departing decisively from the previous eras (in European cultural history), in which the prevailing doctrine explained the origin of society as a handicraft of the divine power, Durkheim turned the picture upside down, showing with his interpretation of totemism that the idea of divine power, and that of the sacred, is derivative of the social nature of human beings and a representation of the imperative of their existing collectively.[21] This was indeed akin to a Copernican revolution in modern social thought, which brought down the laws of movement from the mystical heavens to the actuality of human existence. What Sahlins seems to be arguing is that this foundational revolution in modern social science and its radical humanism was misguided, as it resulted in an overly human-centered, human-directed view of worldmaking. We need to undertake a new revolution, he advocates, to dethrone society from its paradigmatic status in worldmaking so that supernature regains its originary, authoritative place in what he calls "cosmopolitics." His proposition is not, for sure, to return to the *ancien régime*—to the time before the Durkheimian revolution where the cosmopolitical order was centered squarely on the holy spirit and the disposition of the human soul accordingly, rather than on the normativity of human sociality and the religiosity that the construction of this normative order requires. In our view, the proposition is rather an expression of his discontent with how the intellectual revolution by the early French sociological school was conducted and what it missed in carrying out this sociological revolution against theology.[22]

Sahlins is far from alone in expressing discontent with the above genealogy of contemporary social science scholarship, and one keyword for understanding this may be animism. Most of the ethnographic cases and vignettes that Sahlins introduces to his advocacy of a new Copernican revolution in anthropology are broadly animism-related. In fact, Sahlins discusses E. B. Tylor's 1871 *Primitive Culture*, the work that first dealt in a systematic way with the set of religious issues referred to as animism.

It is not an exaggeration to say that the birth of modern social theory, especially within the genealogy of social anthropology, involved an epic battle between two theories of soul. One theory relates closely to the religious form broadly referred to as animism, whereas the other focuses on the social form with a religious aspect called totemism. Curiosities about these forms were strongly present in the early development of modern anthropology. Most prominently, Durkheim brought totemic beliefs to his revolutionary treatise on the nature of society. He did so, however, in critical response to interpretations of animistic beliefs, notably Tylor's.

Tylor defined animism—the human practice of endowing natural objects with the property of soul—as the natural religion.[23] The idea of the natural, for him, was in contrast to that of the moral. Tylor believed that animism was free from questions of morality, which, in his view, constituted the backbone of the doctrines of world religions. One may translate this notion of the natural to the pre-moral or pre-social, following Durkheim, for whom the social order was at once a moral order. The notion appeared profoundly misplaced to Durkheim, who veered decisively away from how Tylor handled the idea of soul.

According to Philippe Descola, although animism and totemism both connect the human world to the natural world, they do so in mutually distinct ways.[24] In animism, the human-cultural world has the upper hand over the natural world in that humans impose on nonhuman species or other natural entities the properties of intentionality and agency similar to those found in the human species. Descola argues that the opposite is true in totemism, in which differences found between natural entities (e.g., between different animal species) are appropriated to explain differences in identity between human groupings. According to Descola, animism speaks of the properties of the human species being extended to the natural environment, whereas totemism infuses the perception and knowledge of the environment into what humans are good at—creating groupings and differentiating their social group from other groupings. The aspect of self-and-other differentiation that Descola highlights originates from Claude Lévi-Strauss's reinterpretation of totemism. Lévi-Strauss's work, as is well known, was a critical response to Durkheim's earlier exposition of totemism, which singularly focused on totemism's power to bind individuals to a group rather than on intergroup differentiation.[25]

For Durkheim, totemism spoke of the birth of society—the question of how individual human souls create a spirit of collective existence. The problem Durkheim had with Tylor was that he placed the question of soul on the wrong trajectory. The proper place for the question was not in the natural world but squarely within the social world. Durkheim's reasoning that follows this challenge is well known: The totem is a symbolic expression of the soul in that it represents the part of the human soul that is social—what Durkheim referred to as collective representation. The work of the totem is principally a means for human individuals to bring themselves together for an existence larger than individual existence. The totem points to the relationship between the two sides of the soul, personal and impersonal, which Durkheim expressed with his powerful idea of *homo duplex*. The totem is concerned with the transformation of the self to a being larger than itself—to part of a family, a clan, a nation, or, following the same logic, humanity as such (and, if necessary, even to a horizon that is called post-human in contemporary scholarship). The concept of soul should be made meaningful to grasp an understanding of human existence along these various institutional and structural layers, from the family to humankind—that is, as a means of scientific inquiry into the human condition. In contrast, Durkheim believed that the idea of soul, as presented in Tylor's interpretation of animism, does not serve the purpose of advancing this science, to which Durkheim himself remained devoted throughout his career. How can you inquire into the life of soul in the context of social science if soul is rendered to have a supposedly natural, pre-moral life? Such questioning formed the background of Durkheim's rejection of animism as a meaningful subject of social scientific enquiry.

We may regard the above episode as the fall of a naturalistic theory of soul in the early history of social science. That is, at least, how Durkheim understood his own project in relation to Tylor's. In contemporary anthropology, there has been a plethora of attempts to go beyond the concept of the scientific that emerges from this story, in the specific sense of the science of the social and the moral, and some of these efforts involve a move back to the largely forgotten prehistory of totemism and what was disregarded in the advent of the totemism-based theory of society.

The French social theorist Bruno Latour delved into the scholarship of a contemporary of Durkheim's, Gabriel Tarde, whose alternative view to social connectivity, in Latour's view, had been unjustly in the shadows of Durkheim.[26] Descola, as mentioned earlier, has been exploring the possibility of bringing back animism as a philosophically meaningful subject on a par with totemism. His strategy is to advance animist and totemic beliefs as contrasting ways to relate society to nature. Descola explains totemism as society's appropriation of nature (society's use of differences found in nature to explain differences between societies). Animism works along the same divide between nature and society but in an opposite trajectory, in which what is distinctly human (the possession of soul) is extended to the realm of nature. Seen in a wider spectrum, other broadly corresponding efforts can be found in contemporary anthropological research. The current interest in everyday ethics is in many ways an effort to go beyond Durkheim's theory of moral order. Totemism, in Durkheim's view, constitutes a moral as well as a symbolic order, in that it involves notions of taboo—that is, what lies beyond the norms of a given society. Contemporary studies on everyday ordinary ethics try to carve out the sphere of human moral practices that are not necessarily neatly patterned according to either the given, collectively shared set of norms or an ideologically dominant moral order.[27] Another relevant development might be contemporary interest in ontology. Scholars actively involved in this development are not satisfied with the idea of culture or cultural difference that has been a hallmark of modern anthropology since the mid-twentieth century.[28] They question whether so-called cultural differences take on, in certain indigenous conceptions, a much more radical character that comes close to "natural" existential differences. Many of the ethnographic facts brought forth in this exciting debate relate to animistic phenomena. Seen from an even broader platform, we may also take note of the currently revived interest in material cultures. This research trend expands the concept of agency from a previously androcentric confinement to broad relational milieu between human actions and the agency of things. The idea is that things may be seen as having social lives just as humans do, not merely in exotic cultural environments but also in modern societies. Sahlins joins in this broad yet diverse debate in contemporary scholarship to go beyond sociocentrism in social science, by raising questions on the idea of collective representation that has been so central to the sociology of religion. If the structure of divinity is not a mirror image of society, the entire scheme of social construction grounded in an analysis of totemism may fall apart. This probably is the bigger picture of Sahlins's essay on "The Original Political Society" and his reflections on the hierarchical, "kingly" political cosmology of some eminently egalitarian societies.[29]

PARALLELISM

Howell raises objections to the way in which the Chewong, who are stubbornly nonhierarchical in their moral worldview and cherish the principle of personal autonomy in their relations with one another, turn into, in the hands of Sahlins, helpless subjects of an all-powerful and encompassing supernatural kingdom.[30] Yim Suk-jay's treatise on Korean shamanic tradition presents a radically different picture of supernature and the universe it makes coactively with human society. Yim argues that here, as in other cultural traditions, the spirit entities take on strong human-like characteristics (i.e., Sahlins's metapersons), some more so than others. He does not refute the fact that relations among these spirit persons may appear to be of a hierarchical order, with the deity of the heavenly realm taking on the supreme authority. He is aware that this impression is held strongly among some experts on Korean folklore.[31] However, he makes it emphatically clear that this impression is valid only to the extent that the observer does not engage with how these spirits are enacted upon in the actual ritual space.

The *kut* invites many different kinds of metaperson to its performative sphere, which consists of a number of separate (yet developmental and sequential) stages—or *gŏri* (ways) as they are called. In each step-like phase, the specific invited spirit-person, whether high or low in formal status, becomes the master of that particular *gŏri*. So the nominally super-majestic deity that holds the movements of the sun, the moon, and all the stars under its authority takes on only one stage and is the master only within this stage. The same is true of the relatively far less majestic, less transcendental, more human-like spirits such as the ancestral spirits, who also are masters of their own stage within the *josang gŏri* (ancestors' way). Even the non-ancestral human-like spirits, which might be called ghosts, have their own stage-realm, within which they are nothing but sovereign identities. Moreover, there is absolutely no indication in this ritual world that some "ways" are more significant and authoritative than others. Doing it right with ghosts is as important as, sometimes more so, than hosting properly the deity of the sun, moon, and stars. Seen within the ritualized world (that is, rather than as an abstract cosmopolitical world), therefore, all spirit-persons are sovereign beings on their own and in their unique spheres, and they are stubbornly self-determining—as in an ideal international society (see later discussion).

In line with Yim's point, noted earlier, about shamanism's embeddedness in everyday life, we may consider the principle of cosmopolitical anti-hierarchy in an ecological perspective (in an ancient sense, where ecology meant household economy at large) and in the context of the domestic space. The traditional Korean house abounds with site-specific spirit-personages. The all-encompassing yet place-specific god of the land (*tŏju* or *tosin*) takes up a place often where the family keeps a collection of earthenware pots in which they store soy-bean sauce, soy-bean paste, and red-pepper paste—

principal elements of Korea's culinary culture, past and present. The all-important god of the built and dwelt house, *sŏngju*, has a number of locations, notably at the main beam supporting the roof. The cooking area is taken up by the kitchen god, *jowang*, and the toilet area has its own master sovereign spirit. All these spirit-persons together guarantee the security and prosperity of the household; yet, each of them has a place and realm, and is independent of the other place-specific spirit-persons.[32] They live collectively and individually at one and the same time, and their collective existence is relevant and meaningful only to the extent that the house exists and that members of the household interact with them on a regular and seasonal basis. When the matron of the house initiates a prayer activity (*bison* or *chisŏng*, an act of prayer by rubbing hands together) on a bowl of fresh water, this can take place at a corner of the main dwelling room, or next to the collection of pots, or at the back of the house. Yim makes it absolutely clear that this humble act of calling spirits is in no way a less authoritative gesture than a full-scale *kut,* overseen by a renowned shaman and lasting three to seven days and nights. When she does this, there is no sense of privileging spirits in the supposedly upper ladders of the supernatural hierarchy over those in the lower. The destination of her prayers may not be clear; it can be a specific sovereign spirit-being or a vaguely conceived collective of spirits. What is crystal clear in this context is rather the sheer empirical and existential fact of an I-and-Thou dialogue unfolding between the human actor and the other-than-human subject.

The political plurality of household gods can be manifested in other myriad circumstances and patterns: A warning against a misfortune possibly in store for the household may emanate from the deity of the land—for instance, through changing color or an unusual odor in the soybean sauce. The warning may be shown instead in the distorted shape of the pumpkins at the corner of the household garden. When the family is planning to move residence elsewhere, the god of the house may appear in a dream of a member of the family to give advice against the move—e.g., in the form of a gigantic spider net that prevents her, in her dream, from leaving the house. In a family whose children live and work in places far away from home, the family's matron may start her day by offering the gesture of *bison* to the kitchen god in the early morning. Occasionally, she may also do the same in her garden and in the thick of the night—toward the god of the mountain that overlooks her home and neighborhood. Madame Yang interacted closely with her kitchen god for many years, in her modest home in Osaka, on behalf of her children in North Korea who had moved there in the 1970s, as well as her other children living elsewhere in Japan and in her natal village of Jeju, an island along Korea's maritime border with Japan. A grandmother moves about, in her garden and in her neighborhood, with her grandchild on her back, reciting her slow-rhythmed lullabies that include a call to the god of fertility to help calm her grandchild's spirit so it can be at peace. Gestures similar to those of *bison* are also typically employed to prepare small rice cakes used for ceremonial offering. When people make them, they may leave a few pieces underneath a tree outside their home or underneath their home's external walls—on behalf of the displaced spirits believed to wander about in the environs.

Recalling her early career in a village in Hwanghae, now in North Korea, Kim Kŭm-hwa says that, at that time, each household was "a world of spirits"—where there were as many spirit-persons as human persons and in which the two groups interacted with each other every day. She makes it clear that the shamanism to which she was first introduced at a tender age was only a small and humble part of this majestic world of cohabitation between humans and spirits. This shamanism remained indistinguishable from the routines of everyday life most of the time, apart from some periodic occasions of a community-wide rite during which she, as the village's *dang'gol*, and her skills were under the spotlight of communal scrutiny. Shamanism then, she concludes, was part of the everyday, rather than some especially festive, formally ritualized occasion as it is typically understood in today's urbanized Korean society.

Yim Suk-jay makes the same point, as noted earlier, with regard to the concept of habitus. He urges us to come to grips with the mundaneness and profanity of shamanism in this regard, which means, in turn, the spirituality and sacredness of the everyday. In this milieu of everyday shamanism, Yim further argues that no particular spirit-personage has more relevance and power than another. There is no discernible power and authority differentiation, for instance, between the eminent god of the land or that of the mountain nearby, on the one hand, and, on the other, the humble kitchen god or even the spirit entity associated with the toilet area. They are simply *there*, he argues, each occupying a particular site as the sovereign dweller of the place. Their place-specific sovereign existence is part of the spirited domestic world, moreover, when the human cohabitants of this world direct their attention to it for their diverse yet concrete social-existential reasons.

Yim captures this evocative portrait of shamanism's spirit-persons and their sociopolitical organization with his theory of parallelism. In linguistics, this idea refers to situations in which various nominal entities and conceptual characters are made to exist in a parallel form and, often, in a long list that does not privilege some against others. In the context of a *kut*, this collective existential form takes on a sequential organization consisting of multiple "ways" and the related association of a particular ritual stage with distinct spirit entities. In the realm of a lived house and the everyday activities occurring within it, the principle is manifested in terms of the specific architectural locations and spatial sites, each of which is identified with the presence of a particular metapersonal entity. Seen together, these spirit-persons may look as though they constitute a distinct society that exists in parallel with the social group of human residents. Taken out of the milieu of active cohabitation with the living and viewed on its own, this society may also appear to have a hierarchical structure, vertical or concentric, in which power, authority, esteem, and fame are distributed varyingly and unevenly. Yim warns against the last impression, arguing that it is an analytical error, a result of failing to consider the spirits as part of a lived social reality and as part of the actually existing world of *mundus duplex*, lived in and enacted in by both spirits and humans.

A similar idea is found, in fact, in the ethnography of the Araweté of the Brazilian rainforest, on which Sahlins draws heavily.[33] This work concentrates on the dualist organization of the Araweté's social world, consisting of the world of spirits, on the one hand, and, on the other, the group of human inhabitants engaged in horticulture and hunting. It allocates considerable space to the work of indigenous shamans, which is, among other things, to mediate between the two distinct yet interconnected worlds. The main focus of this study is, however, on alliance—specifically on the relationship between two forms of alliance—in a way that closely follows Claude Lévi-Strauss's oeuvre on kinship and marriage.[34] One of these alliance relationships takes place between nature and culture, whereas the other is between separate corporate groups of a larger tribal entity, principally through marriage exchanges. Alliance is, as Lévi-Strauss shows, a relationship of reciprocity between parties that are equal to one another, whether it is a restricted one between two partner groups or a complex one involving multiple groups. In the context of indigenous Siberia, which Sahlins also addresses, considerable diversity is found in the shape of cosmopolitical order among many ethnic groups of the region, some of which come quite close to an egalitarian or acephalous social formation. These peoples may refer to the master spirit of the sky or that of the forest, the latter of which is also often regarded as the master of the wild animals on which the indigenous people rely for subsistence. However, the so-called supernatural master can take on a conceptually opposite position in terms of relational hierarchy. As Irving Hallowell shows, bear ceremonialism is traditionally a vital cultural institution across the vast northern territory of Eurasia and North America.[35] Among indigenous groups in eastern Siberia, this ceremonial tradition involves raising a bear cub (taken from the den) as if it were their child, and, when it became mature, conducting a ritually enacted hunt (or sacrifice)—an act intended to renew the environment and wild animal species in it.[36] In this ceremonial context, it is not the all-encompassing power of a kingly master of the forest that regenerates the world. Contrary to Sahlins's view, here it is the collective action of humans (fostering, feeding, and raising the fostered, then returning the child back to nature/supernature) through which only the regenerative power of nature is awakened and brought forward. Moreover, the human power that enables this cosmic renewal is fundamentally social and intersocial (and even international) in character—as the hunters in the bear ritual are typically the ritual-hosting group's affinal partners. Sahlins's discontent with Durkheim notwithstanding, therefore, we may not understand these ceremonial traditions while disregarding Durkheim's central thesis, which is the social nature of religious symbols.

THE ASSEMBLY OF SPIRITS

Yim Suk-jay concentrates on the "king-less," acephalous structure of shamanism, as he believes that this organizational condition of shamanism's supernature provides insights into this religious form's extraordinary longevity and resilience in history. He sees the structural condition more in the prism of a core–periphery concentric hierarchy than of a top-down vertical form, while arguing that the most prominent and distinct property of shamanism is the absence of stratification among its constituent spirit entities. According to him, this ultimately relates to the nonexistence of the core (versus periphery) in shamanism's constitutive order as a whole.[37] He writes:

> It appears that *musok* does not recognize any class difference in its spirits. There are no high or low spirits, nor dominant or dependent spirits in *musok*'s idea of spiritual power. These spirits do not have among themselves such relations of societal character as commanding, cooperating, collaboration or submission and thus maintain a relationship of nonassociation. Each spirit has a particular function of its own and independent from and equal to all others. They associate with each other only in relation to the humans. I will call this organization of spiritual power based on *complete independence and equality* a parallelist worldview.[38]

Therefore, according to him, the majestic "emperor of the heaven" can be, in popular shamanic (and larger-than-shamanic *musok*) culture, only a humble spirit.[39] He says in conclusion:

> The relations among the spirits have no class hierarchy and are instead of *an egalitarian parallelist order*. In other words, there is no core interior in this world, and each spirit is separate and independent. It is due to these qualities that the religious system is not easily to be broken.[40]

In this way, following a series of expositions on shamanism's distinct spatiality (embedded in the broad sphere of everyday life) and temporality (survival across radically different socioeconomic ages from ancient society to the modern industrial age), Yim presents shamanism's internal political organization as the principal condition (as well as a main explanation) for the religious form's unique spatiotemporal features. Concentrating on the question of historical durability, he argues that shamanism's apparently anarchic order (that is, in comparison with the hierarchically instituted supernatural order found in other religions) and the related obviation of a clearly defined normative order (see below) make the religious–social form relatively more resilient in great historical transformations and with regard to influences by other religions involved in these transformative processes. In this light, Yim discusses at length the centuries-old interaction between *musok* and institutional Buddhism in old Korea. As an illustration, he introduces the way in which an ancient shamanic goddess of fertility (having a child-like representation in olden times) gradually came to assimilate the appearance familiar in the Buddhist world (e.g., by taking on the image of a Buddhist monk known as *jesŏk*).

Conversely, institutional Buddhism also brought elements of *musok* into its architectural composition—as can be seen in the shrines that shelter mountain deities (*sansin-gak*) found nearly universally in Korea's Buddhist pagodas today. Yim limits his discussion of religious syncretism mostly to the interaction between indigenous shamanism and Buddhism, which was first introduced into Korea in the fourth century. However, we may extend the discussion to other historical horizons.

The introduction of Confucianism in Korea goes a long way back in Korea's history. However, as Martina Deuchler powerfully shows, since the fourteenth century Confucianism came to assume an explicitly political character in Korea.[41] The neo-Confucian revolution of the era sought to realize a political order grounded on Confucian ethics through a social revolution in the kinship system—from loose bilateral kinship relations to a rigid patrilineal system. This largely elite-driven revolution advanced rituals for ancestors (familial, communal, and stately) as a supreme ethical deed and the moral basis for virtuous human existence, individual and collective. In this milieu, too, as was the case in the encounter with Buddhism, *musok*, the habitus of shamanism, reacted to the mandates of the revolutionary power creatively—for instance, by assimilating this power's central preoccupation, ancestors, into its own ritual order—as can be seen in "the way of ancestors," an important part of a *kut* today. The act of ancestral remembrance in shamanic rituals is distinct from the equivalent in Confucian ritualism, in that it is open to the ego's (ritual host's) intimate memories of the departed, not being bound by the given patrilineal ideology.[42] Partly because of this, the Confucian literati looked down upon *musok*, defining it as *ŭmsa*, or shadowy ritualism—the practice of "offering rite to spirits that are not entitled to rite," according to the legendary text on Korean shamanism by Lee Nŭng-hwa (1869–1943).[43] However, it is also true that the founders of the strongly neo-Confucian Chosun dynasty, which lasted from the end of the fourteenth century till the end of the nineteenth, brought elements of shamanism into the innermost interiority of its state ritualism.[44] One result was the establishment of the Kuksadang (State Shrine) in Namsan, on a hill in the heart of Seoul, although the shrine is now in Inwangsan north of central Seoul, after it was relocated there in 1925 by Japan's colonial power, when they built their prime Shinto shrine on Namsan instead.

The politics of exclusive inclusion continued in the ensuing eras, although this is not to underestimate the rupture in this domain caused by the transition in the beginning of the twentieth century from the neo-Confucian moral order to the colonial political order. We may discuss this transition with relation to two Sino-Korean concepts, *ŭmsa* ("shadow rituals") of the Confucian era versus *misin* ("misguided and misguiding belief"). One key difference between these two concepts is the presence or absence of evolutionary thinking and imagining. *Misin* is Meiji Japan's adaptation of the term "superstition" and, as such, grounded in the ideology of social evolutionism and related civilizational hierarchy that prevailed during the age of empire-building. It projects the cultural form addressed as such in the depth of cultural evolution, in prehistoric or early civilizational times. In the European historical context, the concept is closely associated with many derivative notions such as primitive mentality or magical thought (in opposition to rational thought). As for imperial Japan, the designation of Korea's shamanism as superstition had the crucial function of constructing a cultural evolutionary hierarchy between itself and neighboring Korea and, ultimately, legitimizing its colonial occupation of the latter. The argument is simple: Korea's shamanism is akin to Japan's former popular Shinto beliefs. Whereas in Japan these beliefs have been radically transformed in its modernization experience, and consolidated into a singular, higher state religion during the process, in Korea popular religions remain unchanged, and continue to thrive as diffused local traditions without having developed into a higher unified religious form.

The concept of "shadowy rituals" (*ŭmsa*) existed in the Chosun era among the educated elite of the Confucian sociopolitical system. This referred not only to shamanism but also to a whole host of popular religious customs that the elite regarded as not falling into the order of ritualism as dictated by the neo-Confucian texts. Unlike the concept *misin*, however, *ŭmsa* had no property remotely similar to social-evolutionary ideas that prevailed in colonial politics. The term *ŭmsa* is primarily a spatial reference, separating morally legitimate ritual sites (according to neo-Confucian doctrines) from those that the social elite found in the broad lived milieus that they shared with underclass populations. As such, it resonates somewhat with notions like popular mentality or popular religion that prevailed in Victorian-era England and elsewhere in Europe around the same time. In other words, although it functioned to expunge popular religions from the society's defined normative sphere, the concept was intended more to distinguish highbrow culture from the low, rather than dominate or obliterate the latter (for the simple reason that without the existence of shadowy rituals the elite's self-consciously normative, bright and shining ritualism would lose its clarity).

The semantic power of superstition continued in postcolonial Korea, as discussed earlier with reference to policies of the US Military Government in Korea that privileged those natives whom that they considered like-minded (anti-communist and Christian). The dominant political ethos at this time was to turn the southern half of postcolonial Korea into a garrison state and society as a defense against international communism. This ethos included, in certain circles (for example, many in leadership positions and those displaced from the northern part of Korea), a vision to transform South Korea to an earthly Kingdom of God. Many early American missionaries to Korea at the end of the nineteenth century understood that building this kingdom required an aggressive culture war against, among other things, Korea's *musok* traditions—an approach that was forcefully brought back to Korea in the early Cold War era. The legacies of this era's politics of anti-superstition are far from a thing of the past, but continue to exert considerable influence on Korean society and politics today. Seen in this light, the presence of American power in Korea's religious landscape is both a historical question and an issue of contemporary history. It is a social fact in a literal sense of the term—being vigorously alive in the realm of shamanism as well as in the broad social environment within which this religious tradition dwells today.

On a closing note, let us go briefly back to where we set out in this chapter—to the image of the round table. Recall that the scene depicted MacArthur as present in the council of Lee Jong-ja's spirit-helpers as a fully legitimate member, together with a host of majestic traditional metapersons and eminent ancient hero-deities. This is despite the fact that the American General was a relatively new entry to the world of shamanism, having shallow historical depth and being ungrounded in Korea's traditional spiritual landscape. Following Yim Suk-jay, however, we may conclude that these shortcomings notwithstanding, MacArthur is a sovereign actor and an actor whose status is equal to even that of a majestic nature deity. That this spirit looked somewhat timid, behaving with some modesty and humility (in relation to the other spirits), however, makes us wonder whether even in the structurally anti-hierarchical society of spirits, some form of seniority or other regime of authority is still in play. This is certainly the case in today's international world, where some nations believe that they must have more say in the society of nations against the fact that, in the post–World War II world order, all nations, small or large and weak or strong, are equal to one another and must remain so. Underneath the façade of an acephalous society, therefore, there may lurk an awareness of the reality of differences in authority. Perhaps this disparity between principle and reality applies even to the radically egalitarian society of spirits as seen in Korean shamanism. And perhaps this is not at all unusual. Even in the most egalitarian society, such as that of Australian Aborigines or the Bushmen in central Africa, as the scholarship of hunter-and-gatherer societies amply demonstrates, the society's mature actors who have a lifetime's experience of foraging earn more respect and credulity than some zealous young foragers do.[45] The thing about egalitarian society is not that there is no authoritative voice in it. It is rather that in such a society, these societal authorities do not easily translate into political power (or prestige into privilege).[46] Or it may be the case, as Pierre Clastres argues, that political power is universal, whereas the definition of what power is varies greatly between historical societies and the indigenous worlds.[47] That MacArthur has found a place in the Council of Spirits is not unusual in yet another respect. According to Yim's rendering of Korean shamanism, shamanism as such is only a small part of the larger and much broader spiritual landscape, which is, nevertheless, so ordinary that it does not appear to be a particularly spiritual or religious space. The American General has a firmly established place in the city of Incheon and in the city's war-memorial art. For the townspeople, he has long been an integral part of their lived communal space. In Kim Dong-li's *Portrait of a Shamaness*, the protagonist and established village shaman, Mohwa, undergoes a family crisis, especially with her son, Uk-i, who has converted to Christianity.[48] Uk-i tries to dissuade his mother from her trade, and rescue her from the mud of her superstition. The problem Mohwa faces is not necessarily her son going his way; it is more that he does not allow his mother to go her own way. She is wondering why she can't bring her son's god into the society of gods she is intimate with. She does not understand why this god from America, in order to live in her land, has to first chase the land's old gods away. Yim Suk-jay's political theory of shamanism does not help explain why this has to be the case with Uk-i's new god; however, it does explain the source of Mohwa's confusion and anguish—that her council of spirits, like Lee Jong-ja's, has its doors open to newcomers and is ready to treat them as equal and independent partners.

6

PARALLELISM

A typical *kut* consists of a dozen or more stages, or *gŏri* ("ways"), each involving a distinct spirit-helper category. For instance, *jang'gun gŏri* invokes warrior spirits, whereas *josang gŏri* is exclusively for the hosting family's ancestral spirits. These individual *ways* are both parts of the whole ritual and each a whole in and by itself. Yim Suk-jay explains that each shamanic spirit is a demonstratively sovereign entity within a given sphere and fiercely independent from others.[1] His exposition of shamanism's superstructural political order demonstrates that each *gŏri* is a world on its own, and joins the larger world of *kut* as an independent and sovereign domain. Yim calls this structural condition a "relationship of non-association."[2]

As an analogy, to understand this "parallelistic" cosmopolitical structure, we may think of the modern international system, in which relations among the constituent units (i.e., the states) are governed, nominally speaking, by the principles of individual autonomy and relational equality or parity. It may sound somewhat far-fetched to propose that an arguably archaic religious form may possess within it a political imagination akin to the ideal of modern politics, especially that of international politics. The proposition surely goes against Marshall Sahlins's caricature of political society in supernature in the image of a feudal kingdom (see Chapter 5).[3] With a leap of imagination, however, shamanism's cosmopolitical order can be seen through an analogy of the modern international system—in contrast to that of a feudal monarchical order. Moreover, we argue that this way of seeing worldly affairs—that is, comparing the world of spirits to the world of states—is embedded in the art and aesthetics of shamanism, especially when seen from a historical perspective. This is also the case if approached as a purely conceptual question—for instance, the idea of *alliance*, discussed in the previous chapter as being a key property of some indigenous shamanism practices, is surely a concept concerning international (i.e., intergroup) political relations as well as a language of kinship and marriage. In advancing this somewhat bold argument, in this chapter, we return to the artifact that we introduced early on in this book (see Chapter 2)—the five-nation flags on Chung Hak-bong's spirit shrine at her home in Incheon. Recall that this consists of the flags representing the United States and Japan on one side, China and Russia on the other (the four principal geopolitical powers in Korea's modern history), with the flag of today's South Korea in between these two pairs. We discussed this artifact in relation to the five-color, five-directional flags of *obangki*, an important instrument in today's shamanic rituals, as well as with reference to the identically named emblems of secular territorial integrity and political sovereignty in pre-modern Korea. Here, we will ask whether the secular geopolitical composition represented by the *obangki* can relate to issues of Korean shamanism's supernatural political order discussed in Chapter 5 and, if so, how we can make sense of conversations between these two separate political forms—secular-historical and religious-symbolic. Our discussion will concentrate on the symbol of American power, because among the Hwanghae-origin, Incheon-based ritual actors, which include Chung Hak-bong, one of the most distinct features in their society of helper-spirits today is the presence of General MacArthur. Before going further, however, a few more words are due on Yim Suk-jay's political theory of Korea's popular religious conception.

PARTS AND WHOLES

When spirits are invited to the ritual space of *kut*, the invitation is specific to the rite's temporal or procedural order. It is also a temporary call, starting as each particular ritual stage begins and remaining only as long as that stage continues. Yim Suk-jay observes that one distinct characteristic of Korea's popular religious tradition is that people invite (*chŏngbae*) spirits only when they have a need to do so, and those invited are sent away when the need is no longer there. This observation has far-reaching implications.[4] During the visit of a spirit, the shaman and the spirit meet in an embodied state of dialogue, although the shaman can supplement this dialogic condition with her long-practiced, more formalized performative knowledge and technique. Similar conditions are often referred to as spirit possession in the literature; however, this does not capture what is going on in the *kut*. In Korean shamanic rituals, there is no such thing as "possession" in the sense of possessing a property, monetary wealth, or slaves. The spirit visitor does not possess the body of the ritual performer, nor does the latter take hold of the spirit. The shamanic deities do not have a permanent home: They only occupy the body of the caller on a momentary basis. So when the spirits visit, they do so knowing and expecting that, in due course, they will have to depart, leaving that place free for another visitor.

Italian scholar Antonetta Bruno, an expert on Korean shamanism, makes an interesting observation in this regard.[5] According to Bruno, the shaman who is engaged in *kut* operates in a double-dialogic context: She delivers the hosting family's wishes to the spirit visitor and, at one and the same time, conveys the spirit's messages and instructions to the family. Bruno discovered that when the two-way communication becomes intense, in the thick of the performance, especially when it is about the hosting family's most desired wishes or critical predicaments, the performing shaman sometimes falls into a linguistically confusing condition—demonstrated especially in the complex use of honorifics, a notable phenomenon in Korean language practice. The shaman may speak to the family in the third person (delivering messages from the spirit, addressing the latter with an honorific expression) or in the first person (as if she herself were the spirit, thereby doing without honorifics). Bruno calls this phenomenon double-consciousness on the part of the spirit-inviting ritual performer. This means that even in the context commonly referred to as "spirit possession," the actor is not entirely under the influence of the spirit. It also means the actor's state of being at that instance is, instead, closer in form to what is called in political theory the public sphere or the public world—that is, the space within which a plurality of individual speech-acts takes place freely and with a shared common objective in view.[6]

However, there are, of course, situations that are more akin to the condition of possession. During a *kut*, spirits may visit or occupy the body of a member of the ritual-hosting family rather than that of the shaman. This is especially common during a ritual specifically intended to confront the grievances of the soul of a recently deceased person, especially one who died in tragic or violent circumstances. While this is happening, the spirit (most often an ancestral spirit) may descend to a bamboo branch and then to the person who is holding the twig, through whom it says what it wishes to say. In certain regional traditions, such as of Jindo, an island off Korea's southern coast, the entire family group of the deceased might hold the bamboo, taking turns to become the spirit's means of communication. Compared with this situation, the shaman's body in trance is more of a public space in which spirits and humans can undertake communication. So the *kut* provides a social world that is larger than the usual secular social world, in which participation is extended to both the human persons and the spirit persons; in other words, the acting shaman becomes a fractal image of the ritual space at large, who facilitates, in an embodied way, the enlarged sociality.

As mentioned, a typical *kut* consists of a number of sequential, independent rites involving a plurality of spirit-persons. This means that each specific stage of a *kut* is not a partial segment of the ritual whole but a whole world in itself. We also noted that the composition of the person who performs in these structurally partial yet formally holistic ritual worlds is equivalent, in form, to the composition of the entire ritual space. This is in the sense that as much as the ritual space is a place of meeting between humans and spirits, so is the body of the shaman in which the two ontologically separate groups of beings make contact and engage in dialogue. The composition of the shamanic ritual, then, can be considered in the light of the idea of the fractal person, a theme that has been intensely discussed in certain anthropological research circles as regards individual identity and social structure.

SPIRITS THAT ARE SO HUMAN

Before moving on to debates on the fractal person and society, however, it is perhaps worth briefly returning to Yim Suk-jay and his point about the ephemerality of spirits' presence in the milieu of human existence. As we will see later in this chapter, these two issues—the formal equivalence between the whole and its constitutive parts, on the one hand, and the obviation of permanence (and therefore transcendence) in the concept of supernatural power, on the other—are closely related. Together, the two properties enable the subjectively sovereign and relationally equalitarian political structure of Korean shamanism's supernature.

Yim argues that in the broader habitat of shamanism, which is *musok*, the concept of spirit or god is not conceived of as one cosmically singular sovereign being. Instead, the popular cultural tradition is attentive to "the diverse objects and phenomena, which maintain close and intimate relations with human life, and endow on these various objects and phenomena a plurality of gods or spirits, thereby having them take charge of specific functions."[7] These "functions" point variously to the generation of luck and wealth, protection from misfortunes, achieving fertility or longevity, or enabling less grievous and painful transition to life after death. They also include the prevention and containment of infectious diseases, as was the case with *son'nim-kut* or *mama-kut* that were popular in the past. *Son'nim* (guest) and *mama* (honorific reference to people of high birth and status) refer, in this context, to spirit entities associated with the spread of smallpox. Yim's remark about functional specificity and diversity among shamanic spirit powers leads to another interesting observation. He notes that humans think of spirits' existence only when they feel a need to do so—that is, when they desire a certain state of being, or freedom from a certain negative state of being, and seek help from an external power in order to reach that desired state. According to Yim, when life conditions return to normal momentarily, people leave the spirit's existence "out of the sphere of their interest and attention" as if they had completely forgotten about it.[8] The art of oblivion may also work in a longue-durée context, as is the case with the smallpox *kut* that is no longer performed today. In Korea's modern history, smallpox infections continued to be a critical public issue up until the end of the 1950s (it proliferated during the Korean War), but it has largely disappeared since the 1960s when universal immunization against it became part of public health policy. Consequently, the smallpox ritual has long been forgotten, because the threatening spirit associated with the infectious disease, *mama*, went out of sight.

Yim advances a further observation about the thorough ordinariness of the ephemeral and context-specific character of human–spirit relations. In line with his point about the inseparability of shamanism as a ritual order from the broader milieu of popular practices that we discussed in Chapter 5, he asks the reader to think of two of the most important sacred objects in a traditional Korean village: the communal shrine house (*sindang*) and the stone marker at the village entrance (*ibsŏk*). On occasions of communal festivity, the stone is dressed in colorful clothes and white paper streamers, and the shrine house likewise becomes a focal point of the community's attention, as this is where the village shaman and elders initiate the rite of atonement to the community's protector spirits. When these ritualized events are over, however, the village shrine house falls out of attention and becomes abandoned "with weeds growing around it" until the next ceremonial occasion approaches. As for the stone, he remarks that, while being a sacred site at a certain moment, the stone turns back into a children's plaything when the rite is over. He added that, in some villages, the stone is even used to tie down the village oxen, thereby completely losing its aura of sacredness. Drawing on these observations, Yim makes one of his central points regarding shamanism's distinct conception of spirits and their power, in a way that resonates strongly with the idea of *homo faber* discussed in modern phenomenological thought (see below). He suggests that "an analogy would be the fact that we cannot chop the wood with bare hands or till the soil deep enough [without tools]. In order to do these, we need to fabricate the sickle, axe, or saw and the hoe or the plough so that they can work as extension of our hands."[9] Likewise, in the culture of *musok* in which people aim to generate luck and to deter misfortune by the assistance of spirits, he concludes that the spirits are "so intimate with human beings and so profane."[10]

This statement about intimacy and profanity is significant because it expresses what Kim Seong-nae calls the humanistic foundation of shamanism's religiosity.[11] It is also a call to the reader to imagine a humanistic perspective that is free from its strong grounding, in modern philosophical tradition, in anti-religious movement and secularism.[12] Modern humanist tradition is a worldview that locates the agency and the value of human beings, individual and collective, at the center of worldmaking. Premises of this tradition, or what Raymond Firth explains as "the study of God [that] is included in the study of man," resonate closely with how Yim depicts the milieu in which spirits and humans interact, especially in the realm of the household's life-economic activity (i.e., *oikos*) and along the fluctuating routines of work and life taking place in this realm.[13] The meeting is primarily of a composition that locates human life and human agency as its central structuring principle. The important point is, however, that this principle is manifested in the relational world in which humanity and divinity coexist, which is distinct from the tradition of modern humanism, where the human world is seen as detached and free from the supernatural world. The form of humanism expressed by Korea's shamanism tradition is "natural," as it were—a humanism independent of the rise of modern secular humanism and one that existed long before the latter came into being on the horizons of world history.

This idea of natural humanism is far from unfamiliar in the tradition of modern anthropology. Notable here is the long-lasting research interest in the phenomenon called animism, discussed in Chapter 5. Animism refers to the ways in which, in numerous indigenous or traditional societies, natural objects and environmental phenomena are endowed with animus or the soul, the property unique to humans in the Western theological and philosophical tradition. As is widely known, E. B. Tylor defined animism as natural religion, in distinction to other more institutionalized religions known in human history.[14] The idea of the "natural" is, for Tylor, set against that of the "moral," in that institutional, civilizational religions are basically moral systems, defining what is good and normative versus what is not. Hence, he classifies animism as an "un-moral" religion, which existed before humanity built a moral order and, accordingly, a system of religious concepts to legitimize and sustain this order. As is also widely known, Emile Durkheim brought forward a strong objection to this conceptual scheme in his revolutionary treatise on the social origin of religion.[15] For Durkheim, all religions, even the most archaic, are fundamentally moral systems. Religious concepts and the notions of the sacred are, at an elementary level, about collective existence—the existential condition of human individuals who share their lifeworld with others. If something is regarded as sacred (such as totemic emblems), therefore, this sacred symbol is a social fact *sui generis* before being a religious emblem, in that it speaks, above all, of the imperative of human beings to exist together and share the world together and to express this imperative as a morally sacred principle.

Yim Suk-jay's investigation into the character of spirits in Korean shamanism speaks closely to both of these major streams of thought in the anthropology and sociology of religion. Korea's broad *musok* tradition has a strong animist orientation: Various objects of nature (such as trees, stones, mountains, and water sources) are endowed with spirit properties and related histories and legends. Some of these properties are given explicit representational forms—most often in an anthropomorphic form but not exclusively so. The same is true of some natural phenomena that have direct relevance for the sustainability of human lives—such as the land, wind, or the maritime milieu. Even diseases and objects that are purely artificial can have spirit properties. Regarding diseases, we have already mentioned the spirit of smallpox; as for objects, a good illustration would be *chadae-gam* ("vehicle elder"), a spirit entity identified specifically with cars and two-wheeled vehicles. The vehicle elder can deal with locomotives or airplanes, too. Even the amplifier of a pop music band or the CT scanner in a hypermodern urban medical clinic can have a spirit guardian named as such associated with it. The relationship that humans have with these spirits in their lived environment does not carry with it a clearly defined body of moral principles and directives, unlike in other more institutionalized religions. According to Yim, the multitude of spirits in this animated environment are mostly human-like personalities, which means that they lack the quality of the sacred in the sense of the transcendental. However, as Durkheim rightly points out, it is a category error to exclude morality from the idea of the animated environment entirely. If animism is a way of extending the property of humanity to the realm of nature, as Philippe Descola explains, how can this system of ideas and values be a "un-moral" system?[16] Humanity, whether archaic or modern, is both a moral and an ontological concept. If a system of religious ideas appears to be natural (as against moral), this may mean simply that the system has a distinct normative order, one that is not easily comprehensible if seen from the assumed moral point of view, grounded in the system of ideas deriving from a transcendental religion.

This last point is, in fact, a key message from the currently vibrant anthropology of ordinary ethical life.[17] Although there are several diverging and sometimes mutually conflicting trends in it, this field is very much focused on eliciting normative qualities embedded in human life that are distinct from (or subdued under) the moral directives and dictates emanating from the dominant ideology of a political society. Cases dealt with in this research orientation are often in contexts of religious conversion, or where questions of secularism clash with those of religious purity or different religious traditions collide. However, some influential researchers in the field also confront head-on the vexing issues mentioned above—the exclusion of morality from the so-called natural religions. Notable here are Michael Lambek's work on spirit possession in Mayotte and Janice Boddy's oeuvre on a similar phenomenon in Sudan.[18] Both scholars emphasize the inseparability of spirit phenomena from critical moral issues in the everyday context—as Boddy writes, "[Spirits] are not set apart from the everyday world, [but] are key performers in the most mundane social interactions."[19] Also relevant are studies that belong to the so-called ontological turn in today's scholarship. Many of these studies deal with animism or ideas of the animated environment (or genres of shamanism that present mediation or "diplomacy" between the human world and the broader animate world as its key task).[20] Even though they choose to take on an ontology flag, their ethnographic contents are, in actuality, much about a search for a moral worldview, which, unlike the prevailing ethos of the modern world, celebrates human life that exists in parallel with (rather than in dominance over) other life forms.[21] These exciting new studies amply show that how humans relate to the animals in their environment is richly intertwined with the way in which human groups dwelling in the same environment relate to one another—that is, moral and ontological issues speak to one another. They also show that when a spirit from the past enters a human body of the present and thus creates a condition of spirit possession, the event illustrates a distinct sense of historicity that constitutes the moral backbone of the society's sociopolitical order.[22] Returning to our milieu, we may ask how the act of praying for luck to the mountain god may be considered a natural, other-than-moral religious act—considering the fact the prayer-giver usually enacts the deed on behalf of intimate others, such as those within the milieu of kinship. Moreover, what about the fact, mentioned by Yim, that this humble act of rubbing the palms above a bowl of clear water is equivalent in value to the costly full-scale rite of *kut* that may last several days? Does this not entail that just as the gods are autonomous and self-determining in relation to one another, their human interlocutors, rich or poor, are all equal in this particular realm and instance of interlocution? And what can be a more supremely moral question for human beings than the quest for freedom—freedom from dominance and inequality?

Yim Suk-jay's understanding of the *musok* world strongly resonates with some of the issues explored in modern phenomenology, notably those discussed by Henri Bergson, who famously said that "we are, to a certain extent, what we do." It also speaks closely to contemporary investigations in anthropology influenced by Bergson's *homo faber* idea.[23] Most notably, Tim Ingold states emphatically in his engrossing study of the morphology of lines that "Life is a task."[24] The context-specific, need-based, and distinctly *tool-being*-like character of shamanic spirits comes quite close to the concept of *techne*, which appears prominently in Ingold's recent works. *Techne* is knowledge of the world generated as part of doing and making, or craft-like knowledge embedded in the activity of making and doing, partly in contrast to *episteme*, disinterested or "objective" understanding. As such it is distinct from *a priori* or pre-perceptual truths of the world but is rather knowledge as activity bound to the spectrum of tasks. Because of the last aspect, in the tradition of classical philosophy, *techne* is closely associated with *oikos*, the domestic sphere and life needs in it, defined as against *polis*, the realm of free political life.[25]

The culture of shamanism, as described by Yim Suk-jay, appears to be strongly *techne*-oriented; however, it is important to emphasize once again the fact that this making-and-doing-minded cultural form has also what we would call a religious form, grounded as it is in the extension of human agency to the metaphysical–natural realm in a way that is described by Descola with reference to animism. Descola defines this mode of knowledge as a culture-to-nature extension, or socialization of nature. If *techne*'s doing-and-making-and-knowing is grounded in the materiality of *oikos*, then this aspect of extension may appear to be something akin to a domestication of supernature (not to be confused with "the domestication of nature" idea appearing in the literature of evolutionary biology). The problem is, however, that the concept of the domestic, in this context, is one that incorporates the realm of the supernatural, which is also culturally shared and therefore inherently public. This means that the *oikos*-like supernature of shamanism, unlike the concept of *oikos* appearing in the European intellectual tradition, cannot be set discretely against the public world of *polis* in which political speech and action take place. Despite their being profoundly tool-like and strongly making-and-doing-existent, therefore, we may ask whether the spirits of Korean shamanism have a political order of their own and, following from this, whether these are political beings in their own right. Their political organization is not a kingdom of gods, as we argued earlier. Then, what sort of polity is it?

THE FRACTAL POLITY

According to Yim Suk-jay, in the space of *kut*, each component involving a specific type of spirits is a world in its own right rather than a subordinate part of the ritual whole, just as these spirits are all independent from one another. We discussed also how Yim sees the relationship between the domestic and the cosmic, or *oikos* and *mundus*, in a similar light—that the two mirror each other irrespective of differences in scale. We then proposed that this composition can be considered in the light of the idea of the fractal person and society. This discussion is about the relationship between a whole and the parts of the whole, and how the whole and the parts take on an identical composition. It is, therefore, principally about the question of scale in social analysis.

The idea of fractal identity is discussed especially attentively in the investigation of indigenous Oceania. Within this research sphere, the idea has several notable analytical components. One is a critique of the idea of the individual and the related effort to depart from the dominant concept of society in modern social theory that postulates society as an aggregate of individual persons. This is amply shown in notions such as the composite person, the partible person, and the "dividual" or distributed personhood, which are all widely referred to in the ethnography of indigenous Melanesia. In his seminal essay "The Fractal Person," Roy Wagner highlights "the phenomena [in indigenous Oceania] of equivalent personhood appearing at different scales as a fractal conception of person and world."[26] This statement refers to the distinct way of conceptualizing society and individual prevailing in the region, which Alfred Gell explains as: "The clan is a person at a different scale, so the single person is a fractal equivalent of the clan."[27] In other words, the person and the clan (or the individual and society) have "parallel compositions and move between parallel conditions of personhood."[28] The observed parallelism between self and society is discussed in a number of investigative contexts: notably, bilateral kinship relations, gift exchanges, gender relations and gendered division of labor, and figurative arts and musical tradition. Some investigations bring several of these issues together, as in Marilyn Strathern's integration of kinship, gender, and gift economy in her exposition of the composite personhood as observed in the materiality and spirituality of the gifts exchanged between social and gendered groups.[29] The idea of the composite or non-individual (that is, "dividual") self draws on the specificity of the bilateral kinship system within which the ego's genealogical identity, unlike that in an agnatic or unilineal kinship system, reaches out to an expansive, nearly entire horizon of the social world.[30] The anthropology of Melanesia includes a focused interest in the political structure in such a parallelistic and fractal world. This focus is often on the place of Big Men in society, a position that is distinct from a ruler or a chief; Big Men "operate at both the scale of the individual and the community at once."[31] Although diverse in orientation, and although there are some notable exceptions, researchers in this investigative sphere broadly share the notion that the idea of the individual self, sovereign and irreducible, a key concept in the liberal social and political theories, has little space in indigenous Oceania. If such irreducible selfhood does not hold sway in the ethnographic region, it follows that the concept of society, which in the dominant tradition of modern social theory is grounded in and paired with the idea of the irreducible individual, has to be imagined anew and differently from how it appears in this tradition. Hence, Wagner observes that the fractal person is "never a unit standing in relation to an aggregate, or an aggregate standing in relation to a unit, but always an entity with relationship integrally implied."[32] The issue is, according to him, neither individual nor group but the fractal person, "an entity whose (external) relationships with others are integral (internal) to it. However diminished or magnified, the fractal person, keeping its scale, reproduces only versions of itself."[33]

This statement illustrates how the discussion on fractality in this research sphere is very much focused on the question of personhood. The focus lies with the way in which, in "indigenous social science," as Wagner calls it, what are considered as (external and plural) relations among individuals in conventional Western social science are actually internal to the very singular person.[34] It is important to note at this point, however, that fractal images are far from unfamiliar in conventional (that is, non-indigenous) social science. Most notable is Durkheim's understanding of the process of social construction, which is, in a crucial way, a fractal theory of individual and society. His notion of *homo duplex*, for instance, postulates that the human soul is not a singular, indivisible entity that confronts social forces externally, but rather a duplex entity that keeps the constitutive spirit of society as part of itself. The same is true of the idea of collective representation and the related idea that living individuals are the double of their ancestors (which represents the integrity of the social whole in Durkheim's rendering). In this heritage, common existence is viable only to the extent that the imperative of this existence becomes part of individual moral consciousness, not merely in terms of external symbols. Here too, therefore, the individual takes on fractal images of the society, although in this rendering the composition of the individual is larger than that of the society in that the former has a duplex structure including elements of unique and sovereign individuality as well as those of the common whole of the society. Questions of fractality are also found in other regional ethnographic contexts, which involve a different system of kinship from that which prevails in Oceania.

Notable here is early African anthropology's segmentary descent theory.[35] The growth of segmentation necessarily involves the formation of fractal structure (as with the growth of trees), according to D'Arcy Thompson, whose *On Growth and Form* (1917), in fact, influenced early kinship theorists, notably Meyer Fortes and Claude Lévi-Strauss. Indeed, a typical map of the segmentary descent system can be seen as an inverted image of a growing tree, in which the whole (the entire genealogy of a tribal group) and the parts (e.g., the smaller constituent elements) have the same growth pattern and demonstrative form of bifurcation.

Going back to our principal concern in this chapter, we ask how these renderings of the relationship between the whole and the parts as parallel existence can help us to understand Yim Suk-jay's exposition of parallelism with regard to the multitude of shamanic spirits. Yim asserts that these spirits are ferociously independent of one another and, together, maintain a "relationship of non-association." This is the case not only between different categories of spirits (e.g., between nature spirits and ancestral spirits) but also between those that apparently belong to the same category. For instance, earlier we saw that in the *kut* performance by some Incheon shamans, the spirit of MacArthur is invoked, together with other historically more established warrior spirits, notably Yi Sun-sin and Im Kyŭng-ŏp (see Chapter 2). Although they are called into the ritual space in a group, the spirits of the three generals nevertheless have distinct and separate realms: General Im of the West Sea, General Yi of the South Sea, and General MacArthur of Incheon's coastal water. The question we are concerned with here is about the mode of the "relationship" between these seemingly sovereign, autonomous, and "non-associating" actors. What kind of relationship is it that they have as a whole, if individually they do not associate with each other? Is the life in the world of spirits a life without society? The folklorist Yang Jong-sŭng observes, following Yim, that he finds no class and status difference or discernible hierarchy as such among spirits in Korean shamanism. However, he also argues that these spirits maintain an order in relation to one another, some kind of normative order.[36] What, then, is this *order*?

While proposing a parallelistic picture of this world, Yim concentrates on the spirit participants in a *kut* in multiple and specific stages of *gŏri*, which are, according to him, all parts of the entire ritual process and, at once, each a complete world of its own. When a particular *gŏri* commences, the shaman calls in relevant spirit visitors and changes her dress and in-struments to those that are identified with the particular spirit-beings—for instance, to armor with a spear and a sword, in the case of the Warrior *gŏri*. This does not mean, however, that these various spirit participants have no occasion, during the *kut*, to be treated as a group rather than separately as individuals. At the start of the *kut*, the shaman enacts gestures of *chŏngbae* (invitation) to all the spirit-helper visitors of the day. This is done typically using *sŏnang-ki*, white paper streamers attached to a bamboo stick, with which the shaman makes a gesture of bringing in from outside to the inte-rior ritual space. This act of initiatory invitation may involve an appellation of the identities of the day's spirit visitors. The ritual space, whether this is outdoors or inside a house, also includes a visual display of these visitors' identities. Called *hwan*, these spirit portraits are attached to the wall behind the table of food and drink offerings prepared for the occasion. These por-traits are displayed in a horizontal, parallelistic pattern, often in a way that follows the day's expected sequential order of specific stages. It also happens that when a specific stage is completed, some ritual practitioners choose to take down the portraits of that stage's spirit visitors. In the rituals conducted by Lee Jong-ja, to whom MacArthur is the titular spirit-helper, one often sees a portrait of this general, wearing the officer's uniform of a modern army, next to one of Im Kyŭong-ŏp on horseback. The scenery may be con-sidered, extending Victor Turner's idea of ritual as drama, as the waiting room for a theater performance, in which the day's performing actors are brought in and stand ready before emerging on the stage at an assigned moment—although in the *kut*, there is never a closing ceremony in which all the participating actors reappear at the stage to greet the audience (the last *gŏri* of a *kut* is usually for *japsin* [miscellaneous spirits or ghosts] and held in the exterior, the beings in the spirit world which are not welcome to the ritual's interiority).[37]

One can only imagine how the invited spirits would spend time in the waiting room and how they would relate to one another in it, if they do so at all. The point is rather that there is an imagery of certain associational or cooperative existence of spirit-beings in the ritual context. This is despite the fact that their prevailing existential form is of individual autonomy and self-determination, and that the seemingly associational form is of an ephemeral character, restricted to a particular ritual moment. The dream image of the round-table meeting introduced in Chapter 5 perhaps relates

Kim Kŭm-hwa and her spirit portraits. Photo by Jun Hwan Park.

to this initiatory moment of associational existence. The idea of *hapŭi* (consent or agreement), a frequent notion in the shaman's spirit-calling narratives and songs, also points to a similar state of being. This idea entails that the shaman has reached a consent with a particular spirit-helper on matters concerning the purpose of the ritual. In the ritual action, however, the term can also imply a condition of consensus, although enacted by the shaman, by and among multiple spirit-helpers on the ritual's purpose and on their separate yet collaborative effort for the benefit of the ritual-hosting family. As Yim Suk-jay writes: "Each spirit has a particular function of its own and independent from and equal to all others."[38] However, he also observes that these independent spirits "associate with each other"—"*in relation to* the humans."[39] In this context, *hapŭi* may also entail specifically the prevention of a possible situation in which a specific spirit entity is not pleased, for whatever reasons, and may therefore decide to obstruct the successful execution of the rite. Kim Kŭm-hwa once said, with reference to the last stage of *kut* meant for displaced spirits, "Why do we entertain these spirits? Because if they cause troubles, the whole ritual may turn out to be inutile. No spirit is insignificant in *kut*, not even the ghosts. If some are not willing to help, they should at least not be obstructive." When the shaman sings, "Let us travel to obtain an agreement!", therefore, the purpose of the travel is to purchase consent from a specific spirit entity, which, nevertheless, when done in repetition with regard to diverse entities, ultimately aims to reach a condition in which multiple helper spirits are in agreement with the purpose of the specific rite. The successful completion of a *kut*, in fact, requires a consensual agreement by all helper spirits involved in the rite as a whole as to the wishes of the human group whom they encounter within the ritual space. A good *kut* is one in which all the participating spirits are happy to give support, and which brings together the powers of all these individual supernatural actors.

Seen in the spectrum of a *kut* as a whole, and in view of the coherent and purposeful task taking place in it, therefore, we may conclude that the shaman, within the ritual reality, turns into a powerful actor of fractal personhood. A multitude of spirits comes into her performing body and goes out of it as the rite progresses, thereby creating in it and through it a collective of efficacious powers. At the end of the long ritual procedure, the body becomes an assemblage of many spirits and their separate powers, thus meriting the very status that refers to such activity—*mansin,* or ten thousand spirits. In that instance, in other words, her body is equal, in composition, to the entirety of the spirit world. She becomes a fractal person in the sense that she embodies the ten thousand spirits as well as their gathering place. To borrow Gell's expression, we may even say that, at these moments, the performing person becomes the world of spirits at a different scale, a fractal equivalent of the universe. We may also bring this perspective to the broad realm of *musok*, beyond the narrowly defined ritualized world of *kut*, arguing along the lines of Yim Suk-jay that the house (that is, the living house of *oikos* that keeps many located and task-specific deities) and the universe (the entire supernature consisting of a multitude of *animi*) share the same structure. Here, it is not necessary to employ the idea of microcosm to describe the worldliness of the house in relation to the expansive and majestic outer universe—as the house is already a universe of its own, equal in complexity and magnitude to the outer space, being different only in scale. The same perspective can extend from the house to the community, such as the traditional village space that appears in Kim Kŭm-hwa's recollections of her life in northern Korea, and where she was in charge of the village-wide periodic ritual activity. Last, but not least, we may think of the humble, seemingly solitary act of praying for protection and luck, the practice of *bison*, in the same light. The person who does this in the thick of the night, although she is physically alone, is not doing it as a loner. The idea of praying for luck for oneself is alien to the practice of *bison*. The prayer performs *bison* as a social person, on behalf of someone close to her or for the well-being of the household she is part of. Her performance draws on the household's long historical experience of intimate life with spirits on an everyday basis, and on the fact that the multitude of spirits is part of the household's small yet complete universe. The destination of her prayers and the hoped-for interlocutor of her gestural language may be unclear; nevertheless, it is clear that the encounter is not necessarily between a singular person and a singular metaperson. For this metaperson is, like the prayer-giving person, a sovereign existent, yet, at one and the same time, part of an assembly consisting of many other equally self-determining beings. Indeed, a painting by the renowned eighteenth-century scholar-artist Shin Yun-bok, *Munyŏsinmu* ("A Shamaness and Her Spirit Dance"), locates a woman engaged in the act of *bison* at the center of the scene of a *kut*. According to South Korean anthropologist Chun Kyung-soo, this was an intentional choice grounded in the artist's understanding that in *musok*, the shamaness is not the principal actor. It is instead an ordinary person and an ordinary woman who performs an ordinary act of *bison*.[40]

On a closing note, let us go back to the five-nation flags with which we started our conversation in Chapter 2, and see what insights Yim Suk-jay's take on the political order of shamanism's superstructure can offer to understanding this object's composition. Recall that the flags represent an assembly of five nations in the image of the five-directional flags or *obang'ki*, a key instrument of *kut* as well as an important symbolic cosmopolitical device of premodern Korea. With the national flag of Korea placed in the middle, the other four flags are those of powerful nations and empires, all of which have exerted formative influence on the progression of modern political history in and around the Korean peninsula—China and Russia, on the one side, and the United States and Japan on the other. We say modern history (roughly from the end of the nineteenth century) since the co-presence of these four powers was nonexistent previously in Korea, which was then part of a Sino-centric old international order and a tributary mode of interstate relations. These four states-cum-empires and their influences came together only at the turn of the twentieth century—that is, during what is called the Age of Open Harbor in Korean historical scholarship, or what Andre Schmid aptly calls the era of "Korea between empires."[41] The time was when the forces of imperial politics were knocking loudly at Korea's doors and were doing so in the form of several actors, leading eventually to the triumph of Japanese power in 1905 following its victory in the Russo-Japanese War—the war that had strong ramification well beyond East Asia because of the shock generated by the fact that a European power lost to a non-Western power. As discussed earlier, this was also the onset of the politics against superstition in Korean history, involving American evangelical missions, radical proponents of cultural enlightenment, and the Japanese colonial power in Korea. Crucially for our discussion, this era witnessed the crumbling of Korea's traditional political order within which the symbolic life of the five-directional flags was sustained. Against this background, as also described earlier, shamanism was deployed to the defense of Korea's political sovereignty, notably by Queen Min, who, feeling powerless, took the extraordinary initiative of building shamanic shrine houses in four locations around Seoul as well as in the middle of it. It was in this chaotic, confusing world-changing environment that the iconicity of *obangki* seems to have entered the popular religious domain of shamanism in an explicit way, while losing its relevance as a secular symbol of territorial and political integrity in Chosun, the pre-twentieth-century Korean kingdom.

If *obangki* has shifted its symbolic life from feudal dynastic politics to the sphere of popular religion in the age of empires, the artifact continues to be an important instrument in the shamanic rite today. Consisting of five different colors, each of which points to a specific cardinal direction, and a related body of spirits, the shaman's *obangki* plays a pivotal role during the rite, as a principal means for fortune-telling. MacArthur is no exception to this. In the rituals conducted by the Incheon shamans who take MacArthur as their tutelary spirit, it is typically this spirit-person who is invited to the fortune-telling actions involving the five-color flag as the key instrument. Some of these MacArthur *mansin*, as these ritual actors are sometimes referred to, have replaced the white flag of the bundle of five-directional flags with *taegŭk-ki*, Korea's national flag that displays a set of ancient oracular symbols on a plain white background. We were told that the American General allegedly prefers this flag to the traditional plain-white one during his fortune-telling sessions, and is extremely pleased if a member of the ritual-hosting family has the extraordinary luck to pick this up during the divination. We were also told that, even though he has worked for many years in the world of Korean shamanism, the American General has not yet entirely moved away from his local historical world—the time-space of the Korean War in which he became a major figure in Korean history. We also encountered magical moments of our own in the presence of the American General. On one *kut* occasion, the authors of this book were invited onto the ritual floor. This was when the spirit of MacArthur, in the performance of a shaman for whom MacArthur has long been her principal helper-spirit, was in the thick of fortune-divination by means of the five-color flags. We told him that we were honored to meet him, and the shaman helped to explain to the General the purpose of our visit—that we were hoping to write a report about him. Then the General suddenly burst into tears and said that he was happy to meet us, too. After the day's *kut* was over and the shaman was resting at a corner of the room, we approached her to ask about the General's unusual reaction to our introduction. She said: "Why did he cry? Because the General was so happy. He was happy that at long last, some people came and gave him full recognition. No one but me had ever done so before. Not even my many clients, to whom the General is only a spirit, one among many. You gentlemen were the first visitors to recognize the General as General MacArthur."

Perhaps we can extend this experience to an interpretation of the five-nation flags, the artifact in the spirit shrine of Chung Hak-bong. In Chapter 2, we proposed an ecological view to this artifact's symbolic life, considering it in view of the fate of *kun'ung*—the nameless souls of the dead existing in the old battlegrounds of the Yellow Sea, whose lives had been broken amid and because of the relentless pursuit of power by the political entities represented by the flags. In light of what we discussed in this chapter, we add that an aspirational, proactive property, as well as a recognition of a tragic historical-ecological reality, may be stored in this object. Like MacArthur in the episode above, this object is not in an exactly identical symbolic terrain to the ritual instrument of five-directional flags, although the two objects may share their historical origin in Korea's transition from the old dynastic rule, grounded in the Sino-centric international order, to a modern polity struggling with threats to its sovereign rights within the precarious and violent environment of imperial and colonial politics. The five-nation flags relate to the five-direction flags—they coexist within the same sphere of shamanic religiosity and popular spirituality; however, the meaning of the former object is, in part, exactly what it shows—the coexistence of political entities in and around Korea in the broad space of northeast Asia. In other words, they constitute a religious symbolic object that, nevertheless, has not parted entirely with its representational property in the secular (early modern) political world. Conversely, we may say that they are in touch with the reality of secular geopolitical history, which, nevertheless, within the object that represents it, takes on a relevance that goes beyond secular geopolitics.

If we are permitted to see the object in this way, we can conclude that the five-nation flags illuminate an ideal international order, such as that aspired to by a multitude of people in the turbulent era at the turn of the twentieth century—against the actuality of world affairs characterized by a pursuit of power and the wars of conquest that were unleashed as part of this relentless pursuit of brute power, the ruins of which actors like Chung Hak-bong, in fact, had long had to confront within the ritualized environment of Incheon's coastal waters. Just as does its kindred object of five-directional flags in a *kut*'s most crucial fortune-telling ritual act with respect to the multitude of spirits existing in the universe, the five-nation flags dictate an anti-hierarchy, anti-imperial principle—that all nations depicted in it meet and work together, as sovereign entities, within the space of common tasks involving the augmentation of human well-being. Following Yim Suk-jay's lucid and original exposition of Korea's shamanic culture, we can also conclude that the nations depicted in the five-nation flag are bound by the principle of parallel existence. They are bound by the norms of equality, irrespective of differences in their nominal status and apparent power, each entertaining the same right to sovereign and self-determining existence. A similar vision arose forcefully in the secular political world at the turn of the twentieth century—the vision for an ideal society of nations that developed, in the subsequent era, into a forceful aspiration for decolonization and self-determination. Seen in this way, we may conclude that it is possible to imagine an ideal modern political system within the given order of an arguably ancient religious system—namely, that the artifact of five nations collapses the distance between the condition of *mansin* (i.e., "ten thousand spirits") and that of *mankuk* (i.e., "ten thousand nations" that refers to the ideal of modern international society). We may also think of this obviation of distance in terms of a work of the fractal person and world scheme—on this occasion, in relation to the geopolitical world. The expression "ten thousand nations" was also the original name of the site, Ten Thousand Nations Park in Incheon, to which the spirit of MacArthur is anchored today, before it changed names in the subsequent era of imperial dominance. In the following concluding chapter, we will turn back to the American General to see how this foreign spirit is accommodated by the society of Ten Thousand Spirits and whether the foreignness of this spirit's origin matters at all in the parallelistic universe consisting of the multitude of self-determining spirits.

CONCLUSION

In October 1981, Claude Lévi-Strauss came to South Korea for a three-week visit. Apart from lectures and other social engagements, this giant of modern anthropology was interested in seeing Korea's iconic traditional cultural sites. These included local Confucian academies of the Chosun era, which Monsieur Lévi-Strauss said left a great impression on him, especially because, being located in the countryside, they were quite different from the academic institutions in his native France that are primarily concentrated in the country's urban centers. Interested also in grassroots religious sites, Lévi-Strauss watched a *kut* performance at the national shrine house in the north of Seoul's city center, Kuksadang on Inwang-san. The occasion happened to be a family's rite for their ancestors. After witnessing the rite, the anthropologist remarked on certain differences that he felt existed between shamanism in Korea and the better-known equivalent tradition in indigenous Siberia and among the Inuit in the far north of the American continent.[1] He said that indigenous Siberian shamans were known to be able to travel to the land of the dead, being mediators between the living and the dead (as well as between nature and society).[2] In contrast to this, Lévi-Strauss observed that the focus of Korean shamanism seemed, instead, squarely set on relations among the living. He probably meant relations with the dead who are treated as if they were alive. Following this experience, he went on to take part in another *kut*, this time performed by Kim Kŭm-hwa at her client's home in Seoul's old residential quarter. Soon after his visit to Korea, a portrait of a Korean shamaness found its way to one of Paris's most prominent cultural institutions, UNESCO House in the Place de Fontenoy. Looking somewhat like the portrait of a rite-performing woman drawn by

Nang-i, a protagonist of Kim Dong-li's 1936 *Portrait of a Shamaness* that we saw in the Introduction, this painting is proudly displayed in the corridor that connects the international organization's main conference halls as an artifact representing the indigenous culture of Korea.

Of all the international organizations existing in today's world, UNESCO is probably closest to the discipline of modern sociocultural anthropology in terms of ethos and idealism. The two share a set of ideas and norms that is often glossed as cultural pluralism, and the related vision for human unity based on the celebration of cultural diversity. Since its founding in 1946, in the immediate aftermath of World War II, UNESCO has advocated for the power of education in helping to create this vision of unity through plurality, or, better put, what the great Indian anthropologist Sarat Chandra Roy termed in 1938 "the large *unity-in-diversity-through-sympathy*" that, according to him, "seems to an Indian mind to be the inner meaning of the process of human evolution."[3] According to the organization's charters, this vision constitutes vital groundwork for the prospective realization of lasting peace—a concept that was initiated by the Enlightenment thinkers of the eighteenth century, notably Jean-Jacques Rousseau and Immanuel Kant, and then brought back into the public discourse of interwar Europe and again after 1945.

The connection between anthropology and UNESCO is not limited to the realm of idealism, however. A number of anthropologists and anthropologically minded intellectuals played a formative role in the evolution of UNESCO, especially during the organization's early years. UNESCO's Social Science Department, in particular, was in many ways the brain for the body of the international and intergovernmental organization as a whole, during its many activities to promote intercultural communication, education and science, and to combat poverty. Alfred Métraux, Margaret Mead, Alva Myrdal, Pierre Clastre, and Claude Lévi-Strauss are among those who have engaged with this department at various times; the department also provided financial support for several other anthropologists' pioneering fieldwork projects, including the work of Fredrik Barth. In the 1950s and 1960s, anthropology was at the center of the department's general activity, being then considered a key social scientific discipline in the making of a more peaceful and more egalitarian world society in the post–World War II era. Intimacy between anthropology and the international organization is also visible in UNESCO's international office in Paris. Lucia Allais, a historian of modernist monumental architecture, argues that architecture has become a privileged tool for cultural and political cooperation on the world stage and that this is particularly the case with UNESCO House, completed in 1958.[4] She considers some early monumental initiatives taken after World War I, notably by the League of Nations, and then moves on to the specifics of the World Heritage Convention in 1972. Allais explains that UNESCO House is designed to stand out from its surroundings. Its highly modernist form is detached from the neighborhood of the Place de Fontenoy, which abounds with imposing eighteenth- and nineteenth-century buildings. The composition of UNESCO house is distinct from the particular local tradition of art and architecture in the Parisian context. The building is modernist, not only in the sense that it draws on the fruit of Europe's modernist art and architecture movement, but also in that it was designed to provide a neutral space in which a multitude of other cultural traditions can meet, without some being privileged over the others. We can call this particular version of modernist aesthetics "modernist humanism."[5] Cultural historian Stephen Kern discusses early twentieth-century art and intellectual movements in Europe and highlights two trends in these movements: universalism (humanism as an attempt to locate and cultivate what is essentially and universally human), and perspectivism (the idea that there are as many "realities" as there are views of reality).[6] The shape and structure of UNESCO House bring these two apparently contradictory historical streams of ideas together, thereby aspiring to become a space for universal history (what UNESCO calls "the memory of the world") while also celebrating the reality of radical cultural diversity, past and present.

The celebration of cultural diversity is visible in many corners of UNESCO House, where visitors encounter representative images or material objects from various cultural entities around the world. One of the House's main conference halls, where assemblies on cultural communication and information regularly take place, prominently displays an artwork from the Northwest Coast of North America—as a celebration of what Margaret Mead understood as Boasian internationalism (i.e., bringing Boas's cultural pluralism up to date in response to the changed condition of the world after WWII), referring to the founding figure of American anthropology, Franz Boas, who long studied this region's art and religion after the Jesup North Pacific Expedition of 1897–1902.[7] Along the corridors between the conference halls, where various intergovernmental meetings are regularly held, there are other cultural objects originating from larger cultural and political entities. Examples include a statue of Buddha from Nepal and the painting from Korea depicting *kut*, mentioned earlier. The display of these objects, especially those that represent political entities that became independent after World War II, speaks of the theory of "national characters" or "cultural personalities," which prevailed at the time of the creation of UNESCO. The idea was that world citizens should learn about the diverse cultural relics and heritages existing in the world—a learning process that was regarded as vital to the construction of a peaceful world society after the destruction of 1939–1945. UNESCO's idea of global civic education incorporates not only intercultural learning but also the promotion of science and science education. The latter relates to the other aspect of modernist humanism mentioned above, universalism (rational scientific ideas are universal; all traditional cultural ideas are authentic).

The idea of national character (or "the originality or 'genius' of each people or nation") is closely associated with a group of American anthropologists and social psychologists, including Mead, who actively advanced the idea during World War II and immediately afterward.[8] In the late 1940s and early 1950s, Mead was one of the few anthropologists who was preoccupied with the radical political changes taking place in the global environment at the time, as well as with what these would mean for future anthropological research. These changes consisted, above all, of the advent of decolonization and the related tectonic shift in the composition of global power from the colonial formation to the Cold War formation. Decolonization meant the achievement of self-determination free from colonial subjugation, and equal status in the new postcolonial international environment. This process involved building up new cultural sovereignty and authenticity as part of the pursuit of political independence. In the domestic sphere, however, the key question was instead about integrating the multitude of existing communities and culturally distinct groupings into a unified national political society. In an important article translated from Portuguese by the prominent Amazonist Peter Gow, two Brazilian anthropologists, Federico Neiburg and Marcio Goldman, observe:[9]

The naturalization and universalization of the notion of national character. . . . provide two effects: on the one hand, the mechanisms whereby social and cultural boundaries are made in non-national societies become identical to those that serve to sanction the existence of national frontier, and on the other, the specificity of the processes of the creation of social and cultural boundaries within societies that see themselves as national is annulled.

The display of cultural diversity at UNESCO House is not free from tensions generated by the era's momentous historical transformation—tensions between the idea of plurality understood in a new state-centric sense and a view of plurality that is more traditional to the discipline of social anthropology, involving tribal or stateless societies. The latter dimension is evident in Lévi-Strauss's 1961 essay, published in UNESCO's flagship journal *Courier*: "Today's Crisis in Anthropology."[10] The "crisis" addressed in this essay refers to the challenges to their existence faced broadly by numerous culturally sovereign indigenous or non-state societies of the human world—a crisis that was exacerbated by the process of decolonization and related incorporation of these culturally and politically autonomous societies into the universal political form of state sovereignty. As UNESCO became an overtly intergovernmental organization (rather than an international organization), starting roughly in the 1970s (and coinciding with the establishment of the World Heritage Convention in 1972), the notion of cultural diversity and the related concept of world heritages increasingly became diplomatic concepts, which were tied strongly to the idea of culture and cultural sovereignty in the post-1945 sense and were focused on relations between state entities.[11]

The portrait of the shamaness displayed in UNESCO House captures both of these distinct notions of cultural understanding. On the one hand, it is obvious that the artifact is given a space in the house primarily as a demonstratively representational object of the milieu of history and culture with which it is associated. As such, its relevance is close to what the idea of cultural character or collective personality is meant to convey, and, therefore, seen broadly, relates to Mead's aspiration noted earlier. Margaret Mead saw herself, according to Peter Mandler, "both as the tribune of the great tradition of cultural relativism she had inherited from her mentor Franz Boas, and also as the champion of applying anthropology to international relations and to public service more generally, however hostile the political environment."[12] For her, anthropology's central role in the world after the destruction of World War II was above all "how to make the world safe from differences," or, according to the title of the book she began writing in the summer of 1945 but eventually gave up on, *Learning to Live in One World*.[13] She understood these "differences" in a pragmatic way and primarily in a sense that resonated strongly with the atmosphere of momentous changes in world politics in the mid-twentieth century. Faithful to Boas's legacy, she then defined anthropology's public role as the advocate and educator of the virtues of understanding human differences as cultural differences and of celebrating the condition of human plurality in this sense, departing from the race-based, hierarchical notion of human differences that had prevailed in the earlier era. She emerged out of her Samoan world in this respect to bring the morality of a culturally plural world to the cold world in the mid-twentieth century that came to worship states and nations, and their alliances, in an ideologically bipolarizing global context. In his recent political biography of Mead, Peter Mandler concludes that she failed in this bold undertaking, and was left dispirited and heartbroken.[14] According to him, the outbreak of the Korean War was one major event that made her despair—the war that radicalized and militarized Cold War politics both in international society and on America's home front.[15] In the prevailing condition of decolonization and postcolonial nation-building, moreover, this virtue of pluralism, and the related call for tolerance of differences that she advocated, became increasingly enmeshed in the political idea of cultural authenticity and sovereignty that the emerging state entities in the decolonizing world were bent on engendering as part of their state- and nation-building.

If Mead concentrated on the idea of cultural differences within Boasian internationalism and that of culture as an "anti-concept" of race, now extended to differences between political entities claiming historically constituted unique cultural properties, Lévi-Strauss was preoccupied with the sovereign cultural and cosmological integrity of existing stateless political societies now fast disappearing in a world made of sovereignty-claiming state entities.[16] This is evident not only in his essay introduced earlier but also in his better-known "Rousseau, the Father of Anthropology," which also first appeared in the *UNESCO Courier* as part of a special issue in 1963.[17] This issue of the *Courier* was dedicated to the legacy of Jean-Jacques Rousseau and its relevance for the contemporary world—a legacy that UNESCO holds dear as part of its broad ethos—marking the bicentenary of *Émile* and the *Social Contract* in 1962. Lévi-Strauss made it clear in this essay, as well as on subsequent occasions, that Rousseau's philosophical and spiritual heritage had been influential on his entire intellectual career, as well as on his view of the human world and the place of anthropology in it. He highlighted Rousseau's idea of "natural man" and his critique of modern human "self-love" (*l'amour propre*), among others, as being of particular value for the constitutive spirit of modern anthropology. He later elaborated on the first idea in various treatises on *pensée sauvage*, the natural man's outlook on the world. He explained that the discipline of anthropology is a modern invention created specifically to combat modernity's preponderant drive for self-love. This fight is principally about the notion that "to rediscover one's own image as reflected in others, one should first reject one's image of oneself."[18] It is also about recovering compassion for, and identification with, others, which is a notable property of a natural man, according to Lévi-Strauss's reading of Rousseau. The pursuit of this combat thus requires experiences of deep and radical culture contact, which are, according to Lévi-Strauss, embedded in the anthropologist's vocation.

Going back to the portrait of the shamaness in UNESCO House, it is unavoidable that such an image conveys not merely a sense of distinct cultural specificity (à la Mead) but also an added impression of a unique historical identity in that a modern political society keeps alive the heritage of a supposedly archaic or "natural" religious form (à la Lévi-Strauss).[19] The latter impression is found in the remark by Lévi-Strauss noted earlier, in which he compared the shamanic rite in Korea he was witnessing with his knowledge of shamanism in indigenous Siberia and North America. Similar issues are widely mentioned in the voluminous literature on the extraordinary "survival" of Korea's shamanism and, more broadly, in many ethnographic reports on the vigor of contemporary Asian popular religions.[20] We may also consider these issues in relation to tensions in the concept of cultural plurality and identity described above—that is, tensions between the new state-centric concept, empowered as part of the process of decolonization and nation-building, and the old idea, originating in pre-1945 milieus, in which cultural plurality was a much more localized and far less state-bound notion.

The politics of cultural sovereignty and the broader ethics of cultural plurality are characteristic of the environment of the post-1945 world; they are also an integral element in the transformation of Korean shamanism at large and in the Hwanghae-do shamanic tradition, in particular, in the post–Korean War era. If the portrait of a Korean shamaness in UNESCO House is an emblematic example of the politics of cultural diversity in the international terrain, we argue that the spirit of MacArthur and its place within the world of Korean shamanism can speak loudly about the state politics of cultural sovereignty and some of the vexing contradictions involved in these politics. In the following concluding section, we trace back to where we started in this book, and reiterate the point we made early on, in Chapter 2, that the American General, within the world of Incheon's Hwanghae shamanism, is more a manifestation of the authenticity of Korea's indigenous spirituality than that of American power understood in secular sense. This point goes against the conclusion made by some observers in South Korea that the inception of MacArthur to a certain circle of Korean shamanism testifies to the corruption of national religious culture by encounter with a foreign power. One observer sees the process of inception even as an illustration of *sadaejuŭi*, subservience to big powers.[21] Contrary to this hurried observation and conclusion, we argue that the very fact that this American spirit is able to enter Korea's shamanism world is a testimony to this world's capability to guard its sovereign integrity (of ontological pluralism) and autonomy—that is, in a sense akin to how Lévi-Strauss discusses the issue of sovereignty with reference to the idea of *l'homme naturel*.

Her encounter with Lévi-Strauss was an important event for Kim Kŭmhwa, who kept her photograph taken with the anthropologist prominently displayed in her home. The meeting took place as part of a momentous shift in the moral status of shamanism in South Korea's public understanding of its cultural heritage and identity at the start of the 1980s. We saw this shift through Madame Kim's voyage to Knoxville and elsewhere in the United States as a cultural emissary, to celebrate the centenary of Korean–American friendship. Domestically, the change meant that shamanism was no longer primarily an emblematic legacy of a backward past and a principal focus of the state-driven anti-superstition campaign, becoming instead also a distinct cultural tradition worthy of conversation—a change that Kim recalls in her memoirs as liberating and life-transforming. However, for Kim, the trip to the United States signaled more than relative freedom from persecution and stigmatization at home. For her, the voyage, especially the invitation to one of United States' most eminent cultural institutions, the Smithsonian Institution, was also a powerful encounter with the morality and aesthetics of cultural pluralism (by then, the institution must have long left its early-twentieth-century evolutionist stand against the Boasians) and with the related recognition of her work as a guardian of Korea's traditional cultural integrity. The magnitude of this experience is made evident in the small American flag that Kim brought home from her 1982 trip—first as a souvenir and then used as an emblem of power—that she kept at the very center of her domestic shrine ever after.

The transformation of shamanism from an object of containment politics in the cultural sphere to a meaningful national heritage, and therefore an object of conservation, came with new challenges. The heritization of shamanism involved the state providing entitlements to selected regional ritual forms and to individuals who were believed to preserve these performative arts in the supposedly most authentic form. The notion of "authenticity" in this context was principally historiographical in method, involving the expertise of historians and historically minded folklorists in search of a genuine ritual form in a truly traditional context, on the grounds of which a judgment on contemporary performance was made. The politics of entitlement also involved an intense competition among hopeful ritual specialists, and this competition, being centered on the archetypal notion of cultural authenticity, generated a curious relationship between folklorists and ethnologists who study traditional cultural forms, on the one hand, and their informers who practice and perform these traditional religious forms, on the other. The academic experts heavily depended on the popular practitioners for knowledge and information about the largely untextualized, orally and performatively transmitted ritual form; the practitioners relied on these ethnologists, and the textualization of their performative art in the hands of these academic experts, only through which they could come close to the desired acknowledgment as a holder of an immaterial cultural heritage. A number of informed folklorists questioned these heritage politics and their consequences; some raised concerns about the "fossilization" or mummification of traditional culture.[22]

This question of authenticity becomes critical when it concerns cultural forms such as shamanism, in which convention and invention are both equally important and legitimate properties.[23] It is even more critical in relation to spiritual entities of apparently foreign origin, such as MacArthur. As a historically constituted and history-engaging cultural form, Korean shamanism is grounded in a set of established structural elements, including a composition of spirit-helpers that have mythic origins of unknown historical depth. However, this composition is not a closed society but one that is open to new vitalities whose emergence into the ritual world interacts with changing historical circumstances and remarkable historical events. This coactivity of myth and history (and cosmology and historicity), which is found in all religious forms, is particularly prominent in shamanism, and this artful integration of formal structure and historical agency (and the resulting flexibility in composition), as Yim Suk-jay argues, is probably one of the reasons why shamanism, as a supposedly archaic religiosity, has survived the long course of history and thrives even in a hypermodern society such as today's South Korea.[24]

The assimilation of this historically engaged, organizationally flexible religious tradition to the rigid and bounded notion of cultural heritage has resulted in the revival of a moral hierarchy akin to what is entailed in the concept of ŭmsa ("shadowy rituals"), which prevailed in the neo-Confucian political and social order of Chosun. According to this concept, the state (with its ruling elite) is responsible for properly guiding society's moral disposition and orientation. One supremely important domain of the state's disciplinary action was that of the Rite. The ideology behind this system was both universal and parochial. On the one hand, it was postulated that ritual activity and morality are core properties of being human—something akin to the idea of human beings as ceremonial animals, which is familiar in anthropological research.[25] On the other hand, it was advocated that the social order is maintained principally by a hierarchical ordering of the entitlement to rite. Thus, the sovereign, the ruling elite, and the demos were differentiated from one another through levels of ritual propriety (e.g., the ruling elite restrict their rites to patrilineal ancestry, whereas the people are allowed a certain latitude to be somewhat unruly in this respect and also to attend to Buddhism or shamanism) and by means of their distinct ritual rights (e.g., how deep in ancestral heritage one can go in ritual remembrance). In the political sphere, therefore, the whole system was based on the idea that the state can control society by controlling the society's ritual sites and activities. In addition to the control of the ritual space, the concept of "shadowy rites" also purports to control time. This is evident in the Chosun elite's ruling against the plebeian society's openness to new spirits— that is, the inception of historical personas to spirit beliefs other than those authorized and endorsed by the state and its ruling elite. Although acts of openness were not always punished when they were practiced at the plebeian level, the same acts, if happening closer to the inner circle of moral and political power, were guarded and militated against.

We may extend the idea of *ŭmsa* to the politics of national cultural heritage since the 1980s. Although these heritage politics had parted from the politics of anti-superstition in the previous era and thus provided some space of freedom to practitioners of popular religion, they resulted, as did the old politics of shadowy rituals, in a hierarchy of normative versus non-normative ritual forms. The details of these two political forms, the old Confucian ritualism and the modern heritage politics, vary; however, they both function to sanction against the property of historical adaptability and openness that is crucial to Korea's shamanism tradition. The impact of the politics of authenticity has been far-reaching. In the competitive drive toward a heritage entitlement, it is widely observed among the practitioners of shamanism that they often concealed the actuality of novelty existing in their ritual world, highlighting instead the elements inscribed in the authoritative texts about their traditional ritual forms. The discrimination against historical novelty took many forms. Many Korean shamans underwent their initiatory experience in relation to intimate ancestral spirits (e.g., the spirit of a partner or a family elder, tragically and unjustly killed during the war), whereas these stories were carefully tucked away if the shaman had an ambition to earn an entitlement. If this shaman's society of spirit-helpers included an unconventional persona, it was unlikely that the latter appeared explicitly in her public performance, away from the intimate ritual space she shared with her close and unsuspecting clients. If that unconventional and unorthodox persona happens to be a foreigner in origin (as is the case with MacArthur), the intensity of concealment may be magnified, thereby generating a bifurcated identity on the part of the ritual performer. Hence, in a private *kut* with a client family, General MacArthur takes up a prominent role on the ritual stage that invites warrior spirits, whereas in a public performance at a cultural entertainment event organized by a public authority (which is, in fact, part of a rite of passage toward the acquisition of official heritage entitlement), the American General is invisible in the ritual space, which is taken up, instead, by a group of familiar warrior spirits from old Korean history and ancient mythic-time China. For these ritual actors, therefore, identities such as the spirit of MacArthur are in and out of the ritual space as dictated by the politics of heritage and authenticity. The situation is different with ritual specialists who keep their activity strictly to interactions with their local client families, having no ambition or stake in public heritage politics. In these cases, MacArthur is free to be a demonstrative participant in the ritual milieus and free to act together with many other participants, Korean in origin or otherwise, and mythic or historical in character, as a legitimate member of the society of spirit-helpers. The look of this society is cosmopolitan and that of an open society, and the clients, unlike the spectators of a public performance, would rarely raise questions as to the national origin of the spirit-helper. The singular concern they have would be, instead, the spirit's power and efficacy; there is no place in this for such questions of cultural and esthetic authenticity as dictated by heritage politics.

Seen in this light, we may conclude that the actuality of MacArthur's spirit power in corners of Incheon speaks of the genuine authenticity of Korea's preeminent, ancient popular religious tradition. The spirit's existence in Incheon's Hwanghae shamanism is emblematic of the religious form's openness to history and to new historical events. Of course, the origin of this phenomenon is also inseparable from the legacies of the Korean War, as these are manifested in the monumental and memorial culture of the city. What brought these two separate aspects of the spirit's coming-into-being—historical event and ritual structure—is the historical experience of those who came to recognize the spirit's being in the first place. We discussed earlier that the Korean War resulted in the displacement of Hwanghae shamanism from its home in Hwanghae, and how this experience of displacement and the following process of building a niche in the new place involved nurturing a novel spirit icon. Seen in this light, MacArthur is far from a foreigner or an emissary of American power. It is a local icon and an extension of an old familiar icon back in the original home's ritual and cosmopolitical landscape. This is a story of making a home in an alien place without losing the connectivity with and grounding in the lost home-place.

Would new homemaking have been viable without such an engagement with the local landscape—that is, if the tradition sought to keep its authentic heritage only, despite the experience of displacement and rupture, as the state's cultural policy dictates? Does it matter if the iconic means one makes a home with, in an alien place, is foreign in origin? What is wrong with the modern state that it knows no way other than either expunging from society such a historically grounded yet history-engaging cultural form or keeping it as an unchanging, fossilized tradition? Last but not least, what has happened to the sensibility of modern society that it fails to see the virtues of cosmopolitan openness that is already embedded in the traditional culture while it pursues the ideal of an open, tolerant, and pluralist world? How do these problems relate to the unresolved issues in culture and politics with which Mead was concerned and had frustration—namely, the limits in the ideal of human unity based on the celebration of cultural diversity in the American Century? These questions remain as relevant today as in the past, and it is thanks to the powerful American General in Korea's traditional religion that we came to discover their relevance in the religious history of the Cold War.

On a closing note, let us return briefly to the old Jerusalem of the Orient and its environs to see how conditions are today in the northern half of the Korean peninsula. There has been an explosive growth of fortune-telling in North Korean citizens' everyday lives since the beginning of the 2000s. Nominally an outlawed practice, fortune-telling is now a highly familiar aspect of everyday life decision-making in the country. This phenomenon clearly relates to the generalized radical crisis of economic meltdown and related collapse of the state's food distribution system in North Korea with the end of the Cold War, in the second half of the 1990s, which, referred to as the Arduous March, caused unimaginable pain to ordinary North Koreans and numerous losses of life to hunger and malnutrition.

Long-distance traders consult local fortune-tellers before deciding on the date and direction of their journeys, often employing other modest improvised ritualistic gestures such as throwing a handful of salt behind one's back in the hope of avoiding malignant spirits or bad luck. Some carry a pouch with a handful of dried black beans in it for the same purpose. People who are expected to visit their relatives in China seek help from fortune-tellers— to find the auspicious date and to do small rituals in the hope of augmenting the success of their visit, which usually involves some form of business activity or short-term overseas employment. One middle-aged woman went to see a fortune-teller in her town along North Korea's border with China shortly after her husband passed away and while her family was facing severe economic difficulties. She was told that should she move to a land in the south, new economic prosperity and personal security are to be found. She eventually decided to try a new life in South Korea, after consulting again with the fortune-teller about her two children, who would actually benefit, so she was told, from their mother's being away in the southern land. A number of these fortune-tellers took the difficult decision to move to

South Korea themselves, hoping to practice their trade openly and without fearing punishment. In deciding to do so, some were driven by the commanding desire of their tutelary spirits, according to an informant, "to play in an open space"—that is, to exhibit their power and efficacy in the entertaining public space of a *kut* (rather than in secretive divination sessions), which is not available north of the 38th Parallel yet.

Although complex in background, we may understand this phenomenon in terms of the breakdown of the state as a guarantor of basic subsistence and as part of the society's desperate search for an alternative way to imagine and generate minimal human security. Seventy years after the Korean War and the onset of a militant revolutionary struggle against religions and superstitions in the northern half, therefore, it appears that religion and religious practice are finding their way back in North Korea. Some Christian groups in South Korea and the United States might like to see this returning religion to be the power of the Kingdom of God and this only; as we saw, the evangelization of North Korea has been a vital agenda in the advent of Korea's Protestantism throughout the Cold War. For now, however, what is returning is not yet the message of the Gospel but a host of "seeking good luck" practices—the very old tradition of Korea's spiritual life that had long been considered incompatible with the diffusion of this message. At the end of a long American Century in Korea, we witness a new religious landscape emerging in and around the place where that century began with an especially forceful wave of evangelization. Uk-i had been there and then. He came back to his southern home to share his soul-opening experience with his family. Mohwa refused to do so and took the message her son brought home as the voice of an alien spirit. In between these two, Nang-i struggled to imagine a world in which her brother and her mother could live together and their different worlds could exist alongside each other. Her struggle is as relevant now and in the future as a century ago. The American Century may be coming to a closure.[26] The story of American power in Korean religion, however, is far from over yet.

ACKNOWLEDGMENTS

This book has had a long gestation. We first encountered Incheon's Freedom Park area in 2005 while working on a comparative Cold War social experience project, supported by the UK's Economic and Social Research Council. Professor Cho Hung-yun kindly introduced us to Chung Hak-bong, who subsequently became one of our key interlocutors. Since then, we have visited Incheon on a number of occasions and spent many days in the local and national libraries and archives. The final stage of the project has received generous support from the Academy of Korean Studies (Laboratory Programme for Korean Studies through the Ministry of Education of the Republic of Korea and the Korean Studies Promotion Service of the Academy of Korean Studies, AKS-2016-LAB-2250005). Parts of the book were presented in seminars and lectures held in the London School of Economics, Institute for the Study of Religion at Sogang University, the University of Chicago, Seoul National University's College of Social Sciences, as well as, in 2019, in the Association for Asian Studies in Asia meeting in Bangkok and in the Lévi-Strauss memorial lecture in Paris. Antonetta Bruno, Donald Baker, Kim Seong-nae, and Laurel Kendall have been good companions throughout the years. Carlo Severi, Paolo Fortis, Fenella Cannell, Julie Chu, Gregory Delaplace, and Katherine Swancutt shared with us their interests in the power of magical symbols in modern politics. We are grateful to Thomas Lay, Clara Han, and Bhrigupati Singh for their unfailing support and superb editorial guidance. Above all, this book's tripartite interest in religion, politics, and history owes a lot to what Caroline Humphrey demonstrated in her pioneering work on North Asia, *Shamans and Elders*.

This book is an attempt to reconsider the place of religion in secular world politics, especially the politics of the Cold War. On this, we were fortunate to have Andrew Preston and Peter Mandler as colleagues. It is also an effort to recover the now largely forgotten heritage of modern anthropology in which the discipline was both a scientific study of world cultures and, at one and the same time, a historical investigation of disappearing indigenous cultures. This was certainly the case in the early tradition of anthropological research in the United States as part of the nation's rise to a global power. The same was true in the postcolonial outposts of American power, as in post–Korean War South Korea, where pursuing an anthropological knowledge of the world had never been free from the tensions existing between ethnological studies of familiar yet disappearing past heritages and open inquiries into other dazzlingly diverse human cultural forms. Yim Suk-jay was well aware of this tension and struggled with it all his scholarly life. Roger Janelli (1943–2021), a close colleague of Yim's and his son-in-law, had a lucid understanding of this connectedness between American anthropology and anthropology in Korea. One of Janelli's last essays was about Franz Boas as America's great folklorist, not merely as a founder of American anthropology, who recorded the nation's rich pre-national, indigenous pasts as part of the nation's important historical heritages to be treasured and cherished as such. This book is dedicated to the memory of these two great anthropologists of Korea.

NOTES

INTRODUCTION

1. Michael Shin, *Korean National Identity under Japanese Colonial Rule: Yi Gwangsu and the March First Movement of 1919* (London: Routledge, 2018).

2. Erez Manela, *The Wilsonian Moment: Self-Determination and the International Origins of Anticolonial Nationalism* (New York: Oxford University Press, 2009).

3. Dong-li Kim, *Munyŏdo* [Portrait of a Shamaness] (1936; Seoul: Malŭn Sori, 2010).

4. Among numerous works in this growing genre of research is Comaroff and Comaroff's investigation of South Africa's colonial frontier and the "long conversation" between the Southern Tswana and the nonconformist missionaries: John L. Comaroff and Jean Comaroff, *Of Revelation and Revolution*, vol. 2: *The Dialectics of Modernity on a South African Frontier* (Chicago: University of Chicago Press, 1997), 63. For an emphasis on the radical diversity of this "conversation," see Peter van der Veer, ed., *Conversion to Modernities: Globalization of Christianity* (New York: Routledge, 1994). For an original, stimulating discussion on why some people refuse to convert (while others readily convert), see Robert W. Heffner, ed., *Conversion to Christianity: Historical and Anthropological Perspectives on a Great Transformation* (Berkeley: University of California Press, 1993). Heffner also stresses the need to come to terms with the complex intimate world experience of those undergoing conversion.

5. Seong-nae Kim, "Iljesidae musokdamronŭi hyŭngsŭng'gwa sikminjŏk jaehyŭnŭi jŏngchihak" [The formation of musok discourse and the politics of representation during the Japanese colonial era], *Hankukmusokhak* [Korean folklore studies] 24 (2012): 7–42. See also Seong-nae Kim, *Hankuk mukyoŭi munhwainlyuhak* [Cultural anthropology of Korea's shamanism religion] (Seoul: Sonamu, 2018), 81–114.

6. Youngju Ryu, ed., *Cultures of Yushin: South Korea in the 1970s* (Ann Arbor: University of Michigan Press, 2018). Also Myungseok Oh, "Cultural Policy and

National Culture Discourse in the 1960s and 1970s," *Korean Anthropological Review* 1, no. 1 (2017): 105–129.

7. The phrase is from Donald N. Clark's engrossing study of the intimate experience of the American missionaries in Korea during the first half of the twentieth century, including those in his family: *Living Dangerously in Korea: The Western Experience, 1900–1950* (Norwalk, CT: EastBridge, 2003), 209.

8. Kyung-Koo Han, "Legacies of War: The Korean War—60 Years On," *Asia-Pacific Journal* 8, issue 38, no. 3 (September 20, 2010), available online at https://apjjf.org/-Han-Kyung-Koo/3414/article.html.

9. A prominent example would be Joel Robbins's *Becoming Sinners: Christianity and Moral Torment in a Papua New Guinea Society* (Berkeley: University of California Press, 2004). For an outstanding effort to bring these two separate research strands together, colonial history of religious encounter and ethnographic research on conversion experience, see Webb Keane, *Christian Moderns: Freedom and Fetish in Mission Encounter* (Berkeley: University of California Press, 2007).

10. For a broad discussion of the problematic place of Cold War history in contemporary comparative social research, see Heonik Kwon, *The Other Cold War* (New York: Columbia University Press, 2010).

11. Jürgen Habermas, *The Structural Transformation of the Public Sphere: An Inquiry into a Category of Bourgeois Society*, trans. Thomas Burger (Cambridge, MA: MIT Press, 1989). For a critical assessment of this reductionist tendency of modern ideology, in relation to kinship (as private sphere), see Heonik Kwon, *After the Korean War: An Intimate History* (Cambridge: Cambridge University Press, 2020).

1. RELIGION AND THE COLD WAR

1. This and the other following quotes are from the promotion footage of Graham's visit broadcast at Gŭkdong Bangsong [Far East Broadcasting], available online at https://www.youtube.com/watch?v=UOUzbbHe_lg. See also Hankukgidokgyosŏn'gyohyŏpŭihoi [Korean Christian Mission Society], *Billy Graham jŏnjip: hankukjŏndodaehoit'ŭkjip* [On Billy Graham: special collection on his revival rallies in Korea] (Seoul: Sinkyungsa, 1973).

2. W. Terry Whalin, *Billy Graham: A Biography of America's Greatest Evangelist* (New York: Morgan James Faith, 2014). See also Grant Wacker, *America's Pastor: Billy Graham and the Shaping of a Nation* (Cambridge, MA: Harvard University Press, 2014).

3. These quotes are from "President Meets Graham," *Korea Herald*, May 27, 1973.

4. Cited from Billy Graham's conversation and prayer with his wife, Ruth Bell Graham, featured in the official video footage of '73 Crusade available at https://www.youtube.com/watch?v=UOUzbbHe_lg&t=1813s.

5. For an excellent review of this event, see Helen Jin Kim, "Campus Crusade 'Explosions': Conversions and Conservatism from the US Bible Belt to Cold War South Korea, 1972–1974," *Journal of Korean Religions* 9, no. 1 (2018): 11–41. According to Kim, these events show that "religion is not an epiphenomenal, a second-order variable, but a central and independent category in the historical reconsideration of the global Cold War and US–South Korean relations" (Kim, "Campus Crusade 'Explosions,'" 33).

6. From the official video record, "Segye Kidokgyo Bokŭmhwa Daehoi Explo '74" [World Christian evangelization rally, Explo '74], available online at https://www.youtube.com/watch?v=ahUYa9XVu24.

7. In-cheol Hwang, "Hankuk kyohoi sŏngjang'gwa buhŭng" [The growth and prosperity of Korean church], *Kidoksinmun* [Christian times], February 6, 2012. According to the 1997 report by Gallup Korea, the Protestant population in South Korea grew from 3.19 millions in 1970 to 7.18 million in 1980. Gallup Korea, *Hankukinŭi jong'gyowa jong'gyoŭisik* [Koreans' religions and religious consciousness] (Seoul: Gallup Korea, 1998), 200. These figures are based on information provided by the churches and their denominational associations. In more conservative estimates, the numbers are about two million in 1970 to just under four million in 1980.

8. Available online at https://www.templetonprize.org/laureate-sub/han -acceptance-speech/.

9. Dae-seung Seo, "Sŏngjangjuŭijŏk gyohoiŭi jaesaengsan: jaeminhanin'gyohoiwa infrastrŭkchŏŭi jŏngchi" [Reproduction of the growth-oriented church: Korean American church and the politics of infrastructure], *Bigyomunhwayŏngu* [Journal of comparative cultural studies] 25, no. 2 (2019): 103–143.

10. The expression "Asia's apostles" is quoted from Ju Hui Judy Han, "Shifting Geographies of Proximity: Korean-led Evangelical Christian Missions and the US Empire," in *Ethnographies of US Empire*, ed. Carol McGranahan and John F. Collins (Durham, NC: Duke University Press, 2018), 197. Han approaches South Korea's aggressive World Mission, on the one hand, as an epiphenomenon of the American hegemony within which it takes place and, on the other, in the light of the increasingly influential paradigm of "postcolonial mission"—the South to South diffusion of Good News departing from the previously dominant North to South pattern. See also Sebastian C. H. Kim and Kirsteen Kim, *A History of Korean Christianity* (New York: Cambridge University Press, 2015), 299–315, and Steve Sang-Cheol Moon, "The Protestant Missionary Movement in Korea: Current Growth and Development," *International Bulletin of Missionary Research* 32, no. 2 (2008): 59–64. Since the 1990s, following the fall of the Berlin Wall in 1989 and the disintegration of the Soviet order in 1991, South Korea's overseas mission activities have turned their attention also to former Eastern-bloc societies. Referred to as the Northern Mission [*bukbang sŏngyo*], a prominent activity in this domain

consists of humanitarian intervention and rescue mission on behalf of displaced North Korean refugees in northeast China. The rise of the Northern Mission interacted with South Korea's then active engagement policy with former Eastern-bloc countries (called Northern Diplomacy or Northern Policy, modeled on West Germany's earlier *Ostpolitik*). Again, Reverend Han played an important role in propelling this movement, not least by helping establish the Christian Council of Korea in 1989, an interdenominational organization whose declared two-winged objective was Global Mission and National Evangelization (i.e., bringing the gospel back to Korea's lost northern half). See Jin-Heon Jung, *Migration and Religion in East Asia: North Korean Migrants' Evangelical Encounters* (London: Palgrave Macmillan, 2015); and Ju Hui Judy Han, "Beyond Safe Haven: A Critique of Christian Custody of North Korean Migrants in China," *Critical Asian Studies* 45, no. 4 (2013): 543–547.

11. Melani McAlister, *The Kingdom of God Has No Borders: A Global History of American Evangelicals* (New York: Oxford University Press, 2018), 85.

12. Ibid., 90.

13. Ibid., 88–89.

14. Andrew Preston, *Swords of the Spirit, Shield of Faith: Religion in American War and Diplomacy* (New York: Anchor Books, 2012).

15. Dianne Kirby, "Harry Truman's Religious Legacy: The Holy Alliance, Containment and the Cold War," in *Religion and the Cold War*, ed. D. Kirby (New York: Palgrave Macmillan, 2002), 77.

16. Ibid., 78.

17. See, for instance, Frank J. Coppa, "Pope Pius XII and the Cold War: The Post-war Confrontation between Catholicism and Communism," in *Religion and the Cold War*, ed. D. Kirby (New York: Palgrave Macmillan, 2002), 50–66; Marie Gayte, "The Vatican and the Reagan Administration: A Cold War Alliance?" *Catholic Historical Review* 97, no. 4 (2011): 713–736.

18. Melani McAlister, *Epic Encounters: Culture, Media, and the U.S Interests in the Middle East since 1945* (Berkeley: University of California Press, 2005).

19. Stephen J. Whitfield, *The Culture of the Cold War* (Baltimore: Johns Hopkins University Press, 1991).

20. See Talal Asad, *Formations of the Secular: Christianity, Islam, Modernity* (Stanford, CA: Stanford University Press, 2003).

21. Samuel P. Huntington, *The Clash of Civilizations and the Remaking of World Order* (London: Simon and Schuster, 1997).

22. Robert Buzzanco, "Where Is the Beef? Culture without Power in the Study of US Foreign Relations," *Diplomatic History* 24, no. 4 (2000): 623–632.

23. In his stimulating remark on the subject, Marshall Sahlins traces the difference between the concept of power as in power politics and that which is inclusive of religion and ideology (or culture and history) to the distance between Thucydides

(whom he calls "the darling of contemporary IR realists") and Herodotus's "ethnographically-informed history." Cited from Marshall Sahlins, "Alterity and Autochthony: Austronesian Cosmographies of the Marvelous," The Raymond Firth Lecture, 2008, *HAU: Journal of Ethnographic Theory* 2, no. 1 (2012): 131.

24. Clifford Geertz, *Negara: The Theatre State in Nineteenth-Century Bali* (Princeton, NJ: Princeton University Press, 1980).

25. Clifford Geertz, *The Interpretation of Cultures* (New York: Basic Books, 1973).

26. Heonik Kwon, *The Other Cold War* (New York: Columbia University Press, 2010), 140–148.

27. David Ryan, "Mapping Containment: The Cultural Construction of the Cold War," in *American Cold War Culture*, ed. Douglas Field (Edinburgh: Edinburgh University Press, 2005), 51.

28. Ibid.

29. Andrew J. Rotter, "Christians, Muslims, and Hindus: Religion and US–South Asian Relations, 1947–1954," *Diplomatic History* 24, no. 4 (2000): 594.

30. Ibid. See also the diplomatic historian and Kennedy-era specialist Michael E. Latham's *Modernization as Ideology: American Social Science and "Nation Building" in the Kennedy Era* (Chapel Hill: University of North Carolina Press, 2000), in which he adopts Geertz's idea of ideology as a system of cultural symbols and even a cognitive framework. The way in which historians who study the era's American foreign policies find Geertz useful is, as noted earlier, very much to do with the fact that Geertz advanced his theory of culture and politics in close awareness of the atmosphere of the very era. In short, Geertz's *Interpretation of Cultures* is, to a great extent, a product of the American politics of the 1960s.

31. For a critique of the rendering of the Cold War as an imaginary war, see Kwon, *The Other Cold War*, 153–156.

32. Donald N. Clark, *Living Dangerously in Korea: The Western Experience, 1900–1950* (Norwalk, CT: EastBridge, 2003), 301.

33. Ibid., 116–141.

34. Ibid., 301–304; James E. Hoare and Susan Pares, *North Korea in the 21st Century: An Interpretive Guide* (Folkestone: Global Oriental, 2005); Kim and Kim, *A History of Korean Christianity*, 162–168. For a broad overview of North Korea's changing policies on religion and religious groups from 1945 to the present, see Byung-ro Kim, *Bukhan jong'gyojŏngchaekŭi byŭnhwawa jong'gyosiltae* [North Korea's changing religious policies and its religious reality] (Seoul: Tongilyŏn'guwŏn, 2020). Kim defines North Korea's prewar approach to religious groupings broadly as politics of assimilation and selective exclusion (into and from the political sphere), distinguishing if from the generalized, eliminationist anti-religion politics in the postwar years.

35. Heonik Kwon, *After the Korean War: An Intimate History* (Cambridge: Cambridge University Press, 2020), 28–29.

36. Gurimji pyŏnchan wiwŏnhoi [Editorial committee of Gurim chronicles], *Honam myŏngchon Gurim* [Gurim, a distinguished village in Honam region] (Seoul: Libuk, 2006), 373. Shortly after this tragic incident, on October 17, 1950, the village suffered again, although the village annals mention the second massacre only fleetingly. The perpetrators of this violence were the South Korean combat police, who regarded the village as a whole as a subversive place in sympathy with the communists. See Kwon, *After the Korean War*, 29–30.

37. Ibid., 30.

38. Jeongran Yoon, *Hankukjŏnjaeng'gwa gidokgyo* [The Korean War and Protestantism] (Seoul: Hanul Academy, 2015). See also Jeongran Yoon, "Victory over Communism: South Korean Protestants' Ideas about Democracy, Development, and Dictatorship, 1953–1961," *Journal of American-East Asian Relations* 24 (2017): 233–258.

39. Webb Keane, *Christian Moderns: Freedom and Fetish in the Mission Encounter* (Berkeley: University of California Press, 2007).

40. Kim and Kim, *A History of Korean Christianity*, 176–177.

41. Clark, *Living Dangerously in Korea*, 291–301.

42. Yoon, *Hankukjŏnjaeng'gwa gidokgyo* [The Korean War and Protestantism], 115–148; Yoon, "Victory over Communism," 245–246.

43. On McIntire's career and his role in establishing the International Council of Christian Churches in 1948, in opposition to the World Council of Churches, see Markku Ruotsila, *Fighting Fundamentalist: Carl McIntire and the Politicization of American Fundamentalism* (New York: Oxford University Press, 2015).

44. For an overview of the reshaping of modern evangelicalism in the post-WWII US context, partly in distinction to Christian fundamentalism, we have benefited especially from Frances FitzGerald, *The Evangelicals: The Struggle to Shape America* (New York: Simon & Schuster, 2017). Billy Graham looms large in her story, followed by Jerry Falwell and Pat Robertson. Also useful were William Martin, *With God on Our Side: The Rise of the Religious Right in America* (New York: Broadway Books, 1996); Joel Carpenter, *Revive Us Again: The Reawakening of American Fundamentalism* (New York: Oxford University Press, 1999); and Molly Worthen, *Apostles of Reason: The Crisis of Authority in American Evangelicalism* (New York: Oxford University Press, 2013). Some important anthropological works exist on the subject, too. Notable is Susan Friend Harding's *The Book of Jerry Falwell: Fundamentalist Language and Politics* (Princeton, NJ: Princeton University Press, 2000), which concentrates on textual analysis of evangelical discourses in line with the supremacy of textual authority in the ideology of biblical literalism or realism. Harding makes it clear that contemporary American evangelicalism is a thoroughly modern phenomenon, far from an un-modern

worldview or an anti-modernity movement as it is often seen by the secularists. Vincent Crapanzano, in *Serving the Word: Literalism in America from the Pulpit to the Bench* (New York: New Press, 2000), takes a broad view of literalism and investigates its dogmatic power in both religious and legal-professional spheres. From a different angle, Tanya Luhrmann offers a rich ethnographic account of some middle-class Californians belonging to a fast-growing, contemporary evangelical group, Vineyard Christian Fellowship. Rather than the belief in the inerrancy of Scripture and the transformative experience of being Born Again, which are widely recognized as key constituent elements of being a modern evangelical Christian, Luhrmann highlights the power of intimate interpersonal relationship—the presence of *the* Person (in Billy Graham's terms) felt and experienced by a person in all corners of his or her everyday life. The Person is deeply kind and intimate, and is powerfully present in and around the person, who is therefore never a loner even if she may be physically alone. Tanya M. Luhrmann, *When God Talks Back: Understanding the American Evangelical Relationship with God* (New York: Vintage, 2012). Similarly, Thomas Csordas's investigation of an American Catholic revivalist movement highlights the power of self-discovery and self-transformation in charismatic healing experience: Thomas J. Csordas, *The Sacred Self: A Cultural Phenomenology of Charismatic Healing* (Berkeley: University of California Press, 1997). The sociologist Kelly Chong shows how gendered the making of this sacred self is in South Korea's Pentecostal movement, focusing on the urban middle-class women's spiritual zeal and passionate performance within (and against) the patriarchal order that permeates the church as well as their domestic lives: Kelly H. Chong, *Deliverance and Submission: Evangelical Women and the Negotiation of Patriarchy in South Korea* (Cambridge, MA: Harvard University Press, 2008). Nicholas Harkness's fascinating ethnography of church lives in Seoul describes how music and musical performance contribute to the making of the evangelical selfhood: Nicholas Harkness, *Songs of Seoul: An Ethnography of Voice and Voicing in Christian South Korea* (Berkeley: University of California Press, 2013). In a stimulating essay written from quite a different angle, Tim Ingold approaches biblical literalism as a *closed* Book of Nature, in contrast to the medieval practices of reading that were, according to him, amenable to diverse interpretative discoveries. Ingold also makes a case for some likeness in this respect between the practice of medieval monastic readership and approaches to nature and divinity found in indigenous foraging societies. Tim Ingold, "Dreaming of Dragons: On the Imagination of Real Life," *Journal of the Royal Anthropological Institute* 19, no. 4 (2013): 734–752.

45. Nak-hong Yang, "1959nyŏn hankuk jangrogyoŭi bunyŏl gwajŏng" [An analysis of the schism of the Korean Presbyterian church in 1959], *Hankukgidokgyowa yŏksa* [History of Korean Christianity] 23 (2005): 125–161. See also McAlister, *The Kingdom of God Has No Borders*, 97.

46. Sarah Pulliam Bailey, "'God Has Given Trump Authority to Take Out Kim Jong Un,' Evangelical Adviser Says," *Washington Post*, August 9, 2017. One crucial difference between the Christian Right in the United States and the equivalent movement in South Korea is, however, the near absence of anti-abortion and pro-life preoccupations in the latter—an issue that defines the former.

47. William Inboden, *Religion and American Foreign Policy, 1945–1960: The Soul of Containment* (New York: Cambridge University Press, 2008), 102. See also Rotter, "Christians, Muslims, and Hindus," 595.

48. Ibid., 596.

49. Ibid., 595.

50. David P. Fields, *Foreign Friends: Syngman Rhee, American Exceptionalism, and the Division of Korea* (Lexington: University Press of Kentucky, 2019).

51. Yoon, *Hankukjŏnjaeng'gwa gidokgyo* [The Korean War and Protestantism], 241–245.

52. Chung-Shin Park, *Protestantism and Politics in Korea* (Seattle: University of Washington Press, 2003), 161–167.

53. On the role of the military in South Korea's modernization drive (and, in part, in the theory and ideology of modernization itself), see Gregg Brazinsky, *Nation Building in South Korea: Koreans, Americans, and the Making of a Democracy* (Chapel Hill: University of North Carolina Press, 2007).

54. Carter J. Eckert, *Park Chung Hee and Modern Korea: The Roots of Militarism, 1866–1945* (Cambridge, MA: Harvard University Press, 2016).

55. For the transition in 1960–1961, see Charles R. Kim, *Youth for Nation: Culture and Protest in Cold War Korea* (New York: Columbia University Press, 2017).

56. Michael E. Latham, *The Right Kind of Revolution: Modernization, Development, and US Foreign Policy from the Cold War to the Present* (Ithaca, NY: Cornell University Press, 2011). MIT academics such as Walt Rostow loom large in this story; they viewed changing the postcolonial societies from flawed traditional milieus into a modern, rational order as a vital security question for the United States. So did characters such as Edward Lansdale in another version, who, known as the real-life figure of Pyle, a protagonist of Graham Greene's *The Quiet American* (1955), approached development and modernization as part of a counterinsurgency struggle against radical nationalists in the Philippines and Vietnam. See, for instance, Jonathan Nashel, *Edward Lansdale's Cold War* (Amherst: University of Massachusetts Press, 2005).

57. Kyung-chik Han, "Gŭrisdoin'gwa ban'gong" [Christians and anticommunism], *Saegajŏng* [The new family] 10, no. 3 (1963): 12–13. See also his memoir: Kyung-chik Han, "My Gratitude," in *Kyung-Chik Han Collection*, vol. 1, ed. Eun-seop Kim (Seoul: Han Kyung-Chik Foundation, 2010).

58. Rotter, "Christians, Muslims, and Hindus."

59. Cited from the Templeton Prize's website: https://www.templetonprize.org/.

60. Available online at the website dedicated to his memory: http://hank yungchik.org/Home/bbs/page.php?hid=TempletonPrize.

61. The text is available online at https://www.templetonprize.org/laureate-sub /han-acceptance-speech/.

62. Duk-man Bae, *Hankuk gaesingyo gŭnbonjuŭi* [Korean Protestantism's fundamentalism] (Daejon: Daejangkan, 2010), 31. See also Timothy S. Lee, "Beleaguered Success: Korean Evangelicalism in the Last Decade of the Twentieth Century," in *Christianity in Korea*, ed. Robert E. Buswell Jr. and Timothy S. Lee (Honolulu: University of Hawai'i Press, 2006), 331–333.

63. Bruce Cumings, *The Origins of the Korean War: Liberation and the Emergence of Separate Regimes, 1945–1947* (Princeton, NJ: Princeton University Press, 1981).

64. Sok-Yong Hwang, *The Guest: A Novel*, trans. Kyung-Ja Chun and Maya West (New York: Seven Stories Press, 2008).

65. See Jane Monnig Atkinson, "Religions in Dialogue: The Construction of an Indonesian Minority Religion," *American Ethnologist* 10, no. 4 (1983), 684.

66. William Appleman Williams, *Empire as a Way of Life* (New York: Oxford University Press, 1980).

67. Carol McGranahan and John F. Collins, eds., *Ethnographies of US Empire* (Durham, NC: Duke University Press, 2018).

68. Cited from Raymond Firth, *Religion: A Humanist Interpretation* (London: Routledge, 1996), 79.

2. THE AMERICAN SPIRIT

1. Gap-seng Chun, "Ganghwado·Ongjin chulsinjadŭlŭi gusulesŏ bon hankukjŏnjaengŭi gyŏnghŏmgwa giŏk" [The experience and memory of the Korean War in the testimonies of the settlers from Ganghwa Island and Ongjin], paper presented at the Korean Association for Oral History conference in Incheon (November 21, 2020).

2. This statement accords with Don Baker's observation on religious plurality and the ordinariness of spirituality in Korean society, past and present, as well as his related distinction between spirituality and religiosity. Don Baker, *Korean Spirituality* (Honolulu: University of Hawai'i Press, 2008).

3. Baul Lee, *Gidoro sŭng'lihan MacArthur* [MacArthur who triumphed with prayer] (Seoul: Joŭn, 2014), 362. See also the prayer book and educational material addressed to children: Chi-ho Han, *Janyŏrŭl ŭihan MacArthurŭi gido* [MacArthur's prayers for children] (Seoul: Ilosam, 2008). This pamphlet depicts MacArthur's role in the Korean War also as a revelation of the divine will—that is, as a warrior sent from the Kingdom of God.

4. Myung-hwan Anh, "Chuchŏnsŏ" [Endorsement], in Lee, *Gidoro sŭng'lihan MacArthur* [MacArthur who triumphed with prayer], 16.

5. A close example might be *oboo* religious sites of Inner Asia, especially those referred to as "directional oboos." See Christopher Evans and Caroline Humphrey, "History, Timelessness, and the Monumental: The Oboos of the Mergen Environs of Inner Mongolia," *Cambridge Archaeological Journal* 13, no. 2 (2003): 195–211; and Üjiyediin Chuluu and Kevin Stuart, "Rethinking the Mongol *Oboo*," *Anthropos* 90, no. 4/6 (1995): 550.

6. See Charles Allen Clark, *Religions of Old Korea* (1932; Seoul: Christian Literature Society of Korea, 1961), 177.

7. Ibid.

8. Boudewijn C. A. Walraven, "Popular Religion in a Confucianized Society," in *Culture and the State in Late Chosŏn Korea*, ed. Ja-Hyun Kim Haboush and Martina Deuchler (Cambridge, MA: Harvard University Press, 1999), 160–198. James Huntley Grayson, *Korea: A Religious History* (London: Routledge, 2002).

9. Caroline Humphrey with Urugunge Onon, *Shamans and Elders: Experience, Knowledge, and Power among the Daur Mongols* (Oxford: Clarendon Press, 1996); Caroline Humphrey, "Shamanic Practices and the State in Northern Asia: Views from the Center and Periphery," in *Shamanism, History, and the State*, ed. Nicholas Thomas and Caroline Humphrey (Ann Arbor: University of Michigan Press, 1994), 191–228. See also Jane Monnig Atkinson, *The Art and Politics of Wana Shamanship* (Berkeley: University of California Press, 1992), 297–327.

10. Humphrey and Onon, *Shamans and Elders*, 6.

11. For the place of spirit portraits in *kut* and their changing relevance in time, see Laurel Kendall and Jongsung Yang, "What Is an Animated Image?: Korean Shaman Paintings as Objects of Ambiguity," *HAU: Journal of Ethnographic Theory* 5, no. 2 (2015): 153–175.

12. Chang-mo Anh, "Gaehang'gwa jŏnjaeng, dosiŭi unmyŏngŭl bakkuda" [Shaking up cities since the opening of the ports in 1876], *Gŏnchuksa* [Korean architects], no. 12 (2012): 65–68.

13. Incheon Munhwa Jaedan, *Man'gukgong'wŏnŭi giŏk* [Memories of Ten Thousand Nations Park] (Incheon: Incheon Munhwa Jaedan, 2006).

14. Se-young Lee, "Haebang–hankukjŏnjaeng'ki Incheonjiyŏk wŏlnamminŭi jŏngchakgwa netŭwŏkŭ hyŏngsŏng" [Establishment and networking of Incheon area refugees during the liberation and Korean War periods], *Dongbanghakji* [Journal of Oriental studies], no. 180 (2017): 177–211; Sang-eui Lee, "Hankukjŏnjaeing gusulsa yŏnguwa Incheon" [The Korean War oral history and Incheon], paper presented at the Korean Association for Oral History in Incheon (November 21, 2020).

15. Jeongran Yoon, "Victory over Communism: South Korean Protestants' Ideas about Democracy, Development, and Dictatorship, 1953–1961," *Journal of American–East Asian Relations* 24, no. 2–3 (2017): 233–258.

16. See William M. Leary, ed., *MacArthur and the American Century: A Reader* (Lincoln: University of Nebraska Press, 2001); William Manchester, *American Caesar: Douglas MacArthur, 1880–1964* (Boston: Little, Brown, 1978).

17. Donald W. White, "The 'American Century' in World History," *Journal of World History* 3, no. 1 (1992): 105.

18. Henry R. Luce, "The American Century," *Diplomatic History* 23, no. 2 (1999): 167.

19. William A. Williams, *Empire as a Way of Life* (New York: Oxford University Press, 1980).

20. Michael Schaller, *Douglas MacArthur: The Far Eastern General* (New York: Oxford University Press, 1989).

21. Erez Manela, *The Wilsonian Moment: Self-determination and the International Origins of Anticolonial Nationalism* (New York: Oxford University Press, 2009).

22. Carlo Severi, "On the White Spirits in the Kuna," in *Disturbing Remains: Memory, History, and Crisis in the Twentieth Century*, ed. Michael S. Roth and Charles G. Salas (Los Angeles: Getty Research Institute, 2001), 178–206; Paolo Fortis, *Kuna Art and Shamanism: An Ethnographic Approach* (Austin: University of Texas Press, 2013).

23. Michael Taussig, *Mimesis and Alterity: A Particular History of the Senses* (New York: Routledge, 1993).

24. Ibid., 8.

25. Danilyn Rutherford, *Raiding the Land of the Foreigners: The Limits of the Nation on an Indonesian Frontier* (Stanford, CA: Stanford University Press, 2002).

26. Seong-nae Kim, "The Iconic Power of Modernity: Reading a Cheju Shaman's Life History and Initiation Dream," in *South Korea's Minjung Movement: The Culture and Politics of Dissidence*, ed. Kenneth M. Wells (Honolulu: University of Hawai'i Press, 1995), 155–166.

27. Suk-jay Yim, "Hankukmusokyŏn'gusŏsŏl I" [Introduction to Korean shamanism I], *Aseayŏsŏngyŏngu* (Journal of the studies of Asian women) 9 (1970): 73–90.

28. See Han, *Janyŏrŭl wihan MacArthurŭi gido* [MacArthur's prayers for children].

29. Quoted from Gregory Henderson, "Korea," in *Divided Nations in a Divided World*, ed. in G. Henderson, J. G. Stoessinger, and R. N. Lebow (New York: David McKay, 1974). See also Heonik Kwon, *After the Korean War: An Intimate History* (Cambridge: Cambridge University Press, 2020), 129–130.

30. Bruce Cumings, *The Korean War: A History* (New York: Modern Library, 2010), 290.

31. Jin-wung Kim, "Maekadŏ jang'gunŭi je 2ŭi Inchon sang'ryuk jaksŏn: dong'sang'ŭl dullŏssan bunjaeng'ŭi hamŭi" [General MacArthur's other Inch'on landing: implications of the conflict over his statue], *Yŏksagyoyŭknonjib* [Journal of history education], no. 39 (2007): 415–454.

32. "Jayuhyŭkmyŭngŭi kkotdabal" [Flowers of the revolution for freedom], *Kyunghyang Sinmun* [Kyunghyang Daily], April 30, 1960.

33. See Michael Hyun Choi, "Orijinŏl Mansin: An Ethnography of Shaman Life in South Korea" (PhD thesis, Harvard University, 2010). Also Hong-ku Han, "Maekadŏga ŭninirago?" [Was MacArthur our savior?], *Hankyŏre21*, May 2, 2002.

34. See also Carlo Severi, *The Chimera Principle: An Anthropology of Memory and Imagination* (Chicago: University of Chicago Press, 2015).

35. Jong-sung Yang, "Hwanghaedo majikut hyŭngsikgwa tŭksŏng gochal" [Forms and characteristics of Hwanghae-do kut], in *Hwanghaedokutŭi ihae* [Understanding Hwanghae-do kut], ed. Hankukmusokhakhoi [Korean Association of folklore studies] (Seoul: Minsokwŏn, 2008), 48.

36. Jun Hwan Park, "Money Is the Filial Child. But, at the Same Time, It Is Also the Enemy!: Korean Shamanic Rituals for Luck and Fortune," *Journal of Korean Religions* 3, no. 2 (2012): 39–72.

37. Kŭm-Hwa Kim, *Kim Kŭm-hwa mugajip* [Collection of Kim Kŭm-hwa's ritual songs] (Seoul: Munŭmsa, 1995), 156.

38. Marshall Sahlins, *Islands of History* (Chicago: University of Chicago Press, 1985).

39. Severi, "On the White Spirits in the Kuna."

40. Ibid., 192.

41. Yim, "Hankukmusokyŏn'gusŏsŏl I" [Introduction to Korean shamanism I]; Suk-jay Yim, "Hankukmusokyŏn'gusŏsŏl II" [Introduction to Korean shamanism II], *Aseayŏsŏngyŏngu* (Journal of the studies of Asian women) 10 (1971): 161–217. Also Dawnhee Yim, "Byŭng'lipsin'gwan'gwa hankukmunhwa" [Parallelotheism and Korean culture], *Bigyominsokhak* [Comparative folklore studies] 20 (2001): 55–115; and Jong-sung Yang, "Hankuk musinŭi gujo yŏn'gu" [Studies of the structure of Korean shamanic spirits], *Bigyomunhwayŏngu* [Comparative cultural studies], 5 (1999): 176–177.

42. Yim, "Hankukmusokyŏn'gusŏsŏl I," 88.

43. Bhrigupati Singh, "The Headless Horseman of Central India: Sovereignty at Varying Thresholds of Life," *Cultural Anthropology* 27, no. 2 (2012): 383, 387.

44. Brian Goldstone, "Life after Sovereignty," *History of the Present* 4, no. 1 (2014): 98–99.

45. Ibid., 97.

3. VOYAGE TO KNOXVILLE, 1982

1. See JaHyun Kim Haboush, *The Great East Asian War and the Birth of the Korean Nation* (New York: Columbia University Press, 2016).

2. Chae-hun Rha and Han-seop Park, *Incheon gaehangsa* [Opening of the Incheon port: a history] (Seoul: Miraejisik, 2006). For a broader picture of the era,

see Andre Schmid, *Korea between Empires, 1895–1919* (New York: Columbia University Press, 2002). Also Kirk W. Larsen, "Competing Imperialisms in Korea," in *Routledge Handbook of Modern Korea*, ed. Michael J. Seth (New York: Routledge, 2016), 39–54.

3. Kŭm-hwa Kim, *Mansin Kim Kŭm-hwa* [The shaman Kim Kŭm-hwa] (Seoul: Gungli, 2014).

4. The story told in this chapter unfolds against the background of South Korea's modernization drive of the late 1960s and the 1970s. It is interesting that a transition from this era involved Korea's participation in an international event in the Tennessee Valley in the thick of the genealogy of Cold War anti-communist developmentalism. According to David Ekbladh, the mid-twentieth-century ideology of modernization and development (the "global New Deal") has a deeper background in American history, well beyond the narrow Cold War era, in which the story of the New Deal interventions, especially those in the Tennessee Valley in the 1930s that were centered on power utilities, looms large: David Ekbladh, *The Great American Mission: Modernization and the Construction of an American Order* (Princeton, NJ: Princeton University Press, 2009).

5. Cited from "Hanmi sugyo 100 junyŏn" [Centenary of Korean-American friendship], *Daehan nyusŭ* (Korean news) 1385, May 20, 1982.

6. Kim, *Mansin Kim Kŭm-hwa* [The shaman Kim Kŭm-hwa], 197–208. See also the renowned filmmaker Park Chan-kyung's documentary about her career and life based on this memoir, *Mansin* (2014).

7. Kyung-sun Hwang, "Buknyŭkŭi muhyŭng'yusan: Hwanghaedo kŭnmudangŭi kŭnkut iyagi" [Intangible heritage in North of Korea: story of a great *kut* by a great Hwanghae shaman], *Munhwajae sarang* [Love of cultural heritage, newsletter of Republic of Korea Cultural Heritage Administration], no. 99 (2013): 27.

8. Ibid.

9. Laurel Kendall, *Shamans, Nostalgias, and the IMF: South Korean Popular Religion in Motion* (Honolulu: University of Hawai'i Press, 2009), 1–33.

10. Nŭng-hwa Lee, *Josŏnmusokgo* [Treatise on Chosun musok] (1927; Seoul: Dongmunsŏn, 1991), 105–122. For a fascinating account of the exchange between Lee Nŭng-hwa and the Chicago anthropologist Frederick Starr, see Robert Oppenheim, "'The West' and the Anthropology of Other People's Colonialism: Frederick Starr in Korea, 1911–1930," *Journal of Asian Studies* 64, no. 3 (2005): 677–703. The story depicts Starr moving along sites of interest in Korea, being assisted by American missionaries and the Japanese colonial office. What emerges is not only the co-presence of these two powers, religious and political, in colonial Korea but also tensions generated by the unique character of Japanese colonialism as such—conquering non-distant spaces in terms of historical culture. Having embarked on the journey as a cultural evolutionist and anti-Boasian, according to Oppenheim, Starr comes quite close to being a Boasian internationalist by the

end of it—appreciating the reality and politics of a culturally plural world (see Conclusion to this volume). His friendship with Lee Nŭng-hwa played a role in this transformation.

11. Laurel Kendall, *Shamans, Housewives, and Other Restless Spirits: Women in Korean Ritual Life* (Honolulu: University of Hawai'i Press, 1985).

12. See Roger L. Janelli and Dawnhee Yim Janelli, *Ancestor Worship in Korean Society* (Stanford, CA: Stanford University Press, 1982); and Martina Deuchler, *Under the Ancestors' Eyes: Kinship, Status, and Locality in Premodern Korea* (Cambridge, MA: Harvard University Press, 2015). As for the history of Korea's neo-Confucian revolution that aspired to give birth to a new political and moral order through radical reforms in the ritual activity of the kinship organization (and the limits of this revolution), see Martina Deuchler's masterly *The Confucian Transformation of Korea: A Study of Society and Ideology* (Cambridge, MA: Harvard University Press, 1995).

13. Kun-woo Nam, "Hangukŭi saemaŭl undong'gwa saenghwalbyŭnhwa" [The New Village Movement and changes in everyday life in South Korea], *Ilsang'gwa munhwa* [Everyday life and culture] 5 (2018): 153.

14. For instance, see Hal Hill, *Indonesia's New Order: The Dynamics of Socio-Economic Transformation* (Honolulu: University of Hawai'i Press, 1994); Edward Aspinall, ed., *Soeharto's New Order and Its Legacy: Essays in Honour of Harold Crouch* (Canberra: Australian National University Press, 2011).

15. "Saemaŭl hunpung'e jjotgyŏnan pyesŭp 300onyŏn" [300-year-old rotten customs are blown away by the warm wind of the Saemaŭl movement], *Kyunghyang sinmun* [Kyunghyang daily], February 19, 1973.

16. See Youngju Ryu, Introduction to *Cultures of Yusin: South Korea in the 1970s*, ed. Youngju Ryu (Ann Arbor: University of Michigan Press, 2018).

17. Jong-sung Yang, "Seoul saramdŭlui sarangŭl batatdŏn Sasinsŏnghwangdang" [The Imperial Envoy Shrine that was once loved by the people of Seoul], *Urimunhwasinmun* [Our culture news], October 3, 2018, available online at http://www .koya-culture.com/news/article.html?no=114881.

18. James E. Hoare and Susan Pares, *North Korea in the 21st Century: An Interpretive Guide* (Folkestone, UK: Global Oriental, 2005), 88–89. For a broad overview of the time of the separate military occupation, by the Soviet and the US forces, and what this meant to Korea's Protestant community, see Chung-Shin Park, *Protestantism and Politics in Korea* (Seattle: University of Washington Press, 2003), 158–170.

19. Charles Armstrong, *The North Korean Revolution, 1945–1950* (Ithaca, NY: Cornell University Press, 2004).

20. Park, *Protestantism and Politics in Korea*, 166.

21. According to Andrei Lankov, the *inminban* system was basically an import from Soviet Russia, and it was in place and in operation in the North as early as

1946. The *inminban* network was probably a combination of the Soviet political technology and the legacy of the colonial era—the institution of *aekukban* ("patriotic cells") that Japan imported to the colony during the Pacific War. See Andrei Lankov, *The Real North Korea: Life and Politics in the Failed Stalinist Utopia* (New York: Oxford University Press, 2013), 38–40.

22. Kim, *Mansin Kim Kŭm-hwa* [The shaman Kim Kŭm-hwa], 113–121.

23. See Heonik Kwon, *After the Korean War: An Intimate History* (Cambridge: Cambridge University Press, 2020), 21–36.

24. Don-ku Kang, "Migunjŏngŭi jong'gyojŏngchaek" [US Military Government's religion policy], *Jong'gyohak yŏngu* [Journal of religious studies] 12 (1993): 15–42.

25. *Seoul Sinmun* [Seoul daily], November 20, 1947. Cited in Kang, "Migunjŏngŭi jong'gyojŏngchaek" [US Military Government's religion policy], 39.

26. Yoshinobu Shinzato, "Hankuk musok damronŭi hyŏngsŏng'gwa jŏn'gaee gwanhan yŏngu: 1960nyŏndaebutŏ 8onyŏndaerŭl jungsimŭro" [The development of discourses on Korean shamanism from the 1960s to the 1980s], PhD diss., Seoul National University, 2018.

27. Kendall, *Shamans, Nostalgias, and the IMF*, 19–21.

28. Benedict Anderson, *Imagined Communities: Reflections on the Origin and Spread of Nationalism* (London: Verso, 2006).

29. During the 2010s there has been an attempt to revive the Saemaŭl Movement and to have it relevant for rural development in Asia and Africa. See Asian Development Bank, *The Saemaul Undong Movement in the Republic of Korea: Sharing Knowledge on Community-Driven Development* (Mandaluyog, Philippines: Asian Development Bank, 2012).

30. Youngju Ryu, *Writers of the Winter Republic: Literature and Resistance in Park Chung Hee's Korea* (Honolulu: University of Hawai'i Press, 2015).

31. Kwang-ok Kim, "Jŏhangmunhwawa musokŭirye" [The culture of resistance and the ritual of shamanism], *Hankukmunhwainlyuhak* [Korean cultural anthropology] 23, no. 0 (1992): 131–172.

32. Kwon, *After the Korean War*, 103–104.

33. *Kyunghyang Sinmun* [Kyunghyang daily], May 16, 1981.

34. See Mikhail M. Bakhtin, *The Dialogic Imagination* (Austin: University of Texas Press, 1981); and Victor Turner, *Dramas, Fields, and Metaphors: Symbolic Action in Human Society* (Ithaca, NY: Cornell University Press, 1974).

4. SEEKING GOOD LUCK

1. About historical connections between Incheon and Yokohama, see Young-guk Chae, "Hanilgŭndaehwaŭi ipgu Inchŏn'gwa Yokohama" [Incheon and Yokohama—entry to Korean-Japanese modernity], in *Inchŏnyŏksa ilho* [History of Incheon, vol. 1], ed. Inchŏn'gwangyŏksi Yŏksajaryogwan Yŏksamunhwajŏn'gusil

[Research group on Incheon's history and culture] (Incheon: Inchŏn'gwangyŏksi Yŏksajaryogwan Yŏksamunhwajŏn'gusil, 2004), 239–261.

2. Sebastian C. H. Kim and Kirsteen Kim, *A History of Korean Christianity* (New York: Cambridge University Press, 2015), 63.

3. Even though the arrival of these American missionaries is clearly a formative episode in the history of Korean Protestantism, this does not mean that it was an initiatory event. The northern route was equally important. By the time Underwood and Appenzellers landed in Incheon, Korea's northwest region had already been acquainted with the Evangel through the movement of Korean converts across the Korea-Chinese border and the dissemination of the Korean-translated Bibles they carried. A key figure in building this route was John Ross of the United Presbyterian Church of the Scotland Manchurian mission. According to James Grayson: "Ross believed that Christianity was spread best by convinced converts rather than foreign missionaries. The existence of Protestant communities in Korea before foreign missionaries arrived is an eloquent testimonial to Ross's conviction. Protestantism in Korea, like Catholicism, was self-evangelized from the beginning—evangelism through the distribution of the scripture." However, this story is not the one that was highlighted during the Centenary celebration. James H. Grayson, "Quarter-Millennium of Christianity in Korea," in *Christianity in Korea* , ed. Robert E. Buswell Jr. and Timothy S. Lee (Honolulu: University of Hawai'i Press, 2006), 12–13.

4. B. E. Foster Hall, *The Chinese Maritime Customs: An International Service, 1854–1950* (Bristol: Bristol University Press, 1977).

5. Cited from the webpages of Incheon's Tourism Office: https://itour.incheon .go.kr/.

6. Hyun-joo Lee, "Hwagyoyuipgwa hawai imin" [The influx of the Chinese and the emigration to Hawaii], in *Inchŏnyŏksa ilho* [History of Incheon, vol. 1], ed. Inchŏn'gwangyŏksi Yŏksajaryogwan Yŏksamunhwajŏn'gusil [Research group on Incheon's history and culture] (Incheon: Inchŏn'gwangyŏksi Yŏksajaryogwan Yŏksamunhwajŏn'gusil), 206–210.

7. On this phenomenon, Kenneth Wells describes that "Protestantism began seriously to supplant Confucianism in education, its traditional pride and domain. Protestants were wresting the initiative from neo-Confucianism in education." Kenneth M. Wells, *New God, New Nation: Protestants and Self-Reconstruction Nationalism in Korea, 1896–1937* (Seoul: Voice of the Martyrs Korea, 1990, reprint), 42, 44.

8. William Yoo, *American Missionaries, Korean Protestants, and the Changing Shape of World Christianity, 1884–1965* (New York: Routledge, 2017), 20–59.

9. George W. Gilmore, *Corea of Today* (London: T. Nelson and Sons, 1894), 93.

10. Ibid., 89, 91.

11. Robert Oppenheim, *An Asian Frontier: American Anthropology and Korea, 1882–1945* (Lincoln: University of Nebraska Press, 2016), 37–47.

12. Il-young Park, "Syamŏnijŭme daehan sŏn'gyosadŭlŭi taedonŭn oae daebidŏinŭnga?" [Missionaries' contrasting attitudes to shamanism], in *Syamŏnijŭmgwa tajong'gyoŭi yunghapgwa galdŭng* [Synthesis and conflicts between Shamanism and other religions], ed. Syamŏnijŭm sasangyŏn'guhoi [Research Association for Shamanism] (Seoul: Misonwŏn, 2017), 71–93.

13. Ibid., 88.

14. Cemil Aydin, *The Politics of Anti-Westernism in Asia: Visions of World Order in Pan-Islamic and Pan-Asian Thought* (New York: Columbia University Press, 2007).

15. Adam Kuper, *Anthropology and Anthropologists: The Modern British School in the Twentieth Century* (London: Routledge, 2014), 64–87.

16. Wells, *New God, New Nation*, 27.

17. Edward B. Tylor, *Primitive Culture*, vol. 1 (London: John Murray, 1871).

18. See Heonik Kwon, "Wittgenstein's Spirit, Frazer's Ghost," in *The Mythology in Our Language: Remarks on Frazer's Golden Bough*, ed. Giovanni da Cole and Stephan Palmié (Chicago: University of Chicago Press, 2020), 87–96.

19. For example, Léopold Cadière, *Croyances et pratiques religieuses des viêtnamiens*, vol. 2 (Saigon: École Française d'Extrême-Orient, 1957).

20. This is not to underestimate the forceful introduction of anthropological research method and knowledge practice to the world mission trainings in recent years—as part of what Ju Hui Judy Han calls the formation of "missionary geoscience." See Ju Hui Judy Han, "Shifting Geographies of Proximity: Korean-led Evangelical Christian Missions and the US Empire," in *Ethnographies of US Empire*, ed. Carol McGranahan and John F. Collins (Durham, NC: Duke University Press, 2018), 194–213.

21. For instance, see Max Gluckman, *Custom and Conflict in Africa* (London: Blackwell, 1955).

22. See Christopher Shannon, *A World Made Safe for Differences: Cold War Intellectuals and the Politics of Identity* (Lanham, MD: Rowman and Littlefield, 2000). See also Peter Mandler, *Return from the Natives: How Margaret Mead Won the Second World War and Lost the Cold War* (New Haven, CT: Yale University Press, 2013); and Heonik Kwon, "Anthropology and World Peace," Lévi-Strauss Memorial Lecture, *HAU: Journal of Ethnographic Theory* 10, no. 2 (2020): 279–288.

23. Emile Durkheim, *The Elementary Forms of Religious Life*, trans. Karen E. Fields (New York: Free Press, 1995).

24. Heonik Kwon, "Return to Animism," *Interdisciplinary Science Reviews* 43, nos. 3–4 (2018): 228–236.

25. See, for instance, Joel Robbins, *Becoming Sinners: Christianity and Moral Torment in a Papua New Guinea Society* (Berkeley: University of California Press, 2004).

26. Dale B. Martin, *Inventing Superstition: From the Hippocratics to the Christians* (Cambridge, MA: Harvard University Press, 2004), 93–124.

27. Charles MacKay, *Extraordinary Popular Delusions and the Madness of Crowds* (London: Richard Bentley, 1841).

28. The literature on these historical developments is vast. Here, it suffices to mention two principal points of differentiation between Catholics and Protestants, from the perspective of the latter, that Webb Keane introduces in his majestic study of missionary politics in the Indonesian island of Sumba: "words" and "material objects." In their prayer activities, for instance, the Catholics keep their eyes open (because they have to read the prayer text), whereas the Calvinists have them closed (as they prefer "reading" the words appearing in their interiority). As for material objects, the interiority-preoccupied Calvinist adherents look down upon their Catholic neighbors as victims of fetishism (for instance, the latter take the statues of Virgin Mary, mistakenly, as if they were alive), not to mention the followers of indigenous animist ritualism. Webb Keane, *Christian Moderns: Freedom and Fetish in the Mission Encounter* (Berkeley: University of California Press, 2007), 2–3, 176–196.

29. See the South Korean New Tribes Mission activist's fascinating report of his and his wife's Tribal Church Planting mission to the highland Papua New Guinea over more than twenty years: Seong Mun, *Bŏlgŏbŏtŭn gŭrisdoin* [The naked Christians] (Seoul: Kyobobook MCP, 2019). The report highlights "sinfulness" and "repentance" as two axial ideas of their mission-educational success. For a rich account of how actually one transforms into a sinner in such milieus, see Robbins, *Becoming Sinners*. Robbins notes that the "import of Christianity for the Urapmin is not exhausted by the fact that it is a white religion, however, for of equal importance is the way in which Christianity offers to connect them to the white community from which it comes" (174). The Korean New Tribes missionaries were considered (and referred to as) whites by the locals. For an excellent overview of mission encounters in the region, see Robert W. Robin, "Missionaries in Contemporary Melanesia: Crossroads of Cultural Change," *Journal de la Société des Océanistes*, no. 69 (1980): 261–278.

30. The novel *Son'nim* [The Guest] speaks of a young man who broke his family's ancestral pot into pieces after attending a church meeting in Pyongyang. Sok-Yong Hwang, *Son'nim* [*The Guest*] (Paju: Changbi, 2001), 58.

31. The 1912 colonial edict *Gyŭngchalbŏm chŏbŏl gyuchik* [Rules of punishment against social crimes], sec. 1, art. 22. Don Baker observes that such strivings to make lives more pleasant (or at least less unpleasant) with assistance from supernatural powers are not only so human but also a pronounced aspect of Korea's traditional spirituality as a whole, not merely of its shamanism tradition. If this is indeed the case, we can imagine how radical the implications of such colonial interventions were. See Don Baker, *Korean Spirituality* (Honolulu: University of Hawai'i Press, 2008).

32. Helen Hardacre, *Shinto: A History* (New York: Oxford University Press, 2016), 403–440.

33. Masaaki Aono, *Jekuksintoŭi hyŏngsŏng* [The formation of imperial Shinto], trans. Gwi-duk Bae and Hui-chan Shim (Seoul: Somyŏng Publisher, 2017). Of the reversed flow of ideas and schemes (from colony to metropolis), Aono highlights the concept of "pseudo-religion" that, invented as part of Japan's colonial expansion to Korea, was imported back to the metropolitan realm as a useful social-disciplinary form. See ibid., 376–408.

34. Ibid., 116–126.

35. Wells, *New God, New Nation*, 77–82.

36. The church historian Chung-Shin Park relates this exceptional character of Korea's colonial experience to Korea's unique status in northeast Asia in the religious sphere—as a nation with a strong Christian population unlike China and Japan: *Protestantism and Politics in Korea* (Seattle: University of Washington Press, 2003), 17–18.

37. Ann Stoler and Fredrick Cooper, eds., *Tensions of Empire: Colonial Cultures in a Bourgeois World* (Berkeley: University of California Press, 1997).

38. Chijun Murayama, *Chosunŭi gwisin* [Spirits in Korea], trans. Seong-hwan Rho (Seoul: Minŭmsa, 1990).

39. Seong-nae Kim, "Iljesidae musokdamronŭi hyŭngsŭnggwa jaehyŭnŭi jŏngchihak" [The formation of musok discourse and the politics of representation during the Japanese colonial era], *Hankukmusokhak* (Korean Folklore Studies) 24 (2012): 7–42.

See also her more recent, powerful treatise on Korean shamanism, in which she defines shamanism as a humanist religion (see Chapter 6 of this volume). Kim also confronts squarely contradictions in contemporary perceptions of shamanism among South Koreans on multiple fronts: being familiar and strange, at once, and being close to superstition and emblematic of nostalgia-provoking traditional life: Seong-nae Kim, *Hankuk mukyoŭi munhwainlyuhak* [Cultural anthropology of Korea's shamanism religion] (Seoul: Sonamu, 2018).

40. See, for instance, Bernard Cohn, *Colonialism and Its Forms of Knowledge: The British in India* (Princeton, NJ: Princeton University Press, 1996), 11.

41. Timothy Brooks, *Collaboration: Japanese Agents and Local Elites in Wartime China* (Cambridge, MA: Harvard University Press, 2007).

5. ORIGINAL POLITICAL SOCIETY

1. Marshall Sahlins, "The Original Political Society," *HAU: Journal of Ethnographic Theory* 7, no. 2 (2017): 91–128; and David Graeber and Marshall Sahlins, *On Kings* (Chicago: University of Chicago Press, 2017).

2. Suk-jay Yim, "Hankukmusokyŏn'gusŏsŏl I" [Introduction to Korean shamanism I], *Aseayŏsŏng'yŏn'gu* [Journal of the studies of Asian women] 9 (1970): 73–90; Suk-jay Yim, "Hankukmusokyŏn'gusŏsŏl II" [Introduction to Korean shamanism II], *Aseayŏsŏng'yŏn'gu* [Journal of the studies of Asian women] 10 (1971): 161–217.

3. Michael E. Latham, *The Right Kind of Revolution: Modernization, Development, and US Foreign Policy from the Cold War to the Present* (Ithaca, NY: Cornell University Press, 2011).

4. See also Don Baker, *Korean Spirituality* (Honolulu: University of Hawaiʻi Press, 2008), 19–20. This idea of *musok* that refers to shamanism's embeddedness in the everyday context is traced, according to the South Korean anthropologist Chun Kyung-soo, to the early scholar of Korea's popular religiosity Lee Nŭng-hwa (1869–1943). See Kyung-soo Chun, "'Musok'yŏn'gu baeknyŏnŭi daegang'gwa gulgok—Lee Nŭng-hwa ihu" [Outline of the hundred years of musok studies—after Lee Nŭng-hwa], *Minsokhakyŏn'gu* [Journal of folklore studies], no. 31 (2012): 12–13.

5. Yim, "Hankukmusokyŏn'gusŏsŏl I" [Introduction to Korean shamanism I], 4.

6. Ibid., 3.

7. Eric Hobsbawm and Terence Ranger, eds., *The Invention of Tradition* (Cambridge: Cambridge University Press, 1983).

8. Quoted in William E. Connolly, *A World of Becoming* (Durham, NC: Duke University Press, 2011), 70. As is widely known, Max Weber's view of the disenchanted society had a frightening prophecy to it: "With the progress of science and technology, man has stopped believing in magical powers, in spirits and demons; he las lost his sense of prophecy and, above all, his sense of the sacred. Reality has become dreary, flat and utilitarian, leaving a great void in the souls of men which they seek to fill by furious activity and through various devices and substitutes." Quoted from Daniel Bell, "The Return of the Sacred? The Argument on the Future of Religion," *British Journal of Sociology* 28, no. 4 (1977): 422.

9. For example, see Philip Taylor, ed., *Modernity and Re-enchantment: Religion in Post-revolutionary Vietnam* (Cambridge: Cambridge University Press, 2008).

10. Simon Coleman and Rosaline I. J. Hackett, "Introduction: A New Field?" in *The Anthropology of Global Pentecostalism and Evangelicalism*, ed. S. Coleman and R. I. J. Hackett (New York: New York University Press, 2015), 2. See also Philip Jenkins, *The Next Christendom: The Coming of Global Christianity* (New York: Oxford University Press, 2002); and Paul Freston, *Evangelicals and Politics in Asia, Africa and Latin America* (Cambridge: Cambridge University Press, 2001).

11. Talal Asad, *Formations of the Secular: Christianity, Islam, Modernity* (Stanford, CA: Stanford University Press, 2003).

12. Mark A. Schneider, *Culture and Enchantment* (Chicago: University of Chicago Press, 1993).

13. Christopher Shannon, *A World Made Safe for Differences* (Lanham, MD: Rowman and Littlefield, 2000). See also Heonik Kwon, *The Other Cold War* (New York: Columbia University Press, 2010), 74–79.

14. Rae-ok Choi, "Im Suk-jay sŏnsaengŭi sŏlhwa josawa yŏn'gue daehan gochal" [Thoughts on Im Suk-jay's research into folktales], *Hankukmunhwainlyuhak* [Korean cultural anthropology] 31, no. 2 (1998): 46.

15. Sahlins, "The Original Political Society."

16. Ibid., 95.

17. Ibid., 93. Signe Howell, *Society and Cosmos: Chewong of Peninsular Malaysia* (Oxford: Oxford University Press, 1984).

18. Graeber and Sahlins, *On Kings*, 2.

19. Sahlins, "The Original Political Society," 91. Eduardo Viveiros de Castro, *From the Enemy's Point of View: Humanity and Divinity in an Amazonian Society* (Chicago: University of Chicago Press, 1992).

20. Quoted from Michael Lambek, "Facing Religion, from Anthropology," *Anthropology of This Century*, no. 4 (May 2012). Available online at http://aotcpress.com/articles/facing-religion-anthropology/.

21. Emile Durkheim, *The Elementary Forms of Religious Life*, trans. Karen E. Fields (New York: Free Press, 1995).

22. For an engaging, essentially disapproving, review of this revolution and its consequences from a perspective of theological scholarship, see John Milbank, *Theology and Social Theory: Beyond Secular Reason* (Oxford: Blackwell, 1990), which presents the early French sociological school as being the most noteworthy insurrectionist. For a thoughtful, sympathetic yet critical, response to Milbank, see Joel Robbins, "Anthropology and Theology: An Awkward Relationship?" *Anthropological Quarterly* 79, no. 2 (2006): 288–293.

23. E. B. Tylor, *Primitive Culture*, vol. 1 (London: John Murray, 1871).

24. Philippe Descola, "Societies of Nature and the Nature of Society," in *Conceptualising Society*, ed. Adam Kuper (London: Routledge, 1992), 107–126. See also Morten A. Pedersen, "Totemism, Animism and North Asian Indigenous Ontologies," *Journal of the Royal Anthropological Association* 7, no. 3 (2001): 412–413.

25. Claude Lévi-Strauss, *Totemism*, trans. Rodney Needham (London: Merlin, 1964).

26. Bruno Latour, "Gabriel Tarde and the End of the Social," in *The Social in Question: New Bearings on History and the Social Sciences*, ed. Patrick Joyce (London: Routledge, 2002), 117–132.

27. Webb Keane, *Ethical Life: Its Natural and Social Histories* (Princeton, NJ: Princeton University Press, 2015); Michael Lambek and Janice Boddy, eds., *Ordinary Ethics: Anthropology, Language, and Action* (New York: Fordham University Press, 2010).

28. Martin Holbraad and Morten Axel Pedersen, *The Ontological Turn: An Anthropological Exposition* (Cambridge: Cambridge University Press, 2017); Viveiros de Castro, *From the Enemy's Point of View.*

29. Thus Sahlins argues elsewhere that "all this is to say that the conventional notions of the systematic coherence of the sociocultural totality, these paradigms of 'anthropology-cultures' or 'national-cultures,' whether Marxist, Durkheimian, structural-functional, cultural-materialist, or whatever, supposing as they do in one way or another that the political and spiritual forms of any given society are reflexes of more fundamental social or material realities, are inappropriate." Graeber and Sahlins, *On Kings*, 375. Another larger criticism Sahlins has in mind is addressed to Thomas Hobbes's idea of the natural state—the anarchic world of humans pursuing their self-interests relentlessly with no regulatory power of the state to which these individuals submit part of their natural rights for the common-wealth. In this regard, the idea of "original" in his "original political society" is intended to say that Government (i.e., the princely or kingly rule) can be seen as a cosmological given rather than a result of social contract. It also entails that there is, categorically, no such thing as a "stateless" society—he says emphatically that the state or something akin to it is "the general condition of humankind" (Sahlins, "The Original Political Society," 92). This statement goes against the long-held grains of thought in the tradition of anthropological studies of kinship and politics. Considering that this tradition drew on insights of Lewis Henry Morgan (as well as those of Durkheim), especially his notions of *societas* and *civitas*, we may even say that the revolution Sahlins is advocating is of a post-Morgan character—that there is no such thing as societas and that the origin of human civilization is civitas *tout court*. If this is indeed the case, it needs to be mentioned that for Morgan, societas was far from a pre-political formation. As Meyer Fortes explained it so lucidly, it refers to a political world in its own right, although "politics" here are not the same as those that prevail in the historical world grounded in the ideas of properties and territories (i.e., Morgan's civitas). See Meyer Fortes, *Kinship and the Social Order: The Legacy of Lewis Henry Morgan* (Chicago: Aldine, 1969); Lewis H. Morgan, *Ancient Society* (New York: Henry Holt, 1907). For a discussion of Morgan to Fortes in this regard, see Heonik Kwon, *After the Korean War: An Intimate History* (Cambridge: Cambridge University Press, 2020), 10–14.

30. Signe Howell, "Rules without Rulers?" *HAU: Journal of Ethnographic Theory* 7, no. 2 (2017): 143–147.

31. For an informative overview of debates on this issue among South Korean folklorists, see Jong-sung Yang, "Hankuk musinŭi gujo yŏn'gu" [A study of the structure of Korean shamanic spirits], *Bigyomunhwayŏn'gu* [Comparative cultural studies], no. 5 (1999): 163–193.

32. South Korean anthropologist and a prominent folklorist Kang Jeong Won emphasizes that household spirituality is central to Korea's traditional popular

religious culture as a whole. Jeong Won Kang, "Hyundaihwawa minsokmunhwa, minsoksegye (Modernization, folk-world and folk-culture),"*Hankukminsokhak* (Korean folklore studies) 71 (2020): 34–35.

33. Sahlins, "The Original Political Society," 103–106, 118.

34. Claude Lévi-Strauss, *The Elementary Structures of Kinship* (New York: Beacon Press, 1969).

35. A. I. Hallowell, "Bear Ceremonialism in the Northern Hemisphere," *American Anthropologist* 28, no. 1 (1926): 1–175.

36. Heonik Kwon, "Play the Bear: Myth and Ritual in East Siberia," *History of Religions* 38, no. 4 (1999): 373–387.

37. Yim, "Hankukmusokyŏn'gusŏsŏl I" [Introduction to Korean shamanism I], 87, 90.

38. Ibid., 88; our emphasis. Some observers may focus on only the aspect of functional diversification (for instance, with the idea of functional parity) from Yim's emphatic observation cited here. Yim's interest goes much further, however, and is squarely with the idea of hierarchy (i.e., the obviation of concentric hierarchy).

39. Ibid., 89.

40. Ibid., 90; our emphasis.

41. Korea's old kinship system was primarily bilateral in character before the neo-Confucian revolution of the thirteenth century onward. Deuchler explains that this revolution was both political and social in character, with the aim of realizing a new political order through a radical reform of the existing loose, flexible bilateral kinship order to one that takes patrilineal descent as the singularly relevant ideology. Key to this revolution was the transformation of the ancestral rite to an institution that was exclusively for the patrilateral, patrilineal genealogical past. Martina Deuchler, *The Confucian Transformation of Korea: A Study of Society and Ideology* (Cambridge, MA: Harvard University Press, 1995).

42. Il-byung Park, *Hankuk mugyoŭi ihae* [Understanding Korea's shamanism religion] (Waegwan: Bundo, 1999), 203.

43. Nŭng-hwa Lee, *Josŏnmusokgo* [Treatise on Chosun musok] (1927; Seoul: Dongmunsŏn, 1991), 110.

44. Ibid., 59–72.

45. See Tim Ingold, David Riches, and James Woodburn, eds., *Hunters and Gatherers*, vol. 2: *Property, Power and Ideology* (Oxford: Berg, 1991).

46. See Philip Carl Salzman, "Is Inequality Universal?" *Current Anthropology* 40, no. 1 (1999): 31–61.

47. Pierre Clastres, *Society against the State: Essays in Political Anthropology*, trans. Robert Hurley in collaboration with Abe Stein (New York: Zone Books, 1987).

48. Dong-li Kim, *Munyŏdo* [Portrait of a Shamaness] (1936; Seoul: Malŭn Sori, 2010).

6. PARALLELISM

1. Suk-jay Yim, "Hankukmusokyŏn'gusŏsŏl I" [Introduction to Korean shamanism I], *Aseayŏsŏng'yŏn'gu* [Journal of the studies of Asian women] 9 (1970): 73–90.

2. Ibid., 87.

3. Marshall Sahlins, "The Original Political Society," *HAU: Journal of Ethnographic Theory* 7, no. 2 (2017): 91–128.

4. See also Jong-sung Yang, "Hankuk musinŭi kujoyŏn'gu" [A study of the structure of Korean shamanic spirits], *Bigyomunhwayŏngu* [Comparative cultural studies], no. 5 (1999): 165.

5. Antonetta L. Bruno, *The Gate of Words: Language in the Rituals of Korean Shamans* (Leiden: Research School of Asian, African, and American Studies, 2001).

6. See, for instance, Hannah Arendt, *The Human Condition* (Chicago: University of Chicago Press, 1958).

7. Yim, "Hankukmusokyŏn'gusŏsŏl I" [Introduction to Korean shamanism I], 165.

8. Ibid., 165.

9. Ibid., 164.

10. Ibid., 165.

11. Seong-nae Kim, *Hankuk mukyoŭi munhwainlyuhak* [Cultural anthropology of Korea's shamanism religion] (Seoul: Sonamu, 2018).

12. Raymond Firth, *Religion: A Humanist Interpretation* (London: Routledge, 1996).

13. Ibid., 92.

14. E. B. Tylor, *Primitive Culture*, vol. 1 (London: John Murray, 1871).

15. Emile Durkheim, *The Elementary Forms of Religious Life*, trans. Karen E. Fields (New York: Free Press, 1995).

16. Philippe Descola, *Beyond Nature and Culture* (Chicago: University of Chicago Press, 2013).

17. Most notably, Michael Lambek, ed., *Ordinary Ethics: Anthropology, Language, and Action* (New York: Fordham University Press, 2010).

18. Michael Lambek, *Human Spirits: A Cultural Account of Trance in Mayotte* (Cambridge: Cambridge University Press, 1981); Janice Boddy, *Wombs and Alien Spirits: Women, Men, and the Zar Cult in Northern Sudan* (Madison: University of Wisconsin Press, 1989).

19. Boddy, *Wombs and Alien Spirits*, 308. See also Lambek, *Human Spirits*, 34.

20. The idea of shamanism as essentially a diplomatic career is cited from Eduardo Viveiros de Castro, "The Crystal Forest: Notes on the Ontology of Amazonian Spirits," *Inner Asia* 9, no. 2 (2007): 14.

21. Martin Holbraad and Morten Axel Pederson, *The Ontological Turn: An Anthropological Exposition* (Cambridge: Cambridge University Press, 2017). For a

powerful approach that concentrates on epistemological questions (i.e., ways of knowing) rather than ontological ones (ways of being), see Jane Monnig Atkinson, *The Art and Politics of Wana Shamanship* (Berkeley: University of California Press, 1992), 40–41, 47–51.

22. See Michael Lambek, *The Weight of the Past: Living with History in Mahajanga, Madagascar* (London: Palgrave Macmillan, 2003).

23. Henri Bergson, *Creative Evolution*, trans. A. Mitchell (London: Macmillan, 1911).

24. Tim Ingold, *The Life of Lines* (London: Routledge, 2015), 117.

25. Arendt, *The Human Condition*.

26. Roy Wagner, "The Fractal Person," in *Big Men and Great Men: Personifications of Power in Melanesia*, ed. Maurice Godelier and Marilyn Strathern (Cambridge: Cambridge University Press, 1991).

27. Alfred Gell, "Strathernograms, or the Semiotics of Mixed Metaphors," in *The Art of Anthropology: Essays and Diagrams*, ed. Eric Hirsch (London: Athlone, 1999), 49.

28. Chris Fowler, *The Archaeology of Personhood* (London: Routledge, 2004), 48.

29. Marilyn Strathern, *The Gender of the Gift: Problems with Women and Problems with Society in Melanesia* (Cambridge: Cambridge University Press, 1988).

30. Simon Harrison, *The Mask of War: Violence, Ritual and the Self in Melanesia* (Manchester: Manchester University Press, 1993).

31. Fowler, *The Archaeology of Personhood*, 49.

32. Wagner, "The Fractal Person," 163.

33. Ibid., 159.

34. Ibid.

35. Meyer Fortes and E. E. Evans-Pritchard, eds., *African Political Systems* (London: Oxford University Press, 1940).

36. Yang, "Hankuk musinŭi kujoyŏn'gu" [A study of the structure of Korean shamanic spirits], 187.

37. Victor Turner, *Dramas, Fields, and Metaphors: Symbolic Action in Human Society* (Ithaca, NY: Cornell University Press, 1974).

38. Yim, "Hankukmusokyŏn'gusŏsŏl I" [Introduction to Korean shamanism I], 88.

39. Ibid.

40. Kyung-soo Chun, "'Musok'yŏn'gu baeknyŏnŭi daegang'gwa gulgok— Lee Nŭng-hwa ihu" [Outline of the hundred years of musok studies—after Lee Nŭng-hwa], *Minsokhakyŏn'gu* [Journal of folklore studies], no. 31 (2012): 32.

41. Andre Schmid, *Korea between Empires, 1895–1919* (New York: Columbia University Press, 2002).

CONCLUSION

1. "Lévi-Strauss," *Chungang Ilbo* [Korea JungAng daily], November 5, 2009.

2. Lévi-Strauss had had a long-held interest in religious traditions in these two ethnographic regions, influenced, in part, by two colleagues: Évelyne Lot-Falck, a student of Marcel Mauss's and an ethnologist of indigenous Siberia, and Bernard Saladin d'Anglure, an authority on the Inuit cosmology. See Roberte N. Hamayon, "Ce que les études sibériennes doivent à Claude Lévi-Strauss," in *Claude Lévi-Strauss, un parcours dans le siècle*, ed. Philippe Descola (Paris: Odile Jacob, 2012), 63–91. On differences between shamanism in indigenous Siberia and Korea's popular religious tradition referred to as such, see Boudewijn Walraven, "Korean Shamanism," *Numen* 30, no. 2 (1983): 242–243.

3. Rai Bahadur Sarat Chandra Roy, "An Indian Outlook on Anthropology," *Man* 38 (1938): 150.

4. Lucia Allais, *The Making of International Monuments in the Twentieth Century* (Chicago: University of Chicago Press, 2019).

5. In the anthropological study of religion, the evolution of this positionality is well explained in Raymond Firth, *Religion: A Humanist Interpretation* (London: Routledge, 1996).

6. Stephen Kern, *The Culture of Time and Space, 1880–1918* (Cambridge, MA: Harvard University Press, 1983).

7. Laurel Kendall and Igor Krupnik, *Constructing Cultures Then and Now: Celebrating Franz Boas and the Jesup North Pacific Expedition*, Contributions to Circumpolar Anthropology 4 (Washington, DC: Smithsonian Institution Arctic Studies Center, 2003).

8. Peter Mandler, *Return from the Natives: How Margaret Mead Won the Second World War and Lost the Cold War* (New Haven, CT: Yale University Press, 2013). The cited phrase is from Federico Neiburg and Marcio Goldman, "Anthropology and Politics in Studies of National Character," trans. Peter Gow, *Cultural Anthropology* 13, no. 1 (1998): 60.

9. Ibid., 61.

10. Claude Lévi-Strauss, "Today's Crisis in Anthropology," *UNESCO Courier* (November 1961): 12–17.

11. Chloé Maurel, "L'UNESCO de 1945 à 1974" (PhD diss., Université Paris 1, 2006).

12. Peter Mandler, "One World, Many Cultures: Margaret Mead and the Limits to Cold War Anthropology," *History Workshop Journal* 68, no. 1 (2009): 149.

13. Ibid., 154. See also Christopher Shannon, *A World Made Safe for Differences* (Lanham, MD: Rowman and Littlefield, 2000).

14. Mandler, *Return from the Natives.*

15. Mandler, "One World, Many Cultures," 151, 167. See also Heonik Kwon, *The Other Cold War* (New York: Columbia University Press, 2010), 77.

16. The expression of culture as an anti-concept of race is cited from Robert Oppenheim, "'The West' and the Anthropology of Other People's Colonialism: Frederick Starr in Korea, 1911–1930," *Journal of Asian Studies* 64, no. 3 (2005): 691.

17. Claude Lévi-Strauss, "Rousseau, the Father of Anthropology," *UNESCO Courier* (March 1963): 10–15.

18. Ibid., 12.

19. It can be argued that Mead's interest encompassed both of these. Mead came to have a duplex scholarly interest by the late 1940s, as Mandler rightly shows, in a small-scale indigenous world (e.g., New Guinea and Manus) as well as large national societies (notably, Indonesia). Mandler, "One World, Many Cultures," 162.

20. Hung-yun Cho, *Hankukmuŭi segye* [The world of Korean shamanism] (Seoul: Minjoksa, 1997), 172.

21. See, for instance, Hong-ku Han, "Maekadŏga ŭninirago?" [Was MacArthur our savior?], *Hankyŏre21*, May 2, 2002.

22. Myungseok Oh, "Cultural Policy and National Culture Discourse in the 1960s and 1970s," *Korean Anthropological Review* 1, no. 1 (2017): 106–107.

23. For excellent examples that delve into the innovative potential of contemporary Korean shamanism, see Kyoim Yun, *The Shaman's Wages: Trading in Ritual on Cheju Island* (Seattle: University of Washington Press, 2019), and Liora Sarfati, *Contemporary Korean Shamanism: From Ritual to Digital* (Bloomington: Indiana University Press, 2021).

24. Suk-jay Yim, "Hankukmusokyŏn'gusŏsŏl I" [Introduction to Korean shamanism I], *Aseayŏsŏngyŏngu* [Journal of the studies of Asian women] 9 (1970): 73–90.

25. Wendy James, *The Ceremonial Animal: A New Portrait of Anthropology* (Oxford: Oxford University Press, 2003).

26. Steven Miller contends that the rise of evangelicalism as a political force in American society and politics, since the late 1970s (Jimmy Carter's time), relates to the American Century coming to a close and the anxieties this generates: *The Age of Evangelicalism: America's Born-Again Years* (New York: Oxford University Press, 2014).

BIBLIOGRAPHY

Allais, Lucia. *The Making of International Monuments in the Twentieth Century.* Chicago: University of Chicago Press, 2019.

Anderson, Benedict. *Imagined Communities: Reflections on the Origin and Spread of Nationalism.* London: Verso, 2006.

Anh, Chang-mo. "Gaehang'gwa jŏnjaeng, dosiŭi unmyŏngŭl bakkuda" [Shaking up cities since the opening of the ports in 1876]. *Gŏnchuksa* [Korean Architects], no. 12 (2012): 63–68.

Anh, Myung-hwan. "Chuchŏnsŏ" [Endorsement]. In Baul Lee, *Gidoro sŭng'lihan MacArthur* [MacArthur who triumphed with prayer], 15–17. Seoul: Joŭn, 2014.

Aono, Masaaki. *Jekuksintoŭi hyŏngsŏng* [The formation of imperial Shinto]. Translated by G. Bae and H. Shim. Seoul: Somyŏng Publisher, 2017.

Arendt, Hannah. *The Human Condition.* Chicago: University of Chicago Press, 1958.

Armstrong, Charles. *The North Korean Revolution, 1945–1950.* Ithaca, NY: Cornell University Press, 2004.

Asad, Talal. *Formations of the Secular: Christianity, Islam, Modernity.* Stanford, CA: Stanford University Press, 2003.

Asian Development Bank. *The Saemaul Undong Movement in the Republic of Korea: Sharing Knowledge on Community-Driven Development.* Mandaluyog, Philippines: Asian Development Bank, 2012.

Aspinall, Edward, ed. *Soeharto's New Order and Its Legacy: Essays in Honour of Harold Crouch.* Canberra: Australian National University Press, 2011.

Atkinson, Jane Monnig. "Religions in Dialogue: The Construction of an Indonesian Minority Religion." *American Ethnologist* 10, no. 4 (1983): 684–696.

Atkinson, Jane Monnig. *The Art and Politics of Wana Shamanship.* Berkeley: University of California Press, 1992.

Aydin, Cemil. *The Politics of Anti-Westernism in Asia: Visions of World Order in Pan-Islamic and Pan-Asian Thought.* New York: Columbia University Press, 2007.

Bae, Duk-man. *Hankuk gaesin'gyo gŭnbonjuŭi* [Korean Protestantism's funda-mentalism]. Daejon: Daejangkan, 2010.

Bailey, Sarah Pulliam. "'God Has Given Trump Authority to Take Out Kim Jong Un,' Evangelical Adviser Says." *Washington Post*, August 9, 2017.

Baker, Don. *Korean Spirituality.* Honolulu: University of Hawai'i Press, 2008.

Bakhtin, Mikhail M. *The Dialogic Imagination.* Austin: University of Texas Press, 1981.

Bell, Daniel. "The Return of the Sacred? The Argument on the Future of Religion." *British Journal of Sociology* 28, no. 4 (1977): 419–449.

Bergson, Henri. *Creative Evolution.* Translated by A. Mitchell. London: Macmillan, 1911.

Boddy, Janice. *Wombs and Alien Spirits: Women, Men, and the Zar Cult in Northern Sudan.* Madison: University of Wisconsin Press, 1989.

Brazinsky, Gregg. *Nation Building in South Korea: Koreans, Americans, and the Making of a Democracy.* Chapel Hill: University of North Carolina Press, 2007.

Brooks, Timothy. *Collaboration: Japanese Agents and Local Elites in Wartime China.* Cambridge, MA: Harvard University Press, 2007.

Bruno, Antonetta L. *The Gate of Words: Language in the Rituals of Korean Shamans.* Leiden: Research School of Asian, African, and American Studies, 2001.

Buzzanco, Robert. "Where Is the Beef? Culture without Power in the Study of US Foreign Relations." *Diplomatic History* 24, no. 4 (2000): 623–632.

Cadière, Léopold. *Croyances et pratiques religieuses des viêtnamiens*, vol. 2. Saigon: École Française d'Extrême-Orient, 1957.

Carpenter, Joel. *Revive Us Again: The Reawakening of American Fundamentalism.* New York: Oxford University Press, 1999.

Chae, Young-guk. "Hanilgŭndaehwaŭi ipgu Inchŏn'gwa Yokohama" [Incheon and Yokohama—entry to Korean-Japanese modernity]. In *Inchŏnyŏksa, ilho* [History of Incheon, vol. 1], edited by Inchŏn'gwangyŏksi Yŏksajaryogwan Yŏksamunhwayŏn'gusil [Research group on Incheon's history and culture], 239–261. Incheon: Inchŏn'gwangyŏksi Yŏksajaryogwan Yŏksamunhwayŏn'gusil, 2004.

Cho, Hung-yun. *Hankukmuŭi segye* [The world of Korean shamanism]. Seoul: Minjoksa, 1997.

Choi, Michael Hyun. "Orijinŏl Mansin: An Ethnography of Shaman Life in South Korea." PhD diss., Harvard University, 2010.

Choi, Rae-ok. "Im Suk-jay sŏnsaengŭi sŏlhwa josawa yŏn'gue daehan gochal" [Thoughts on Im Suk-jay's research into folktales]. *Hankukmunhwainlyuhak* [Korean cultural anthropology] 31, no. 2 (1998): 45–69.

Chong, Kelly H. *Deliverance and Submission: Evangelical Women and the Negotiation of Patriarchy in South Korea.* Cambridge, MA: Harvard University Press, 2008.

Chuluu, Üjiyediin, and Kevin Stuart. "Rethinking the Mongol *Oboo.*" *Anthropos* 90 (1995): 544–554.

Chun, Gap-seng. "Ganghwado·Ongjin chulsinjadŭlŭi gusulesŏ bon hankukjŏn-jaengŭi gyŏnghŏmgwa giŏk" [The experience and memory of the Korean War in the testimonies of the settlers from Ganghwa Island and Ongjin]. Paper presented at the Korean Association for Oral History conference in Incheon (November 21, 2020).

Chun, Kyung-soo. "'Musok'yŏn'gu baeknyŏnŭi daegang'gwa gulgok—Lee Nŭng-hwa ihu" [Outline of the hundred years of musok studies—after Lee Nŭng-hwa]. *Minsokhakyŏngu* [Journal of folklore studies], no. 31 (2012): 5–44.

Clark, Charles Allen. *Religions of Old Korea.* 1932. Seoul: Christian Literature Society of Korea, 1961.

Clark, Donald N. *Living Dangerously in Korea: The Western Experience, 1900–1950.* Norwalk, CT: EastBridge, 2003.

Clastres, Pierre. *Society against the State: Essays in Political Anthropology.* Translated by Robert Hurley in collaboration with Abe Stein. New York: Zone Books, 1987.

Cohn, Bernard. *Colonialism and Its Forms of Knowledge: The British in India.* Princeton, NJ: Princeton University Press, 1996.

Coleman, Simon, and Rosaline I. J. Hackett. "Introduction: A New Field?" In *The Anthropology of Global Pentecostalism and Evangelicalism,* edited by S. Coleman and R. I. J. Hackett, 1–37. New York: New York University Press, 2015.

Comaroff, John L., and Jean Comaroff. *Of Revelation and Revolution,* vol. 2: *The Dialectics of Modernity on a South African Frontier.* Chicago: University of Chicago Press, 1997.

Connolly, William E. *A World of Becoming.* Durham, NC: Duke University Press, 2011.

Coppa, Frank J. "Pope Pius XII and the Cold War: The Post-war Confrontation between Catholicism and Communism." In *Religion and the Cold War,* edited by D. Kirby, 50–66. New York: Palgrave Macmillan, 2002.

Crapanzano, Vincent. *Serving the Word: Literalism in America from the Pulpit to the Bench.* New York: New Press, 2000.

Csordas, Thomas J. *The Sacred Self: A Cultural Phenomenology of Charismatic Healing.* Berkeley: University of California Press, 1997.

Cumings, Bruce. *The Korean War: A History.* New York: Modern Library, 2010.

Cumings, Bruce. *The Origins of the Korean War: Liberation and the Emergence of Separate Regimes, 1945–1947.* Princeton, NJ: Princeton University Press, 1981.

Descola, Philippe. *Beyond Nature and Culture.* Chicago: University of Chicago Press, 2013.

Descola, Philippe. "Societies of Nature and the Nature of Society." In *Conceptualising Society,* edited by A. Kuper, 107–126. London: Routledge, 1992.

Deuchler, Martina. *The Confucian Transformation of Korea: A Study of Society and Ideology.* Cambridge, MA: Harvard University Press, 1995.

Deuchler, Martina. *Under the Ancestors' Eyes: Kinship, Status, and Locality in Premodern Korea.* Cambridge, MA: Harvard University Press, 2015.

Durkheim, Emile. *The Elementary Forms of Religious Life.* Translated by Karen E. Fields. New York: Free Press, 1995.

Eckert, Carter J. *Park Chung Hee and Modern Korea: The Roots of Militarism, 1866–1945.* Cambridge, MA: Harvard University Press, 2016.

Ekbladh, David. *The Great American Mission: Modernization and the Construction of an American Order.* Princeton, NJ: Princeton University Press, 2009.

Evans, Christopher, and Caroline Humphrey. "History, Timelessness, and the Monumental: The Oboos of the Mergen Environs of Inner Mongolia." *Cambridge Archaeological Journal* 13, no. 2 (2003): 195–211.

Fields, David P. *Foreign Friends: Syngman Rhee, American Exceptionalism, and the Division of Korea.* Lexington: University Press of Kentucky, 2019.

Firth, Raymond. *Religion: A Humanist Interpretation.* London: Routledge, 1996.

FitzGerald, Frances. *The Evangelicals: The Struggle to Shape America.* New York: Simon & Schuster, 2017.

Fortes, Meyer. *Kinship and the Social Order: The Legacy of Lewis Henry Morgan.* Chicago: Aldine, 1969.

Fortes, Meyer, and E. E. Evans-Pritchard, eds. *African Political Systems.* London: Oxford University Press, 1940.

Fortis, Paolo. *Kuna Art and Shamanism: An Ethnographic Approach.* Austin: University of Texas Press, 2013.

Fowler, Chris. *The Archaeology of Personhood.* London: Routledge, 2004.

Freston, Paul. *Evangelicals and Politics in Asia, Africa and Latin America.* Cambridge: Cambridge University Press, 2001.

Gallup Korea. *Hankukinŭi jong'gyowa jongyoŭisik* [Koreans' religions and religious consciousness]. Seoul: Gallup Korea, 1998.

Gayte, Marie. "The Vatican and the Reagan Administration: A Cold War Alliance?" *Catholic Historical Review* 97, no. 4 (2011): 713–736.

Geertz, Clifford. *The Interpretation of Cultures.* New York: Basic Books, 1973.

Geertz, Clifford. *Negara: The Theatre State in Nineteenth-Century Bali.* Princeton, NJ: Princeton University Press, 1980.

Gell, Alfred. "Strathernograms, or the Semiotics of Mixed Metaphors." In *The Art of Anthropology: Essays and Diagrams,* edited by Eric Hirsch, 29–75. London: Athlone, 1999.

Gilmore, George W. *Corea of Today.* London: T. Nelson and Sons, 1894.

Gluckman, Max. *Custom and Conflict in Africa.* London: Blackwell, 1955.

Goldstone, Brian. "Life after Sovereignty." *History of the Present* 4, no. 1 (2014): 97–113.

Graeber, David, and Marshall Sahlins. *On Kings*. Chicago: University of Chicago Press, 2017.

Grayson, James Huntley. *Korea: A Religious History*. London: Routledge, 2002.

Grayson, James Huntley. "Quarter-Millennium of Christianity in Korea." In *Christianity in Korea*, edited by Robert E. Buswell Jr. and Timothy S. Lee, 7–25. Honolulu: University of Hawai'i Press, 2006.

Gurimji pyŏnchan wiwŏnhoi [Editorial committee of Gurim chronicles]. *Honam myŏngchon Gurim* [Gurim, a distinguished village in Honam region]. Seoul: Libuk, 2006.

Habermas, Jürgen. *The Structural Transformation of the Public Sphere: An Inquiry into a Category of Bourgeois Society*. Translated by Thomas Burger. Cambridge, MA: MIT Press, 1989.

Hall, B. E. Foster. *The Chinese Maritime Customs: An International Service, 1854–1950*. Bristol: University of Bristol, 1977.

Hallowell, A. I. "Bear Ceremonialism in the Northern Hemisphere." *American Anthropologist* 28, no. 1 (1926): 1–175.

Hamayon, Roberte N. "Ce que les études sibériennes doivent à Claude Lévi-Strauss." In *Claude Lévi-Strauss, un parcours dans le siècle*, edited by Philippe Descola, 63–91. Paris: Odile Jacob, 2012.

Han, Chi-ho. *Janyŏrŭl wihan maekadŏŭi gido* [MacArthur's prayers for children]. Seoul: Ilosam, 2008.

Han, Hong-ku. "Maekadŏga ŭninirago?" [Was MacArthur our savior?]. *Hankyŏre21*, May 2, 2002.

Han, Ju Hui Judy. "Beyond Safe Haven: A Critique of Christian Custody of North Korean Migrants in China." *Critical Asian Studies* 45, no. 4 (2013): 533–560.

Han, Ju Hui Judy. "Shifting Geographies of Proximity: Korean-led Evangelical Christian Missions and the US Empire." In *Ethnographies of US. Empire*, edited by Carol McGranahan and John F. Collins, 194–213. Durham, NC: Duke University Press, 2018.

Han, Kyung-chik. "Gŭrisdoin'gwa ban'gong" [Christians and anti-communism]. *Saegajŏng* [The new family] 10, no. 3 (1963): 10–15.

Han, Kyung-chik. "My Gratitude." In *Kyung-Chik Han Collection*, vol. 1, edited by Eun-seop Kim. Seoul: Han Kyung-Chik Foundation, 2010.

Han, Kyung-Koo. "Legacies of War: The Korean War—60 Years On." *Asia–Pacific Journal* 8, issue no. 38, no. 3 (2010). https://apjjf.org/-Han-Kyung-Koo/3414/article.html.

Hankukgidokgyosŏn'gyohyŏpŭihoi [Korean Christian Mission Society]. *Billy Graham jŏnjip: hankukjŏndodaehoit'ŭkjip* [On Billy Graham: special collection on his revival rallies in Korea]. Seoul: Sinkyungsa, 1973.

Hardacre, Helen. *Shinto: A History*. New York: Oxford University Press, 2016.

Harding, Susan Friend. *The Book of Jerry Falwell: Fundamentalist Language and Politics*. Princeton, NJ: Princeton University Press, 2000.

Harkness, Nicholas. *Songs of Seoul: An Ethnography of Voice and Voicing in Christian South Korea*. Berkeley: University of California Press, 2013.

Harrison, Simon. *The Mask of War: Violence, Ritual and the Self in Melanesia*. Manchester: Manchester University Press, 1993.

Heffner, Robert W., ed. *Conversion to Christianity: Historical and Anthropological Perspectives on a Great Transformation*. Berkeley: University of California Press, 1993.

Henderson, Gregory. "Korea." In *Divided Nations in a Divided World*, edited by G. Henderson, J. G. Stoessinger, and R. N. LeBow. New York: David McKay, 1974.

Hill, Hal. *Indonesia's New Order: The Dynamics of Socio-Economic Transformation*. Honolulu: University of Hawai'i Press, 1994.

Hoare, James E., and Susan Pares. *North Korea in the 21st Century: An Interpretative Guide*. Folkestone, UK: Global Oriental, 2005.

Hobsbawm, Eric, and Terence Ranger, eds. *The Invention of Tradition*. Cambridge: Cambridge University Press, 1983.

Holbraad, Martin, and Morten Axel Pedersen. *The Ontological Turn: An Anthropological Exposition*. Cambridge: Cambridge University Press, 2017.

Howell, Signe. "Rules without Rulers?" *HAU: Journal of Ethnographic Theory* 7, no. 2 (2017): 143–147.

Howell, Signe. *Society and Cosmos: Chewong of Peninsular Malaysia*. Oxford: Oxford University Press, 1984.

Humphrey, Caroline. "Shamanic Practices and the State in Northern Asia: Views from the Center and Periphery." In *Shamanism, History, and the State*, edited by N. Thomas and C. Humphrey, 191–228. Ann Arbor: University of Michigan Press, 1994.

Humphrey, Caroline, with Urugunge Onon. *Shamans and Elders: Experience, Knowledge, and Power among the Daur Mongols*. Oxford: Clarendon Press, 1996.

Huntington, Samuel P. *The Clash of Civilizations and the Remaking of World Order*. London: Simon and Schuster, 1997.

Hwang, In-cheol. "Hankuk kyohoi sŏngjang'gwa buhŭng" [The growth and prosperity of Korean church]. *Kidoksinmun* [Christian times], February 6, 2012.

Hwang, Kyung-sun. "Buknyŭkŭi muhyŭng'yusan: Hwanghaedo kŭnmudangŭi kŭnkut iyagi" [Intangible heritage in North of Korea: story of a great *kut* by a great Hwanghae shaman]. *Munhwajae sarang* [Love of cultural heritage, newsletter of Republic of Korea Cultural Heritage Administration], no. 99 (2013): 26–27.

Hwang, Sok-Yong. *Son'nim* [*The Guest*]. Paju: Changbi, 2001.

Hwang, Sok-Yong. *The Guest: A Novel*. Translated by Kyung-Ja Chun and Maya West. New York: Seven Stories Press, 2008.

Inboden, William. *Religion and American Foreign Policy, 1945–1960: The Soul of Containment*. New York: Cambridge University Press, 2008.

Incheon Munhwa Jaedan. *Mangukgong'wŏnŭi giŏk* [Memories of Ten Thousand Nations Park]. Incheon: Incheon Munhwa Jaedan, 2006.

Ingold, Tim. "Dreaming of Dragons: On the Imagination of Real Life." *Journal of the Royal Anthropological Institute* 19, no. 4 (2013): 734–752.

Ingold, Tim. *The Life of Lines*. London: Routledge, 2015.

Ingold, Tim, David Riches, and James Woodburn, eds. *Hunters and Gatherers*, vol. 2: *Property, Power and Ideology*. Oxford: Berg, 1991.

James, Wendy. *The Ceremonial Animal: A New Portrait of Anthropology*. Oxford: Oxford University Press, 2003.

Janelli, Roger L., and Dawnhee Yim Janelli. *Ancestor Worship in Korean Society*. Stanford, CA: Stanford University Press, 1982.

Jenkins, Philip. *The Next Christendom: The Coming of Global Christianity*. New York: Oxford University Press, 2002.

Jung, Jin-Heon. *Migration and Religion in East Asia: North Korean Migrants' Evangelical Encounters*. London: Palgrave Macmillan, 2015.

Kang, Don-ku. "Migunjŏng'ŭi jong'gyojŏngchaek" [US Military Government's religion policy]. *Jong'gyohak yŏn'gu* [Journal of religious studies] 12 (1993): 15–42.

Kang, Jeong Won. "Hyundaihwawa minsokmunhwa, minsoksegye" [Modernization, folk-world and folk-culture]. *Hankukminsokhak* [Korean folklore studies] 71 (2020): 7–45.

Keane, Webb. *Christian Moderns: Freedom and Fetish in the Mission Encounter*. Berkeley: University of California Press, 2007.

Keane, Webb. *Ethical Life: Its Natural and Social Histories*. Princeton, NJ: Princeton University Press, 2015.

Kendall, Laurel. *Shamans, Housewives, and Other Restless Spirits: Women in Korean Ritual Life*. Honolulu: University of Hawai'i Press, 1985.

Kendall, Laurel. *Shamans, Nostalgias, and the IMF: South Korean Popular Religion in Motion*. Honolulu: University of Hawai'i Press, 2009.

Kendall, Laurel, and Igor Krupnik. *Constructing Cultures Then and Now: Celebrating Franz Boas and the Jesup North Pacific Expedition*. Contributions to Circumpolar Anthropology 4. Washington, DC: Smithsonian Institution, Arctic Studies Center, 2003.

Kendall, Laurel, and Jongsung Yang. "What Is An Animated Image?: Korean Shaman Paintings as Objects of Ambiguity." *HAU: Journal of Ethnographic Theory* 5, no.2 (2015): 153–175.

Kern, Stephen. *The Culture of Time and Space, 1880–1918*. Cambridge, MA: Harvard University Press, 1983.

Kim, Byung-ro. *Bukhan jong'gyojŏngchaekŭi byŭnhwawa jong'gyosiltae* [North Korea's changing religious policies and its religious reality]. Seoul: Tongil-yŏn'guwŏn, 2020.

Kim, Charles R. *Youth for Nation: Culture and Protest in Cold War Korea*. New York: Columbia University Press, 2017.

Kim, Dong-li. *Munyŏdo* [Portrait of a Shamaness]. 1936. Seoul: Malŭn Sori, 2010.

Kim Haboush, JaHyun. *The Great East Asian War and the Birth of the Korean Nation*. New York: Columbia University Press, 2016.

Kim, Helen Jin. "Campus Crusade 'Explosions': Conversions and Conservatism from the US Bible Belt to Cold War South Korea, 1972–1974." *Journal of Korean Religions* 9, no. 1 (2018): 11–41.

Kim, Jin-wung. "Maekadŏ jang'gunŭi je 2ŭi Inchŏn sangryuk jakjŏn: dongsang'ŭl dullŏssan bunjaeng'ŭi hamŭi" [General MacArthur's other Inch'on landing: implications of the conflict over his statue]. *Yŏksagyoyŭknonjib* [Journal of history education], no. 39 (2007): 415–454.

Kim, Kŭm-hwa. *Mansin Kim Kŭm-hwa* [The shaman Kim Kŭm-hwa]. Seoul: Gungli, 2014.

Kim, Kŭm-Hwa. *Kim Kŭm-hwa mugajip* [Collection of Kim Kŭm-hwa's ritual songs]. Seoul: Munŭmsa. 1995.

Kim, Kwang-ok. "Jŏhangmunhwawa musokŭirye" [The culture of resistance and the ritual of shamanism]. *Hankukmunhwainlyuhak* [Korean cultural anthropology] 23, no. 0 (1992): 131–172.

Kim, Sebastian C. H., and Kirsteen Kim. *A History of Korean Christianity*. New York: Cambridge University Press, 2015.

Kim, Seong-nae. *Hankuk mukyoŭi munhwainlyuhak* [Cultural anthropology of Korea's shamanism religion]. Seoul: Sonamu, 2018.

Kim, Seong-nae. "The Iconic Power of Modernity: Reading a Cheju Shaman's Life History and Initiation Dream." In *South Korea's Minjung Movement: The Culture and Politics of Dissidence*, edited by Kenneth M. Wells, 155–166. Honolulu: University of Hawai'i Press, 1995.

Kim, Seong-nae. "Iljesidae musokdamronŭi hyŭngsŭng'gwa sikminjŏk jaehyŭnŭi jŏngchihak" [The formation of musok discourse and the politics of representation during the Japanese colonial era]. *Hankukmusokhak* [Korean folklore studies] 24 (2012): 7–42.

Kirby, Dianne. "Harry Truman's Religious Legacy: The Holy Alliance, Containment and the Cold War." In *Religion and the Cold War*, edited by D. Kirby, 77–102. New York: Palgrave Macmillan, 2002.

Kuper, Adam. *Anthropology and Anthropologists: The Modern British School in the Twentieth Century*. London: Routledge, 2014.

Kwon, Heonik. *After the Korean War: An Intimate History*. Cambridge: Cambridge University Press, 2020.

Kwon, Heonik. "Anthropology and World Peace." Lévi-Strauss Memorial Lecture. *HAU: Journal of Ethnographic Theory* 10, no. 2 (2020): 279–288.

Kwon, Heonik. *The Other Cold War.* New York: Columbia University Press, 2010.

Kwon, Heonik. "Play the Bear: Myth and Ritual in East Siberia." *History of Religions* 38, no. 4 (1999): 373–387.

Kwon, Heonik. "Return to Animism." *Interdisciplinary Science Reviews* 43, nos. 3–4 (2018): 228–236.

Kwon, Heonik. "Wittgenstein's Spirit, Frazer's Ghost," In *The Mythology in Our Language: Remarks on Frazer's Golden Bough*, edited by G. da Cole and S. Palmié, 87–96. Chicago: University of Chicago Press, 2020.

Lambek, Michael. "Facing Religion, from Anthropology." *Anthropology of This Century*, no. 4 (May 2012). http://aotcpress.com/articles/facing-religion -anthropology/.

Lambek, Michael. *Human Spirits: A Cultural Account of Trance in Mayotte.* Cambridge: Cambridge University Press, 1981.

Lambek, Michael. *The Weight of the Past: Living with History in Mahajanga, Madagascar.* London: Palgrave Macmillan, 2003.

Lambek, Michael, and Janice Boddy, eds. *Ordinary Ethics: Anthropology, Language, and Action.* New York: Fordham University Press, 2010.

Lankov, Andrei. *The Real North Korea: Life and Politics in the Failed Stalinist Utopia.* New York: Oxford University Press, 2013.

Larsen, Kirk W. "Competing Imperialisms in Korea." In *Routledge Handbook of Modern Korea*, edited by Michael J. Seth, 39–54. New York: Routledge, 2016.

Latham, Michael E. *Modernization as Ideology: American Social Science and "Nation Building" in the Kennedy Era.* Chapel Hill: University of North Carolina Press, 2000.

Latham, Michael E. *The Right Kind of Revolution: Modernization, Development, and US Foreign Policy from the Cold War to the Present.* Ithaca, NY: Cornell University Press, 2011.

Latour, Bruno. "Gabriel Tarde and the End of the Social." In *The Social in Question: New Bearings on History and the Social Sciences*, edited by Patrick Joyce, 117–132. London: Routledge, 2002.

Leary, William M., ed. *MacArthur and the American Century: A Reader.* Lincoln: University of Nebraska Press, 2001.

Lee, Baul. *Gidoro sŭnglihan MacArthur* [MacArthur who triumphed with prayer]. Seoul: Joŭn, 2014.

Lee, Hyun-joo. "Hwagyoyuipgwa hawai imin" [The influx of the Chinese and the emigration to Hawaii]. *Inchŏnyŏksa ilho* [History of Incheon, vol. 1], edited by Inchŏn'gwangyŏksi Yŏksajaryogwan Yŏksamunhwajŏn'gusil [Research group on Incheon's history and culture], 195–220. Incheon: Inchŏn'gwangyŏksi Yŏksajaryogwan Yŏksamunhwajŏn'gusil, 2004.

Lee, Nŭng-hwa. *Josŏnmusokgo* [Treatise on Chosun musok]. 1927. Seoul: Dongmunsŏn, 1991.

Lee, Sang-eui. "Hankukjŏnjaeng gusulsa yŏn'guwa Incheon" [The Korean War oral history and Incheon]. Paper presented at the Korean Association for Oral History in Incheon (November 21, 2020).

Lee, Se-young. "Haebang–hankukjŏnjaeng'ki Incheonjiyŏk wŏlnamminŭi jŏngchakgwa netŭwŏkŭ hyŏngsŏng" [Establishment and networking of Incheon area refugees during the liberation and Korean War periods]. *Dongbanghakji* [Journal of Oriental studies], no. 180 (2017): 177–211.

Lee, Timothy S. 2006. "Beleaguered Success: Korean Evangelicalism in the Last Decade of the Twentieth Century." In *Christianity in Korea*, edited by Robert E. Buswell Jr. and Timothy S. Lee, 330–350. Honolulu: University of Hawai'i Press.

Lévi-Strauss, Claude. *The Elementary Structures of Kinship*. New York: Beacon Press, 1969.

Lévi-Strauss, Claude. "Rousseau, the Father of Anthropology." *UNESCO Courier* (March 1963): 10–15.

Lévi-Strauss, Claude. "Today's Crisis in Anthropology." *UNESCO Courier* (November 1961): 12–17.

Lévi-Strauss, Claude. *Totemism*. Translated by Rodney Needham. London: Merlin, 1964.

Luce, Henry R. 1999. "The American Century." *Diplomatic History* 23, no. 2 (1999): 159–171.

Luhrmann, Tanya M. *When God Talks Back: Understanding the American Evangelical Relationship with God*. New York: Vintage, 2012.

MacKay, Charles. *Extraordinary Popular Delusions and the Madness of Crowds*. London: Richard Bentley, 1841.

Manchester, William. *American Caesar: Douglas MacArthur, 1880–1964*. Boston: Little, Brown, 1978.

Mandler, Peter. "One World, Many Cultures: Margaret Mead and the Limits to Cold War Anthropology." *History Workshop Journal* 68, no. 1 (2009): 149–172.

Mandler, Peter. *Return from the Natives: How Margaret Mead Won the Second World War and Lost the Cold War*. New Haven, CT: Yale University Press, 2013.

Manela, Erez. *The Wilsonian Moment: Self-Determination and the International Origins of Anticolonial Nationalism*. New York: Oxford University Press, 2009.

Martin, Dale B. *Inventing Superstition: From the Hippocrates to the Christians*. Cambridge, MA: Harvard University Press, 2004.

Martin, William. *With God on Our Side: The Rise of the Religious Right in America*. New York: Broadway Books, 1996.

Maurel, Chloé. "L'UNESCO de 1945 à 1974." PhD diss., Université Paris 1, 2006.

McAlister, Melani. *Epic Encounters: Culture, Media, and the US Interests in the Middle East since 1945.* Berkeley: University of California Press, 2005.

McAlister, Melani. *The Kingdom of God Has No Borders: A Global History of American Evangelicals.* New York: Oxford University Press, 2018.

McGranahan, Carol, and John F. Collins, eds. *Ethnographies of US Empire.* Durham, NC: Duke University Press, 2018.

Milbank, John. *Theology and Social Theory: Beyond Secular Reason.* Oxford: Blackwell, 1990.

Miller, Steven. *The Age of Evangelicalism: America's Born-Again Years.* New York: Oxford University Press, 2014.

Moon, Steve Sang-Cheol. "The Protestant Missionary Movement in Korea: Current Growth and Development." *International Bulletin of Missionary Research* 32, no. 2 (2008): 59–64.

Morgan, Lewis H. *Ancient Society.* New York: Henry Holt, 1907.

Mun, Seong. *Bŏlgŏbŏsŭn gŭrisdoin* [The naked Christians]. Seoul: Kyobobook MCP, 2019.

Murayama, Chijun. *Chosunŭi gwisin* [Spirits in Korea]. 1929. Translated by Seong-hwan Rho. Seoul: Minŭmsa, 1990.

Nam, Kun-woo. "Hangukŭi saemaŭl undong'gwa saenghwalbyŭnhwa" [The New Village Movement and changes in everyday life in South Korea]. *Ilsang'gwa munhwa* [Everyday life and culture] 5 (2018): 153–166.

Nashel, Jonathan. *Edward Lansdale's Cold War.* Amherst: University of Massachusetts Press, 2005.

Neiburg, Federico, and Marcio Goldman. "Anthropology and Politics in Studies of National Character." Translated by Peter Gow. *Cultural Anthropology* 13, no. 1 (1998): 56–81.

Oh, Myungseok. "Cultural Policy and National Culture Discourse in the 1960s and 1970s." *Korean Anthropological Review* 1, no. 1 (2017): 105–129.

Oppenheim, Robert. *An Asian Frontier: American Anthropology and Korea, 1882–1945.* Lincoln: University of Nebraska Press, 2016.

Oppenheim, Robert. "'The West' and the Anthropology of Other People's Colonialism: Frederick Starr in Korea, 1911–1930." *Journal of Asian Studies* 64, no. 3 (2005): 677–703.

Park, Chung-Shin. *Protestantism and Politics in Korea.* Seattle: University of Washington Press, 2003.

Park, Il-byung. *Hankuk mugyoŭi ihae* [Understanding Korea's shamanism religion]. Waegwan: Bundo, 1999.

Park, Il-young. "Syamŏnijŭme daehan sŏn'gyosadŭlŭi taedonŭn oae daebidŏinŭnga?" [Missionaries' contrasting attitudes to shamanism]. In *Syamŏnijŭmgwa tajong'gyoŭi yunghapgwa galdŭng* [Synthesis and conflicts between Shamanism and other religions], edited by Syamŏnijŭm sasangyŏnguhoi [Research association for shamanism], 71–93. Seoul: Misonwŏn, 2017.

Park, Jun Hwan. "Money Is the Filial Child. But, at the Same Time, It is also the Enemy!: Korean Shamanic Rituals for Luck and Fortune." *Journal of Korean Religions* 3, no. 2 (2012): 39–72.

Pedersen, Morten A. "Totemism, Animism and North Asian Indigenous Ontologies." *Journal of the Royal Anthropological Association* 7, no. 3 (2001): 411–427.

Preston, Andrew. *Swords of the Spirit, Shield of Faith: Religion in American War and Diplomacy.* New York: Anchor Books, 2012.

Rha, Chae-hun, and Han-seop Park. *Incheon gaehangsa* [Opening of the Incheon port: a history]. Seoul: Miraejisik, 2006.

Robbins, Joel. "Anthropology and Theology: An Awkward Relationship?" *Anthropological Quarterly* 79, no. 2 (2006): 285–294.

Robbins, Joel. *Becoming Sinners: Christianity and Moral Torment in a Papua New Guinea Society.* Berkeley: University of California Press, 2004.

Robin, Robert W. "Missionaries in Contemporary Melanesia: Crossroads of Cultural Change." *Journal de la Société des Océanistes*, no. 69 (1980): 261–278.

Rotter, Andrew J. "Christians, Muslims, and Hindus: Religion and US–South Asian Relations, 1947–1954." *Diplomatic History* 24, no. 4 (2000): 593–613.

Roy, Rai Bahadur Sarat Chandra. "An Indian Outlook on Anthropology." *Man* 38 (1938): 146–150.

Ruotsila, Markku. *Fighting Fundamentalist: Carl McIntire and the Politicization of American Fundamentalism.* New York: Oxford University Press, 2015.

Rutherford, Danilyn. *Raiding the Land of the Foreigners: The Limits of the Nation on an Indonesian Frontier.* Stanford, CA: Stanford University Press, 2002.

Ryan, David. "Mapping Containment: The Cultural Construction of the Cold War." In *American Cold War Culture*, edited by Douglas Field, 50–68. Edinburgh: Edinburgh University Press, 2005.

Ryu, Youngju. Introduction to *Cultures of Yusin: South Korea in the 1970s*, edited by Y. Ryu, 1–20. Ann Arbor: University of Michigan Press, 2018.

Ryu, Youngju. *Writers of the Winter Republic: Literature and Resistance in Park Chung Hee's Korea.* Honolulu: University of Hawai'i Press, 2015.

Ryu, Youngju, ed. *Cultures of Yushin: South Korea in the 1970s.* Ann Arbor: University of Michigan Press, 2018.

Sahlins, Marshall. "Alterity and Autochthony: Austronesian Cosmographies of the Marvelous." The Raymond Firth Lecture. *HAU: Journal of Ethnographic Theory* 2, no. 1 (2008): 131–160.

Sahlins, Marshall. *Islands of History.* Chicago: University of Chicago Press, 1985.

Sahlins, Marshall. "The Original Political Society." *HAU: Journal of Ethnographic Theory* 7, no. 2 (2017): 91–128.

Salzman, Philip Carl. "Is Inequality Universal?" *Current Anthropology* 40, no. 1 (1999): 31–61.

Sarfati, Liora. *Contemporary Korean Shamanism: From Ritual to Digital.* Bloomington: Indiana University Press, 2021.

Schaller, Michael. *Douglas MacArthur: The Far Eastern General.* New York: Oxford University Press, 1989.

Schmid, Andre. *Korea between Empires, 1895–1919.* New York: Columbia University Press, 2002.

Schneider, Mark A. *Culture and Enchantment.* Chicago: University of Chicago Press, 1993.

Seo, Dae-seung. "Sŏngjangjuŭijŏk gyohoiŭi jaesaengsan: jaemihanin'gyohoiwa infrastrükchŏŭi jŏngchi" [Reproduction of the growth-oriented church: Korean American church and the politics of infrastructure]. *Bigyomunhwayŏn'gu* [Journal of comparative cultural studies] 25, no. 2 (2019): 103–143.

Severi, Carlo. *The Chimera Principle: An Anthropology of Memory and Imagination.* Chicago: University of Chicago Press, 2015.

Severi, Carlo. "On the White Spirits in the Kuna." In *Disturbing Remains: Memory, History, and Crisis in the Twentieth Century,* edited by Michael S. Roth and Charles G. Salas, 178–206. Los Angeles: Getty Research Institute, 2001.

Shannon, Christopher. *A World Made Safe for Differences: Cold War Intellectuals and the Politics of Identity.* Lanham, MD: Rowman and Littlefield, 2000.

Shin, Michael. *Korean National Identity under Japanese Colonial Rule: Yi Gwangsu and the March First Movement of 1919.* London: Routledge, 2018.

Shinzato, Yoshinobu. "Hankuk musok damronŭi hyŏngsŏng'gwa jŏn'gaee gwanhan yŏn'gu: 1960nyŏndaebutŏ 8onyŏndaerŭl jungsimŭro" [The development of discourses on Korean shamanism from the 1960s to the 1980s]. PhD diss., Seoul National University, 2018.

Singh, Bhrigupati. "The Headless Horseman of Central India: Sovereignty at Varying Thresholds of Life." *Cultural Anthropology* 27, no. 2 (2012): 383–407.

Stoler, Ann, and Fredrick Cooper, eds. *Tensions of Empire: Colonial Cultures in a Bourgeois World.* Berkeley: University of California Press, 1997.

Strathern, Marilyn. *The Gender of the Gift: Problems with Women and Problems with Society in Melanesia.* Cambridge: Cambridge University Press, 1988.

Taussig, Michael. *Mimesis and Alterity: A Particular History of the Senses.* New York: Routledge, 1993.

Taylor, Philip, ed. *Modernity and Re-enchantment: Religion in Post-revolutionary Vietnam.* Cambridge: Cambridge University Press, 2008.

Turner, Victor. *Dramas, Fields, and Metaphors: Symbolic Action in Human Society.* Ithaca, NY: Cornell University Press, 1974.

Tylor, Edward B. *Primitive Culture,* vol. 1. London: John Murray, 1871.

Van der Veer, Peter, ed. 1994. *Conversion to Modernities: Globalization of Christianity*. New York: Routledge.

Viveiros de Castro, Eduardo. "The Crystal Forest: Notes on the Ontology of Amazonian Spirits." *Inner Asia* 9, no. 2 (2007): 13–33.

Viveiros de Castro, Eduardo. *From the Enemy's Point of View: Humanity and Divinity in an Amazonian Society*. Chicago: University of Chicago Press, 1992.

Wacker, Grant. *America's Pastor: Billy Graham and the Shaping of a Nation*. Cambridge, MA: Harvard University Press, 2014.

Wagner, Roy. "The Fractal Person." In *Big Men and Great Men: Personifications of Power in Melanesia*, edited by Maurice Godelier and Marilyn Strathern, 159–173. Cambridge: Cambridge University Press, 1991.

Walraven, Boudewijn. "Korean Shamanism." *Numen* 30, no. 2 (1983): 240–264.

Walraven, Boudewijn C. A. "Popular Religion in a Confucianized Society." In *Culture and the State in Late Chosŏn Korea*, edited by Ja-Hyun Kim Haboush and Martina Deuchler, 160–198. Cambridge, MA: Harvard University Press, 1999.

Wells, Kenneth M. *New God, New Nation: Protestants and Self-Reconstruction Nationalism in Korea, 1896–1937*. Reprint. Seoul: Voice of the Martyrs Korea, 1990.

Whalin, W. Terry. *Billy Graham: A Biography of America's Greatest Evangelist*. New York: Morgan James Faith, 2014.

White, Donald W. "The 'American Century' in World History." *Journal of World History* 3, no. 1 (1992): 105–127.

Whitfield, Stephen J. *The Culture of the Cold War*. Baltimore: Johns Hopkins University Press, 1991.

Williams, William Appleman. *Empire as a Way of Life*. New York: Oxford University Press, 1980.

Worthen, Molly. *Apostles of Reason: The Crisis of Authority in American Evangelicalism*. New York: Oxford University Press, 2013.

Yang, Jong-sung. "Hankuk musinŭi gujo yŏn'gu" [A study of the structure of Korean shamanic spirits]. *Bigyomunhwayŏn'gu* [Comparative cultural studies], no. 5 (1999): 163–193.

Yang, Jong-sung. "Hwanghaedo majikut hyŭngsikgwa tŭksŏng gochal" [Forms and characteristics of Hwanghae-do kut]. In *Hwanghaedokutŭi ihae* [Understanding Hwanghae-do kut], edited by Hankukmusokhakhoi [Korean association of folklore studies], 25–62. Seoul: Minsokwŏn, 2008.

Yang, Jong-sung. "Seoul saramdŭlui sarangŭl batatdŏn Sasinsŏnghwangdang" [The Imperial Envoy Shrine that was once loved by the people of Seoul]. *Urimunhwasinmun* [Our culture news] (October 3, 2018). http://www.koya-culture.com/news/article.html?no=114881.

Yang, Nak-hong. "1959nyŏn hankuk jangrogyoŭi bunyŏl gwajŏng" [An analysis of the schism of the Korean Presbyterian church in 1959]. *Hankukgidokgyowa yŏksa* [History of Korean Christianity] 23 (2005): 125–161.

Yim, Dawnhee. 2001. "Byŭnglipsin'gwan'gwa hankukmunhwa" [Parallelotheism and Korean culture]. *Bigyominsokhak* [Comparative folklore studies] 20 (2001): 55–115.

Yim, Suk-jay. "Hankukmusokyŏn'gusŏsŏl I" [Introduction to Korean shamanism I]. *Aseayŏsŏng'yŏn'gu* [Journal of the studies of Asian women] 9 (1970): 73–90.

Yim, Suk-jay. "Hankukmusokyŏn'gusŏsŏl II" [Introduction to Korean shamanism II]. *Aseayŏsŏng'yŏn'gu* [Journal of the studies of Asian women] 10 (1971): 161–217.

Yoo, William. *American Missionaries, Korean Protestants, and the Changing Shape of World Christianity, 1884–1965.* New York: Routledge, 2017.

Yoon, Jeongran. *Hankukjŏnjaeng'gwa gidokgyo* [The Korean War and Protestantism]. Seoul: Hanul Academy, 2015.

Yoon, Jeongran. "Victory over Communism: South Korean Protestants' Ideas about Democracy, Development, and Dictatorship, 1953–1961." *Journal of American–East Asian Relations* 24, no. 2–3 (2017): 233–258.

Yun, Kyoim. *The Shaman's Wages: Trading in Ritual on Cheju Island.* Seattle: University of Washington Press, 2019.

NEWSPAPERS AND OTHER MEDIA

Gŭkdong Bangsong [Far East Broadcasting]. Available online at: https://www.youtube.com/watch?v=UOUzbbHe_lg; and https://www.youtube.com/watch?v=UOUzbbHe_lg&t=1813s

"Hanmi sugyo 100 junyŏn" [Centenary of Korean-American friendship]. *Daehan nyusŭ* [Korean news] 1385, May 20, 1982.

"Jayuhyŭkmyŭng'ŭi kkotdabal" [Flowers of the revolution for freedom]. *Kyunghyang Sinmun* [Kyunghyang daily], April 30, 1960.

Kyunghyang Sinmun [Kyunghyang daily], May 16, 1981.

"Lévi-Strauss," *Chungang Ilbo* [Korea JungAng daily], November 5, 2009.

Mansin. Documentary film by Chan-kyung Park, 2014.

"President Meets Graham." *Korea Herald*, May 27, 1973.

"Saemaŭl hunpung'e jjotgyŏnan pyesŭp 300nyŏn" [300-year-old rotten customs are blown away by the warm wind of the Saemaŭl movement]. *Kyunghyang sinmun* [Kyunghyang daily], February 19, 1973.

"Segye Kidokgyo Bokŭmhwa Daehoi Explo '74" [World Christian evangelization rally, Explo '74]. Available online at https://www.youtube.com/watch?v=ahUYa9XVu24.

Seoul Sinmun [Seoul daily], November 20, 1947.

INDEX

Note: Illustrations are indicated by page numbers in *italics*.

fractal identity, 145–146
Frazer, James G., 99–100
Freedom Park, 8, 45–49, 47, 53–54, 57, 60, 64, 66, 71, 104
fundamentalism, 19, 27–29, 178n44

Geertz, Clifford, 21–22, 37, 177n30
Gell, Alfred, 146
Ghana, 97
Gilmore, George, 95–96
Goldman, Marcio, 160–161
Goldstone, Brian, 67–68
gŏri, 126, 136
Gow, Peter, 160
Graham, Billy, 5, 13–14, 15, 15–18, 23, 28, 32, 92, 178n44
Grayson, James, 43, 188n3
Great Asian Co-prosperity, 105
Great East Asian War, 70
Greene, Graham, 180n56
Guan Yu cult, 69–70. *See also* Gwan-u cult
Guest, The (Son'nim) (Hwang), 37
Gurim, 25, 178n36
Gwan-u cult, 69–70. *See also* Guan Yu cult

Habermas, Jürgen, 11
Hackett, Rosaline, 118
Hallowell, Irving, 130
Han, Ju Hui Judy, 189n20
Han Kyung-chik, 14–16, 15, 23–24, 28, 32–35, 40, 91–92, 94, 175n10
Han Kyung-Koo, 6
hapŭi, 150
Harding, Susan Friend, 178n44
Harkness, Nicholas, 179n44
Hawaii, 49
Henderson, Gregory, 52
Hermit Kingdom, 46
Hobbes, Thomas, 67

household gods, 126–129
Howell, Signe, 120
Humphrey, Caroline, 43
hwan, 88, 149
Hwang Sok-young, 37

"Ideology as a Cultural System" (Geertz), 22
idolatry, 2, 5, 34–35, 38, 103–106
Imjin War, 70
Im Kyŏng-ŏp, 55–57, 56, 58–59, 64–65, 70, 149
imperialism, 43–44, 104. *See also* colonialism
Inboden, William, 30
Incheon, 6–7, 39–40, 45, 47–48, 58, 61–62, 66, 71, 72, 90–93
Incheon Landing, 7, 52, 64
India, 33, 67
inequality, 17, 20–21, 68, 144
Ingold, Tim, 144, 179n44
inminban, 80, 186n21
International Bible Museum, 93
Interpretation of Cultures (Geertz), 177n30
Inuit, 120
Irian Jaya, 51

jang'gun, 61–64. *See also* warrior spirits
Japan, 23, 44, 54, 66, 90, 97, 113, 185n10; anti-Westernism and, 106–107; colonialism and, 103–104; Imjin War, 70; imperialism and, 104–105; MacArthur in, 49–50; shamanism and, 3–4, 42–43, 107–108
Jeffress, Robert, 30
Jeil Church, 93–94
Jeju, 24, 36–37, 51, 128
Jemulpo Club, 92–93
Jesup North Pacific Expedition, 159
John Paul II, Pope, 19

Reformation, 103

religion, 2, 4–5, 7–10; Cold War and, 13–38, 41; New Village Movement and, 76–79. *See also* Christianity; fetishism; Protestantism; shamanism

Rhee Syngman, 27–28, 31, 81–82

Robertson, Pat, 178n44

Roman Catholicism, 103

Ross, John, 188n3

Rostow, Walt, 4, 180n56

Rotter, Andrew, 22, 32–33

Rousseau, Jean-Jacques, 162–163

"Rousseau, the Father of Anthropology" (Lévi-Strauss), 162–163

Roy, Sarat Chandra, 158

Rusk, Dean, 52

Russia, 66, 79, 137, 152, 186n21

Russo-Japanese War, 44, 66, 104

Rutherford, Danilyn, 51

Ryan, David, 22

Ryu, Youngju, 85

Sahlins, Marshall, 64, 120–121, 129, 136, 176n23

Sasin-dang (the Shrine for Envoys), 77

Schmid, Andre, 153

Schneider, Mark, 118

Scranton, Mary F., 106

Scranton, William B., 106

Second Sino-Japanese War, 3, 97

segmentary descent theory, 148

Severi, Carlo, 65

shadowy rituals, 75, 132–134, 166–167

shamanism, 3–4, 9–12, 37; Buddhism and, 108–109; Confucianism and, 108–109; as cultural heritage, 87; as evil, 115; heritization of, 165; hierarchy and, 113–114; Japan and, 107–108; Korean War and, 62, 64;

Kuna, 50; *kut,* 37, 41, 48, 55, 60–61; MacArthur and, 44–45, 54, 65, 69, 163–164, 167–168; neo-Confucianism and, 75; New Village Movement and, 74–79; *obangki* divination in, 41, 44–45; Protestantism and, 54; structure in, 113–114; as superstition, 133; suppression of, 82–83; in Yim Suk-jay, 125–126; Yim Suk-jay and, 115–117

Shin Chae-ho, 109

Shintoism, 97, 104–107, 109

Shin Yun-bok, 152

Shinzato Yoshinobu, 83

Shufeldt, Robert W., 92

Shufeldt Treaty, 92

Sinchŏn, 36

Singh, Bhrigupai, 67

Sin Hŏn, 92

Song of Saemaŭl, 84

son-nim kut, 37

sonoli-kut, 86

sovereignty, 12, 51, 53, 58–59, 67–68

spirit portraits, 44, 56, 63, 149, 150, 157–158

spirit possession, 138, 143–144

Spirits in Korea (Murayama), 107

Stages of Economic Growth, The: A Non-Communist Manifesto (Rostow), 4

Starr, Frederick, 185n10

Steger, G., 97, 104–105

Strathern, Marilyn, 146

Sudan, 143

Sungsil Academy, 94

superstition, 70, 74–83, 87, 103, 133

surveillance, 80–81, 186n21

symbolic coercion, 21

Taegŭk-ki Army, 29–30

Taiwan, 70

Heonik Kwon is Senior Research Fellow of Social Anthropology at Trinity College, University of Cambridge, and a member of the Mega-Asia research group at Seoul National University Asia Center. He is the author of *After the Korean War: An Intimate History* (2020, winner of James Palais Prize), *The Other Cold War* (2010), *Ghosts of War in Vietnam* (2008, George Kahin Prize), and *After the Massacre: Commemoration and Consolation in Ha My and My Lai* (2006, Clifford Geertz Prize).

Jun Hwan Park is an expert on Hwanghae shamanism. He has published widely on the symbolism of luck and the morality of money in Korea's shamanic rituals.

THINKING FROM ELSEWHERE

9 780823 299911